About the Author
David Weiss Halivni is Professor of Religion
at Columbia University.

Peshat and Derash

PESHAT AND DERASH

Plain and Applied Meaning in Rabbinic Exegesis

DAVID WEISS HALIVNI

New York   Oxford
OXFORD UNIVERSITY PRESS
1991

Oxford University Press

Oxford   New York   Toronto
Delhi   Bombay   Calcutta   Madras   Karachi
Petaling Jaya   Singapore   Hong Kong   Tokyo
Nairobi   Dar es Salaam   Cape Town
Melbourne   Auckland

and associated companies in
Berlin   Ibadan

Copyright © 1991 by David Weiss Halivni

Published by Oxford University Press, Inc.,
200 Madison Avenue, New York, New York 10016

Oxford is a registered trademark of Oxford University Press

Library of Congress Cataloging-in-Publication Data
Halivni, David Weiss
Peshat and derash : plain and applied meaning
in Rabbinic exegesis / by David Weiss Halivni.
p. cm. Includes bibliographical references.
ISBN 0-19-506065-2
1. Bible. O.T.—Criticism, interpretation, etc., Jewish.
2. Midrash. I. Title. II. Title: Rabbinic exegesis.
BS1186.H28 1991   221.6′088296—dc20   90-31375

2 4 6 8 9 7 5 3 1

Printed in the United States of America
on acid-free paper

Preface

This book reflects the confluence of complementary interests: scholarly and theological. It is divided into two parts that are related but not necessarily substantively continuous. The structure of the book thus mirrors its central theological proposition—that rabbinic exegesis and halakha (legal norms) are integrally, but not always inextricably, linked. Though always related, Jewish exegesis and behavior do not always coincide or converge. The continuity of religious behavioral norms can withstand the occasional uncoupling of praxis and intellect. This conclusion is borne out by a rigorous scholarly exploration of relevant rabbinic materials, but its theological underpinnings will not ultimately be slighted or concealed.

The relationship between the scholarship and theology embodied in this book, like that between Jewish exegesis and behavior, is intimate but not inviolate. The matters of exegesis and theology to be discussed, though arranged consecutively, may certainly be understood and assessed separately. In fact, the fate of the relationship between parts one and two lie in the reader's hands; they may be read productively either continuously or disjunctively. I realize that the scholarly and theological sections of the book may appeal to distinct audiences. My hope is that, to some extent at least, these audiences may overlap.

The relationship between scriptural peshat (i.e., the plain meaning) and rabbinic derash (i.e., the applied meaning), is the generative and axial issue of the book. It binds the scholarly and theological halves of the book to each other while nourishing the discussion in each. The aim of the book as a whole is to delineate and grapple with the tension that occasionally arises between what is perceived by the contemporary reader of the Bible to be the straightforward, austere sense of a scriptural text and the more creative, seemingly artificial interpretation that the rabbinic tradition has affixed to it. This goal lends the book a holistic coherence, even though the discrepancy between peshat and derash is addressed from scholarly and theological perspectives. Underlying and propelling the book as an entirety is the question: can we elucidate the dynamics of classical rabbinic exegesis, from talmudic through medieval till modern times, in a way that will explain, and thus alleviate, the tension between peshat and derash—between what Scripture seems to denote and what traditional rabbinic exegetes have claimed that it implies? Is rabbinic exegesis, when it deviates from peshat, simply capricious and contrived, or is it in fact more responsible and accountable than first appears, once its exegetical commitments have been identified and labeled?

The first part of the book tackles these questions from a scholarly standpoint. That is, it is not my intention in the first part to be apologetic or condemnatory vis-à-vis rabbinic derash that strays from scriptural peshat. My challenge is to *explain* this phenomenon on scholarly grounds through an internal evaluation of the workings of rabbinic hermeneutics based on a close reading of rabbinic texts. The approach to the problem of the discrepancy of peshat and derash that is fashioned in the first chapter is one that does not pass sentence on the apparent rabbinic violation of peshat, but that seeks to understand it. An honest investigation of rabbinic exegesis will expose the conflict of peshat and derash, and an objective analysis will rationalize this phenomenon, that is, make it seem reasonable. The fact that the rabbis of the talmudic period did not possess the same exegetical sensibility that we modern readers do, and were not as dedicated to the plain sense of a text as we have been trained to be, will not be used as evidence in the condemnation of rabbinic midrash. We are engaged in a hearing, not a trial, with rabbinic exegesis the main character witness for its own defense. Rabbinic sources will be read in terms of their proper historical, theological, and exegetical contexts. It will be conceded that the rabbis did not share our allegiance to peshat, but no value judgment will flow from this scholarly conclusion.

The first chapter will thus establish the scholarly agenda for the remainder of the book, and will present the book's most important, and perhaps provocative, scholarly thesis, that of timebound exegesis. The notion that exegesis, rabbinic included, is timebound and historically conditioned, and thus must be historically contextualized, frees us of the need, or temptation, to provide a valuative critique of our subject matter. Talmudic exegesis will only be fixed within a context of historical time, not arranged within a hierarchy of exegetical sensibilities.

Our aim will be to trace the historical origins and contours of the path toward peshat, for it will indeed be our claim that rabbinic exegesis has developed through time an increasing preference for peshat. We will seek to establish when and why this preference for the simple meaning of the scriptural text developed, in light of the fact that initially the penchant for derash was so pronounced. The second chapter will substantiate our theory of timebound exegesis and validate our claim that the tendencies of rabbinic exegesis did not remain static or uniform. A linear development in the direction of greater respect for the integrity of the text, be it Scripture, Mishnah, or Talmud, the classic religious documents of Judaism, extending from the late biblical through the modern periods, will be tracked. It will be seen that the incompatibility of peshat and derash became an increasingly thorny problem for Jewish exegetes, and increasingly objectionable.

The third chapter will suggest an alternative meaning of the noun *peshat* in talmudic literature to the one traditionally provided by scholars. It will be demonstrated that the definition of peshat as "plain meaning" was introduced by the medieval exegetes and was not operative during the talmudic period. The talmudic understanding of peshat was, rather, the "context" of a phrase or verse. The context, but not necessarily the plain meaning, of the text was hallowed, and generally shielded from the devices and designs of derash. This chapter is the most technical in the book, the one most laden with scholarly accoutrements, although the concluding section, which deals with the medieval period, is less so. The first section of this chapter, which deals with the talmudic period, may not be easy going for readers with little patience for scholarly minutiae, but it is crucial to a proper and thorough appreciation of the evolving interconnection of peshat and derash.

With part two, we embark on a theological exploration of some of the implications of the scholarly conclusions reached in the first part of the book. After a brief interlude to discuss the methodological strategies that will be employed in the concluding two chapters, several theological issues that reverberated within our scholarly analysis of the relationship of peshat and derash will be addressed. Our discussion of the problem of the deviation of derash from peshat will become, consciously and purposefully, theologically charged. No attempt is made to camouflage the implicit theological motivations or considerations. Scholarly aloofness is abandoned as we set out to work through the theological consequences of the notion of timebound exegesis. Does timebound exegesis imply timebound religious behavior? Does the variability of Jewish exegesis through time entail the mutability of legal norms? The fourth chapter answers these questions negatively and asserts that there is talmudic theological precedent for our contemporary standpoint. It is shown that the rabbis of the Talmud were not averse to the occasional dissolution of the ties that bind exegesis and practice. This cleavage between the realms of intellect and praxis is refracted through the talmudic depictions of the conflict between minority and majority halakhic positions. As we shall see, these realms may contradict each other, but they also complement each other. The historical reality of the changing orientations and commitments of traditional Jewish exegesis through time does not demand a correlative agenda of halakhic reform. Religious behavior need not keep pace with exegesis, for practice does not always conform to the rigorous dictates of intellectual truth.

The fifth and concluding chapter offers a theological, though historically grounded, resolution to the occasional collision of peshat and derash. It yields the theological dividend for the religious Jew that rabbinic derash may be embraced without the necessary abandonment of scriptural peshat. Sustained by an analysis of relevant rabbinic materials, and contingent upon particular historical conceptions of the First Temple period and of Ezra the Scribe, this theological resolution champions the causes of both peshat and derash. Our exegetical commitment to peshat is certainly not sacrificed as we pave the way for the acceptability, and indeed necessity, of rabbinic derash. The rabbinic midrashic tradition, it will be argued, has preserved, rather than violated, the integrity of the scriptural text. It has restored and preserved rather than transgressed peshat.

The division of the book into two distinct parts is perhaps a bit artificial, for the orbits of scholarship and theology often collide, and the roles of historian and theologian sometimes merge. Historiography and scholarship can never completely transcend subjective concerns or even conceal theological undercurrents. These basic traits of scholarship may be evident in this work, for my efforts as scholar and theologian could not always be successfully segregated. The point at which a scholar may become a theologian or philosopher of religion is, in any event, uncertain and wavering. The accusation of subjectivity is thus often a banal one.

The genesis of the scholarly section of the book was, however, decidedly different from that of the theological section. My analysis of the dynamic history of rabbinic exegesis is a fluid and organic continuation of my lifelong preoccupation with the sources and traditions of rabbinic literature. I have come to believe that the problem of peshat and derash lies at the nerve center of rabbinic interpretation and that its examination therefore is a prime desideratum of Jewish scholarship. Exegesis is the religious pipeline of Judaism, and its genuine character must be investigated in a methodical manner and in a critical mode.

The genesis of the theological section was more existential in character. In the heat of the debate, less than a decade ago, concerning the enactment of religious reforms in regard to the rabbinate—which I opposed—the leader of the proreform group accused me of, at the very least, gross inconsistency. This charge was based on the assumption that the scientific, critical study (and teaching) of the Talmud is inconsistent with the maintenance of a conservative stance in matters of halakhic observance. The critical apperception of Jewish history and literature, so the argument was formulated, should have an enlightening and liberating impact upon the halakhic process. In the eyes of my accuser, my progressive scholarly program and my conservative halakhic platform were incongruous.

I realized then that there is a widespread belief that an advocate of the critical study of religious texts, whether the text be the Bible or the Talmud, must also by logical necessity be a proponent of religious reform, at least of the more modest variety. I soon recognized that this erroneous belief was the product of a faulty understanding of the character of rabbinic exegesis and of the nature of the halakhic process. The scholarly section of this work seeks to dispel some of the illusions about and mischaracterizations of rabbinic exegesis, while the theological section presents the results of my reflections on the issue of the congruity of critical scholarship and halakhic conservatism. Just as in the relationship of peshat and derash, I maintain that critical scholarship and halakhic conservatism can ultimately be embraced simultaneously and harmoniously, precisely because they need not, and should not, impinge on each other. They should be perceived as parallel lines which can never converge, for the workings of each are distinct. My goal in the second part of this book is not necessarily to convince the reader of the truth of a certain theological perspective, but to convince him or her of the viability and reasonableness of the theological position that sequesters matters of halakhic practice from critical historical scholarship. Only to the detriment of both scholarship and halakha are the two realms conjoined. The affiliation of scholarship and theology may be hazardous, but the convergence of scholarship and halakha cannot be other than dangerous and damaging. The problem of the relationship of peshat and derash can become for us, then, a conduit of understanding into the dynamics of rabbinic exegesis as well as a vehicle of appreciation for a sensitive and controversial—and contemporary—Jewish theological issue.

Finally, I would be remiss if I did not publicly record my thanks to Mr. Marc Ashley, my teacher's assistant. His contribution to chapter 5 and to the Introduction was more than stylistic. He reformulated some of their ideas, added connecting tissue, and strengthened them contextually. The book is a better book because of him.

New York City   D. W. H.
April 1990/Nissan 5750

Contents

I

ON MATTERS OF EXEGESIS

1

Timebound Exegesis

Reading In and Allegorizing

The realization that the rabbis of the Talmud in their interpretation of the Bible occasionally deviated from the "simple" literal meaning of the text provoked condemnation from those outside the rabbinic tradition and puzzled insiders. Spinoza[1] criticized Maimonides for sanctioning deviation from the literal meaning and called such a practice "rash and excessive." Two hundred years later, A. Geiger[2] chastised the rabbis of the Talmud for having abandoned "the natural meaning" of the text; he attributed this lapse to their "deficient sense of exegesis." Insiders since the time of Saadya[3] (882–942), one of the most important Jewish scholars of the early Middle Ages, have agonized over the conflict between what the text seems to say and the way it was understood by the rabbis of the Talmud. The discrepancy was particularly pronounced when it affected a matter of law, when a mode of behavior was demanded on the basis of an interpretation that was not congruous with the literal meaning of the text. An aggadic, nonlegal passage could easily be converted into a metaphor or an allegory,[4] blunting the troublesome edges of the literal meaning. In legal matters, however, conversion into metaphor or allegory is inappropriate, indeed forbidden. One faces the dilemma of choosing, in the words of a recent traditional scholar,[5] between "assuming that the Torah expressed itself—God forbid—in an unsuitable manner and accepting the binding result of the rabbinic interpretation, or accepting the literal

3

meaning of the text and rejecting the rabbinic tradition"—neither a very comforting alternative to the traditionalist.[6]

Several examples will suffice to indicate the frequent disparity between the meaning of a scriptural verse and its rabbinic interpretation. The simple, literal reading of Exod. 21:24 is "an eye for an eye," implying physical compensation; the rabbis changed it to mean monetary compensation.[7] In another case, biblical law enjoins a woman whose husband died without children to marry one of the deceased husband's brothers (levirate marriage): "And the first son whom she bears shall succeed to the name of his brother who is dead, that his name may not be blotted out of Israel" (Deut. 25:6). The simple, literal meaning of the verse implies that the living brother is a surrogate father for the deceased. He lends his seed to the deceased brother who is considered the "real" father of the firstborn of the levirate marriage. The rabbis changed the meaning of the verse to refer not to the firstborn child, as the literal meaning suggests, but to the firstborn brother, that is the oldest brother of the deceased, who shall perform the levirate marriage.[8] A third example is Exod. 22:6–12, which deals with the obligations of custodianship. Literally understood, the Bible distinguishes between giving "silver or chattels for safekeeping" and giving "an ass, an ox, a sheep or any beast into his neighbor's keeping" with respect to culpability if the object is stolen. If the object that was stolen was inanimate (such as silver or chattels) the keeper is absolved from payment; if it was animate, he is responsible. The rabbis totally ignored the distinction of the simple, literal meaning, and instead distinguished between one who is a "gratuitous bailee" and one who is a "bailee for hire." If he does not get paid for safekeeping and the object was stolen he is absolved from payment; if he was paid to watch the object and then it was stolen, he is responsible.[9] In these instances the rabbis negated both the meaning and the content of the verses: you never extract an eye for an eye; there is no father other than the biological father; and there is absolutely no difference whether the object given for safekeeping was animate or inanimate. There are instances where the rabbis' changes did not affect the practical outcome implied by the simple literal meaning. However, that was because another verse fulfilled that function, allowing the verse in question to convey other, nonliteral information. For example, in Deut. 24:16, we read: "Fathers shall not be put to death for the children, nor shall the children be put to death for the fathers; every man shall be put to death for his own sin." The rabbis interpret the phrase "fathers shall not be put to death for the children" to mean that fathers cannot testify (pro or con) in a case involving their children nor can children testify (pro or con) in a case involving their father.[10] To the rabbis, not to kill parents because of crimes committed by their children, or children for their parents, is implied in the second half of the verse: "every man shall be put to death for his own sin." The superfluous exhortation "fathers shall not be put to death for their children" conveys additional information that relatives cannot be witnesses. The simple meaning here is already included in the second part of the verse.

To be sure, the rabbis of the Talmud were not the only ones[11] who on occasion abandoned the plain meaning of a text (the meaning that scrupulously follows the tenor of the words and the thrust of the context).[12] A similar criticism may be leveled against Christian theologians whenever they have extracted christological predictions from the Old Testament, or when during the medieval period they regarded the writings of pagan authors like Homer and Vergil as Christian allegories. The wavering attitude of the church throughout the ages regarding the divine nature of the Old Testament (so ably documented by J. S. Preus),[13] was due to its vacillation in deciding the proper exegetical posture to be adopted vis-à-vis the Old Testament. What ultimately defeated Marcionism and saved the Old Testament for the church was the willingness of the church fathers to interpret the contents of the Old Testament in a manner spiritually edifying to a Christian. They could do so—though not without quarrels and differences of opinion—only because they did not adhere to simple meaning, although they protested all the while that they were following the *sensus litteralis*.[14] When the fifteenth-century chancellor of the University of Paris, Jean Gerson (d. 1429) asserted[15] (with ostensible support from Thomas Aquinas) that *sensus litteralis* is only what the church, as the official, authoritative interpreter of Holy Writ, declares it to be, he was not living up to the standards of textual exegesis later systematized by Spinoza.

However, rabbinic exegesis is distinct from the church's method of interpretation. The church, for instance, when confronting texts that it wanted to utilize or even adopt and integrate into its system but whose surface meanings were not truly consistent with its theology, allegorized their meaning (or turned them into metaphors, figures of speech, etc.). The rabbis of the Talmud, in contrast, when confronting a legal text whose surface meaning needed to be revised, changed it, *read in* a different meaning.[16]

The difference between *reading in* and allegorizing is crucial. Allegorization or metaphorization preserves the surface meaning; reading in displaces the surface meaning. In allegory and the like the simple meaning is retained, albeit transformed; in reading in, the simple meaning is rejected. Allegorization burdens the text, strains it; reading in changes the text. Allegorization *adds to* the text (*superadditio*).[17] In the celebrated example of the four senses of meaning given by the medieval Christian exegetes,[18] Jerusalem stands for both the physical city of Jerusalem (the simple, literal meaning) and the church (the allegorical meaning). Its tropological meaning is the soul, and its anagogical meaning is the heavenly city. These meanings are not mutually exclusive. Reading in, however, excludes the simple, literal meaning. The rabbis also allegorized the nonlegal sections of the Bible (or metaphorized or treated them as figures of speech). An entire book, the Song of Songs, was interpreted by some rabbis as an allegory of man's love for God.[19] They also *added to* texts, indeed quite frequently. They are the distinguished authors of that fascinating, rich and multifaceted genre called aggada,[20] whose legitimacy[21]—though not its reliability[22] as a mode of interpretation—was never questioned. Aggada contains all the means and modes of interpretation employed by the church fathers, and scholars have duly noted that it is similar to the way the church fathers interpret the Bible.[23] However, in law in general and in rabbinic law in particular, allegorization and the like are inadmissible. When modification is called for, there is often no choice but to "read in," changing the simple meaning. Since law is so dominant in rabbinic thought and dependence on the Bible so fundamental, the process of reading in is more pronounced and prominent in rabbinic literature. But it is not entirely unique to it. Those who claim that capital punishment is unconstitutional because it violates the Eighth Amendment's guarantee against "cruel and unusual punishment" are reading into the constitutional text which says: "no person shall be deprived of life or liberty without due process of law," clearly implying that with due process of law a life may be deprived. One may still argue, however, given the present climate of opinion and the ethnicity of most of those who are awaiting the death penalty, that no due process of law is possible.[24] This argument does not read into the text. It does, however, add to it, giving new meaning to "due process" that most likely was not intended by its framers. Adherence to any system of written law may on occasion stimulate reading in. When that system is justified as an expression of the will and desire of a higher being, like the Bible, reading in is almost endemic. That is why rabbinic exegesis, centered as it is on law, is more exposed than any other kind of exegesis to the charge that it does not strictly adhere to the "natural" meaning of a text.

Interpretive States of Mind

What were the reactions to the charges against the rabbis? They were generally of two kinds: one, put forward most forcefully by what can best be termed apologists,[25] denied that the rabbis violated the simple, literal meaning of the biblical text; the other response was the denial by certain exegetes of the Middle Ages[26] that the Rabbis *intended* to do away with simple, literal meaning. The former claimed that the rabbis, more than any other exegetes, were committed to the simple literal meaning, called *peshat* in later Hebrew, which they perfected and studied systematically and comprehensively. What appears to us as applied (in the sense of "forced, worked") meaning is actually "peshat-in-depth," based on rules of grammar known to the rabbis of the Talmud and subsequently forgotten. Not all apologists subscribe to this extreme position, nor do they all reduce the problem of peshat and derash to matters of knowledge of syntax and grammar. Yet all of them maintain that fundamentally the rabbis of the Talmud did not violate the simple, literal meaning (i.e., the peshat) except in a few instances where they say so themselves. It is because of an inability of the critics of the rabbis to comprehend properly the divine text of the Bible that many an exposition of the rabbis, called in later Hebrew *derasha*, appears inconsistent with the simple, literal meaning, while in fact it is not. Most apologists lived in or close to the modern era, a period whose "interpretive state of mind" encourages adherence to the simple literal meaning. Their own commitment to peshat is therefore understandable. What is problematic, however, is the transference of this conviction retroactively to talmudic times, making the rabbis experts in peshat.

Medieval exegetes, on the other hand, claimed that the scriptural verses which the rabbis cite in cases of applied meaning (derash) are merely an *asmakhta*, a support, a kind of Biblical ornament, for laws (or beliefs) whose authority was not actually the verses quoted, but either a tradition or a rabbinic ordinance. Unlike the apologists, they admit that many talmudic *derashot* (expositions) are not in line with the simple, literal meaning. They claim, however, that the rabbis never intended with these *derashot* to replace the "natural" meaning of *peshat*. The *derashot* come only to add richness and texture to the text, and reciprocally to endow the laws (or beliefs) with greater authority by associating them with the Bible. Association, however, should not be confused with derivation. If a verse is to function as a true biblical source, it must flow from the simple, literal meaning. Laws and beliefs that do not emerge from the peshat are not entitled to be designated as scriptural, and must be classified as either traditional or rabbinic. The medieval exegetes' position assumes that *derashot* do not contradict the peshat. However, their view cannot explain those instances where, as in the case of an eye for an eye, the simple meaning and the applied meaning, the peshat and the derash, are mutually exclusive. You cannot logically have both a physical eye for an eye and an eye in pecuniary compensation. There the *derasha* replaces the simple meaning. In those instances, the medieval exegetes, like the apologists, were desperately trying to elevate the applied meaning to the rank of simple meaning.

I would like to suggest a different approach: to recognize that rabbinic deviation from simple meaning is a historical fact, and to see it as a stage in the development of the interpretation of texts in general, without assigning either praise or blame. This shifts the focus of the debate from concentrating on rabbinic violation of peshat to the development of rabbinic *attitudes* towards peshat. The view presented here denies the two assumptions made by the aforementioned schools, that is, that our sense of peshat is universal, and that the rabbis shared this valuation. It is my contention that the rabbis did not share our devotion to the simple literal meaning. Exegesis is "timebound." Each interpretive state of mind has its own system of exegesis, and the rabbis' interpretive state of mind did not dictate to them that the simple, literal meaning was inherently superior to the applied meaning. Although they generally began their interpretations of the Bible with the simple, literal meaning of the text, they did not feel committed to it. The slightest provocation, most often an apparently superfluous word or letter, moved them to abandon it.

This position is difficult for a modern exegete to grasp. The modern state of mind demands a greater faithfulness to the simple, literal meaning (to the peshat), and a greater obligation to preserve it. Only in the face of virtually insurmountable problems is this approach abandoned. The presence of an extra word, letter, or even an entire phrase can be easily seen as a stylistic peculiarity. Peshat, from this point of view, is synonymous with exegetical truth, and one does not abandon truth lightly. But to the rabbis of the Talmud, deviation from peshat was not repugnant. Their interpretive state of mind saw no fault with an occasional reading in. It was not against their exegetical conscience, even though it may be against ours.

We are thus necessarily more historically conscious, inasmuch as we hold that the commitment to the literal meaning of a text is a product of historical development. This development will be more fully appreciated after one has read chapter 2, which traces the history of rabbinic exegesis and which, together with chapter 3, constitutes the major proof for this position. The remainder of this chapter will be devoted to removing possible objections that may occur to a learned reader upon hearing the notion of timebound exegesis for the first time (in the course of which material from these two chapters will be utilized, hence, the slight duplication) and to making this notion intellectually more palatable. Only after the reader has overcome his natural resistance to this notion will he be susceptible to evidence.

Miscellaneous Objections

First we have to establish when a preference for simple, literal meaning over applied meaning, peshat over derash, first emerged in rabbinic literature. If it can be shown that this preference existed already in the early talmudic period, any deviation from it must be attributed to negligence or knowing violation of that principle. On the other hand, if it can be shown that the rabbis of the Talmud were aware of the distinction between peshat and derash, yet at the slightest provocation switched from simple meaning to applied meaning, one must conclude that they simply did not have the absolute aversion to reading in that is so characteristic of the modern exegete. A widespread and pervasive resort to reading in cannot be attributed to ignorance, but to a collective interpretive state of mind that had not conceded absolute superiority to simple, literal meaning.[27]

Of critical importance in proving that rabbinic exegesis did not subscribe to the modern sense of literal meaning is the analysis of the famous dictum in the Babylonian Talmud,[28] *ein mikra yotze middei peshuto* (No text may be deprived of its *peshat*). The crux of the matter is the meaning of the word *peshat*, both in this dictum and in other places (in different inflectional forms) where the context indicates that the term is being used as a mode of interpretation. Is it—as it has been understood at least since the time of R. Samuel ben Chofni (d. 1013)[29]—similar or equivalent to the simple, literal meaning, in contrast with derash, which generally designates applied meaning? In that case, the rabbis of the Talmud themselves, by asserting the permanency and inviolability of the simple meaning, made it superior to the applied meaning; and their occasional abandonment of the simple meaning could not be explained as reflecting a state of mind. If, however, peshat means "context"—as I hope to prove in chapter 3—then all this dictum asserts is that any meaning ascribed to the verse must cover the full text, including what is said before and what is said after it. Etymologically, the root *p-sh-t* means extension, continuation, context. If this is the word's meaning, there is no evidence that the rabbis of the Talmud gave precedence to literal meaning. Indeed, from some places[30] in the Talmud where the root *p-sh-t* is not employed, it can be proven that the rabbis of the Talmud did not always prefer simple over applied meaning. They possessed no built-in sense of the superiority of *peshat*. Peshat did not take hold of them at their time.

A striking example of the rabbis' not honoring our modern sense of peshat is the observation made by two rabbis, one from the sixteenth century and one from the nineteenth century,[31] pertaining to Lev. 19:14: "Thou shall not put a stumbling block before the blind." Nowhere in the Talmud, observed these scholars, does it say that to put a physical stumbling block before a physically blind person is a violation of this injunction. The Talmud does say in several places[32] that if anyone knowingly gives false advice to another person, the giver violates the above injunction. It goes even further and says[33] that if a person abets the wrongdoing of another person, the abettor violates the above injunction. It is putting a spiritual stumbling block before a spiritually blind man. But it does not say that the same is true if a person has put an actual stumbling block before a physically blind man. This silence is not due to the rabbis' ignorance of the literal meaning of the injunction, as if it did not occur to them that when the law says "Thou shall not put a stumbling block before the blind" it means a physical stumbling block before a physically blind man. Maimonides himself, in his book on the commandments, surprisingly seems to say just that, that the simple meaning of this injunction is not to give false advice (commandment no. 299). However, the rabbis of the Talmud knew very well what the literal meaning of this injunction was. They explicitly say (*b. Nid.* 57a) that the Samaritans (and the Sadducees), who do not believe in the oral law as the authoritative interpretation of Scripture, and who explain every verse in the Bible literally, understand the above injunction to refer only to a physical stumbling block put before a physically blind man. Giving false advice or abetting wrongdoing is not included in the literal meaning. The rabbis of the Talmud, for reasons unknown, rejected the simple, literal meaning of the phrase and preferred the applied meaning. Not that putting a physical stumbling block before a physically blinded man was permitted, according to the rabbis of the Talmud. There is another verse that forbids it: "Cursed be he that makes the blind go astray in the way" (Deut. 27:18). (By relegating it to the other verse in Deuteronomy, they made it less of a crime, only a curse. Removing redundancy, therefore, is not the motive. When the rabbis perceived a redundancy, it was usually the less severe that is exposited.)

What makes this example unique is not the abandonment of the simple meaning as such—there are many instances where the rabbis of the Talmud abandoned the literal meaning—but that they did so in a case where the abandonment was least expected. And what is more, they did not even find it necessary to explain why, unlike the Samaritans (and the Sadducees), they did not subsume the placing of a physical stumbling block before an actual blind man under the biblical injunction. We would have expected them to include all three categories under this injunction: placing a physical stumbling block, giving false advice, and abetting wrongdoing. They were completely silent about this. In the other instances an explanation, usually based on a redundancy of a word or a letter, is given for the abandonment of the simple, literal meaning. Here, it is simply ignored. The attachment to the simple, literal meaning, which is so unflinching in the modern exegete, held no special allure for the rabbis of the Talmud. They easily dispensed with it, sometimes, as in this instance, not even explaining its absence.[34]

One ought not, however, deduce from the above example that the rabbis of the Talmud were aware of the simple, literal meaning as we understand it, and always attributed such a view to the Samaritans (and the Sadducees). Our sense and the rabbis' sense of what constitutes simple, literal meaning do not always agree. Their sense of the simple, literal meaning was more inclusive.[35] They felt less committed to our limited sense of peshat, seeing it instead as larger and wider in scope. To the rabbis, there was less of a distinction between simple and applied meaning with respect to both scope and primacy of peshat than there is to us. Scope, too, is subject to the respective differences in the interpretive state of mind between the rabbis and the modern exegete, and it is reflected accordingly. We have a narrower definition of, and a greater commitment to, the simple, literal meaning. For the rabbis, the Samaritans (and Sadducees) were the representatives par excellence of the simple literal meaning. Yet, on the same page where the Talmud transmits the Samaritans' (and the Sadducees') interpretations of the verse in Lev. 19:14 (with respect to the stumbling block), it also attributes to them in a slightly different context an exposition of Deut. 19:14 that even by rabbinic standards is farfetched. Thus the rabbis did not equate peshat with simple, literal meaning as we know it, but with a wider scope of expositions. Indeed, most, if not all of the rebuttals offered (in the *b. Menach.* 65a–66a and parallels) against the Sadducees' interpretation of "the morrow of the Sabbath" (Lev. 23:15) do not coincide with our sense of what constitutes the simple, literal meaning.[36] That could be said also about other biblical expositions attributed to the Samaritans (and the Sadducees) in other places in the Talmud (particularly in *b. Hor.* 4a). The rabbis clearly do not conform to our sense of the simple, literal meaning. If one assumes that the rabbis subscribed to our sense of peshat, then these examples may cause us to view the rabbis as inconsistent in their perception of Samaritan (and Sadducean) laws. In fact, however, they were quite consistent. Those laws that the rabbis, not necessarily we today, considered explicitly stated they thought ought to be binding even on the Samaritans (and Sadducees); whereas those laws that they considered derived from reading in (or adding to), though equally binding on themselves, were nevertheless treated as nonexplicit and therefore not binding on the Samaritans (and Sadducees).

Asmakhta: Biblical Support for Rabbinic Law

Aside from understanding the meaning of peshat, one also has to reconcile the thesis that rabbinic exegesis is timebound, that the rabbis of the Talmud viewed peshat differently than we do today, with the history and employment of the concept of *asmakhta* (support), found frequently in the Talmud. Some medieval scholars[37] applied this term to the relationship between peshat and derash, asserting that the rabbis of the Talmud knew, if not in all cases, at least in most of them, that reading in does *not* represent the genuine meaning of the text, that the content occasioned by reading in is either rooted in tradition or is rabbinically instituted. The biblical verses quoted are not the sources of content, only their "support." They were cited either to add authority to the tradition by showing that it was already vaguely hinted at in the written law or to facilitate memorization. (Later laws are more easily remembered when they are studied and remembered together with the Bible.)[38] If this is true there is no need to posit timebound barriers between the rabbis of the Talmud and the modern exegete. The mindset remains more or less the same, but now that the oral law is also written and visibly separated from the written law, the need to "ornament" rabbinic (or traditional) ordinances with biblical verses (the condiment of authority) or to facilitate memorization through some connection to the Bible is not as urgent or pressing. The modern exegete may avail himself less of the *asmakhta* than the rabbis did in halakha. In principle, however, he understands it. In a similar situation he might even duplicate it. In fact, modern preachers do much the same in aggada, using Scriptural verses for ornamental purposes in their sermons. The rabbis may have overdone it; they did not misdo it.

I do not believe that the rabbis considered reading in extraneous to the "true" meaning, nor were the verses of the Bible they used intended to be a merely decorative support. The word *asmakhta* (first used relatively late, in the fifth century) is never employed in talmudic sources as a means of explaining the repugnance of reading in, since the rabbis of the Talmud, unlike the rabbis of medieval times, did not consider reading in offensive. The word is exclusively used in a situation where a law contains a biblical prooftext, yet is treated as though it were rabbinically instituted. There are differences with respect to severity of observance between a law which is biblically commanded and a law which is rabbinically ordained.[39] When practical behavior (based on respected authority) treats a law as being of the second category, while the official formulation of the law attaches it to a biblical verse, the rabbis may declare that the verse is *asmakhta*, implying that the verse is not really the source of the law and that the law rightly behaves as a rabbinically instituted one. *Asmakhta* arose in the early fifth century because of the increasing number of rabbinic ordinances having biblical prooftexts. Prior to that time rabbinic ordinances or their equivalent were considered biblically charged since, according to the interpretation prevalent throughout Jewish history, the Bible (Deut. 17:8–12) gave the sages the right to institute new laws. In effect, the sages were acting on behalf of the Bible. Sectarians knew no difference between what was later called *de-oraita* (biblical) and *de-rabbanan* (rabbinic). The list of prohibitions in Jubilees 49–50, for instance, contains both laws that are written in the Bible and laws that were added later (presumably by the scholars) without a discernible difference. The Babylonian Talmud (*Yevam.* 90b, *Sanh.* 46a) reports that during the Hellenistic rule (pre-Hasmonean) a man was put to death by stoning for having ridden a horse on the Sabbath— a rabbinic prohibition. There was no difference between biblical and rabbinic. The blessing recited to this day before the performance of a rabbinic ordinance is the same as the one recited before the performance of a biblical commandment, namely: "Blessed be Thou, O Lord our God, King of the universe, who has sanctified us with your commandments and bid us to. . . ." Biblical and rabbinic ordinances are both divine commandments. The origin of the blessing is pretannaitic, and it was equally applied to both, biblical and rabbinic. The difference in severity between a biblical injunction and a rabbinic ordinance most likely emerged during the tannaitic period. The first clear distinction we hear made between biblical and rabbinic is by sages contemporaries of R. Joshua (*m. Yad.* 3:2), a late first century Palestinian scholar. Subsequently, the number of rabbinic ordinances increased not only because the rabbis added new ordinances,[40] but also because gradually a great many laws previously considered biblical (with prooftexts) now became rabbinic. For a while it looked as if some rabbinic ordinances were both biblical and rabbinic, rabbinic in nature and biblical in their scriptural justification.

Ultimately, the question arose how can a rabbinic law be accompanied by a biblical prooftext and remain rabbinically ordained. It took approximately three hundred years from the time of R. Joshua until R. Ashi (d. in 427)[41] to suggest the term *asmakhta*. He in turn most likely was influenced by Rava (died c. 353) who is quoted in three places in the Babylonian Talmud (*Sukk.* 28b, *Kid.* 9a, *Nid.* 32a–b) to the effect that certain laws, though contained within biblical expositions, are traditions (presumably given to Moses on Mount Sinai, not yet rabbinic) which the rabbis later attached to verses of the Bible. It is mentioned in the Talmud only once (*Yev.* 52b) that R. Ashi used the term *asmakhta*. The term spread, however, quite rapidly; for the *stammaim*—the anonymous authors of sections of the Talmud, who flourished soon after R. Ashi—utilized it close to twenty-five times. By the eleventh century the notion of *asmakhta* had come to mean any biblical exposition that did not live up to current standards of exegesis. This meaning is medieval, not talmudic. Nowhere does the Talmud use the word *asmakhta* in connection with an exposition that has overstepped the boundaries of interpretation and violated what seems to be the genuine meaning of the text. Nowhere in the Talmud[42] do we find the word *asmakhta* (or any other word or phrase for that matter) used as an apology for reading in.[43] The rabbis of the Talmud, unlike their colleagues of the Middle Ages, did not consider reading in a violation of the integrity of the text as long as the whole verse was involved and no part of it was taken out of context. That may not suit our exegetical sensibilities, but it cannot be denied.

A good illustration is the passage in *b. Chul.* 17b. It reads as follows:

> R. Hisda said: Whence do we learn from Scripture that it is necessary to examine the slaughtering knife? from the verse (in 1 Sam. 14:34): "And slaughter with this and eat" ("with this" means the knife examined and checked). But is it not obviously necessary to do so since if the gullet is perforated the animal is *terefa*, unkosher? [will not a knife with a notch most certainly perforate and tear the gullet, asks the *stam*, the anonymous author, and answers:] We mean, whence do we learn from Scripture that it is essential that the knife be examined by a sage? [And that is from the verse: "And slaughter with this (the knife examined by the sage) and eat."] But surely does not R. Yochanan say that the ruling that one must present the knife to a sage for examination was laid down only out of respect to the sages? The rule is actually rabbinic, and the verse adduced is an *asmakhta*, merely a support.

The simple, literal meaning of "and slaughter with this" has nothing to do with examining the knife by the sage or by anybody else. It means slaughter the animal here on the stone (referred to in 1 Sam. 14:33). Nevertheless, the *stammaim* were willing to accept R. Hisda's exposition of that verse in 1 Samuel, even though it is against the simple, literal meaning. They categorized it as asmakhta only because R. Yochanan declared the examination of the slaughter knife by a sage to be rabbinically ordained. The discrepancy between the text and the exposition did not bother them.

Talmudic Attitudes Toward Reading In

But, the perceptive reader may wonder, is not the very need for an *asmakhta* to resolve the contradictory nature of rabbinic ordinances having biblical prooftexts an indication that the process of reading in was gradually weakening during the talmudic period? Were it in full force, rabbinic ordinances with biblical prooftexts—

at least some of them—would have been integrated into the text through reading in and would have constituted a bona fide biblical exposition. And, is not the tendency toward a sharp distinction between what is biblical and what is rabbinic a sign that a greater consciousness of what the text really says was slowly emerging? Because the text is no longer saying what was attributed to it, the law that was derived from the text is no longer part of the text, and hence no longer biblical. If so, reading in was not so prevalent during the talmudic period and the rabbis' interpretive state of mind with respect to peshat was not after all much different from our own, at least not in the fifth century when *asmakhta* arose and rabbinic ordinances proliferated.

My answer to this is: similar signs and indications can be found already at the end of the first century. When R. Joshua, a first century Palestinian scholar, used the Hebrew word *vadai*[44] in the sense of simple, literal meaning, when he is purported to have said that a certain biblical verse ought to be understood *bevadai* (literally), against the view of his colleague, R. Eleazar of Modi'im who interpreted the verse nonliterally, R. Joshua attached a value judgment to the simple, literal meaning. The word *vadai* in rabbinic literature overwhelmingly appears in contrast to *safek* (doubt). *Vadai* means "certain, real." When used as a synonym for simple, literal meaning, it conveys the notion that the simple, literal meaning is truer, more certain, more real than any other meaning. Preferability of peshat over derash is implied. Are we to assume that already in the first century reading in was in a state of irresolution?

No. Neither the need for an *asmakhta* nor the increase of rabbinic ordinances in the fifth century nor the use of the word *vadai* in the sense of simple, literal meaning at the end of the first century constitute a break with the past. They represent intimations of what was to come, stirrings of new ideas. R. Joshua and those that followed him in the use of the word *vadai* in the sense of simple, literal meaning continued their biblical exposition in a manner undifferentiated from their predecessors. Despite the implication of the word *vadai* when used in that sense, they remained unaffected by it. Their biblical expositions did not change because of it. They remained the same expositors. This explains why Rava, the father of *asmakhta* (who in criticizing his colleague Abaye's interpretation of Num. 27:11 expresses [*b. B. Ba.* 111b] a modern sentiment against rabbinic midrash in general, namely that they "take a sharp knife and dissect biblical verses") is offering an alternative interpretation of the verse in a way that is jarring to a modern ear.[45] The old and new intermingled. Among the rebuttals offered (in *b. Menach.* 65b–66a and parallels) against the Sadducees' interpretation of "the morrow of the sabbath," Rava does not choose the one that is to our taste, the closest to the simple, literal meaning.[46] Rava sensed what was coming in the future but remained anchored in the past. And it continued that way until medieval times.

This is not to say that the rabbis' interpretive state of mind remained static, until medieval times. The entirety of chapter two is devoted to proving the contrary, that there was a linear development stretching from the late biblical books to our own times in the direction of greater respect for the integrity of the text. This respect can be partially equated with the simple, literal meaning. I say partially only because staying closer to the integrity of the text does not necessarily imply also staying closer to authorial intention, which is commonly identified with the simple, literal meaning. "Integrity of the text" means no violence to the substantive meaning of the text, no twisting of the text. A certain type of adding to the text, for example, may not be congruous with authorial intention, yet not violate the tenor of the text. Making earlier texts refer to later events may run counter to authorial intention but not necessarily to the words and context of the text. In the following chapter, we also state that reading in, in the more technical sense of displacing the simple, literal meaning as a mode of interpretation, was discontinued in the third century if not earlier. From the third century on, rabbinic exegesis displays a noticeable trend away from reading in (used here as an inclusive term for any interpretation that requires straining the words or the context of the text). Rabbinic exegesis was far from being static.

What I have been saying up to this point is that neither the need for *asmakhta* nor the increase of rabbinic ordinances (certainly not the use of the word *vadai*, which took place in the first century) indicates that the rabbis of the Talmud emphasized peshat to the extent of retroactively interpreting earlier expositions (*derashot*) to make them compatible with their sense of the value of peshat. This was done only during the Middle Ages. In talmudic times, even as late as the fifth century, the simple, literal meaning had not yet acquired such an authority. Instead, the rabbis of the Talmud sanctioned earlier *derashot* that were not in line with their own sense of interpretive priority.[47] They recognized the validity of such *derashot* only if they were composed in the past. The authority of the past overcame their internal opposition and they accepted these *derashot* without trying to explain them away. The exegetical policy of explaining away the *Derashot* of the past became a hallmark of medieval interpretation.

Metaphor as Plain Meaning

I ought to remark that throughout I am using the word *literal* as a synonym for *peshat* (plain meaning). It is not intended to exclude metaphors or allegories, etc. from being *peshat*. Sometimes, in fact, a metaphorical or allegorical interpretation is the plain meaning, the peshat, borne out by the text. Rather, the terms *literal* and *peshat* exclude an interpretation which is not implied by the extant literature, an interpretation which is extraneous to the text, which is being read into it from the outside. An interesting example is the putting on of the phylacteries. The rabbis and apparently also the sectarians were convinced that the verses in Exod. 13:9 ("This shall serve you as a sign on your hand and as a reminder on your forehead") and in Deut. 6:8 ("Bind them as a sign on your hand and let them serve as a frontlet on your forehead") command the placing of actual boxes, containing certain biblical passages, on the forehead and on the hand.[48] They interpreted the verses "literally," not metaphorically. However, the plain meaning, the peshat, supports the contention that the verses, particularly the verse in Exodus, ought to be understood metaphorically.[49] Here the rabbis deviated from the peshat by being literal. They, on the other hand, did not even find it necessary, either in the tannaitic *Mekhilta* on Exodus or in the tannaitic *Sifrei* on Deuteronomy, to raise and reject the possibility of a metaphorical interpretation. It is characteristic of midrash to posit untenable expositions and reject them. In connection with the putting on of the phylacteries, the possibility of a metaphorical interpretation was not even offered as an exposition, so convinced were the rabbis of the literal meaning of these verses. Only in medieval times, when the exegetical temper had changed, was the possibility of a metaphorical interpretation seriously considered. The Karaites[50] advocated it; and even some Rabbanites, like the Rashbam, thought that the peshat favored a metaphorical interpretation. With the new state of mind closer to what we today call peshat, the tendency was more toward a metaphorical interpretation, the literal being ruled out as not according with the peshat.

Changing Mindsets: A Homeric Analogy

Conventionally, historians allow for a broad intellectual understanding of earlier periods. Even when they posit irreversible trends, permanent changes, newly emergent qualities, etc., they do not assume radical breaks. Some level of continuity remains, allowing the intelligent person from any period to comprehend the intellectual activity of another period. Applied to the realm of exegesis, that would mean that an interpretation of a text offered in an earlier period should be comprehensible to a person of a later period, though he may not necessarily agree with that interpretation. He at least should be able to conceive of the earlier exposition as an exegetical possibility. However, if we accept the notion that the rabbis of the Talmud occasionally considered reading in as reflective of the true meaning of the text, we are positing a distinct discontinuity in exegetical tradition. A modern exegete cannot comprehend reading in as conveying the intention of the author. In order to understand the rabbis' mentality, the modern exegete must accept that what is exegetically impossible for him and his contemporaries was actually quite possible two thousand years ago. Moreover, he must both posit and overcome distance. Recognizing that he is far removed from the rabbis' mode of exegesis, that he is, so to speak, operating on different interpretive wavelengths, he must yet try to grasp their state of mind, appreciate their exegetical flavor. To do this is not easy. Paradoxical relationships are not accepted easily. Direct explanation will not help, since the terms that go into the explanation, the components that are supposed to make the explanation intelligible, are not transferable from period to period. Unlike the conventional view, the periods remain distinct, each one with its own mode of cognition, not necessarily accessible to people from another period.

An analogy may help explain this difference between periods. By showing that there are more instances like the one I posited in connection with reading into a text, drawn from totally different subjects, but sharing similar intellectual patterns, the modern exegete may become more credulous. Admittedly, analogies do not elucidate the inner reason of the object under question; they do, however, make it more believable, undermining the logical objections. For retaining paradoxes as paradoxes, that is without dissolving their contradictory content, nothing is as efficacious as analogy. It keeps the paradox intact, protects it from objections. Analogy is anchored in fact, whereas the logical objections are based on reason. Therefore, the former always has the right of way. To support the notion that reading in was once considered to be the true, more palpable meaning, I will quote an analogy from Homeric studies. The subject is distant enough yet demands a similar exertion on the part of the exegete to abandon his present mode of thinking in order to grasp the state of mind of an earlier period. I am referring to Bruno Snell's thesis that the Greeks of Homer's day had no conscious idea of a unified human self or a unified human body.[51]

For a modern man, it is difficult to conceive of someone who describes in great detail the different human limbs and their multiple functions without being aware of the body as a whole; or of someone who depicts with depth and insight various intellectual activities without being aware of the intellect as such; or of someone who know life's intricacies but not the soul. Yet that is what Homeric man was, according to Snell. The *Iliad* and the *Odyssey* never refer to, nor even have words for, the soul, the intellect, or the body. This trio's disparate actions fill the pages of these epic poems, but they themselves are never mentioned as such. To us parts must add up to a whole; limbs, functions and activities imply something larger, more inclusive, an abstract unifier, an organic whole. Not so to those ancient Greeks. Their state of mind did not necessitate the concept of unified wholes. They saw everything as aggregates, as constituents, not unity—a phenomenon incomprehensible to a modern man. Therein lies the analogy to the reading in into a text of the rabbis. In both instances, modern man's incomprehension is due not to a lack of information, nor to not knowing all the pertinent facts, but to a chronological, timebound barrier. Were the ancient Greeks asked (given all the relevant evidence) to explain how they can ignore the unified body, unified intellect, and the unified soul; or were the rabbis asked (given all the relevant evidence) to account for their acceptance of reading in as reflecting the genuine intention of the author, they would respectively answer that they do not feel these tensions, that they do not see them. What separates modern man from the Homeric lack of a concept of the whole and from the exegesis of the rabbis is not the higher degree of knowledge accumulated in the course of generations, or a more complete set of reliable data, but the inexorable clock of universal time. Little can be done to change it other than to try to empathize, to lift oneself out of one's contemporary mindset, if only for a while, in order not to cavalierly dismiss the thoughts of an earlier period, or, what is worse, to distort them apologetically, denying a priori that people could have had such conceptions.[52]

It should be noted that according to our approach, the choice is not between acceptance or rejection of rabbinic exegesis. It is both acceptance and rejection. It is rejection because for a person today to read into a text is tantamount to falsifying that text. It is acceptance because on our account, we do not attribute falsification to the rabbis. Their reading into the text was as authentic then as is our aversion to it today. There is no single exegetical criterion, no single interpretive state of mind uniting all periods. This, however, does not necessarily imply that the criterion of a particular generation is entirely arbitrary. Exegesis from one generation to the next has inexorably evolved in one direction—that of diminishing textual yield. As time marched on, the text per se seems to have yielded less and less. That process is far from being concluded.

2

The Direction of
Rabbinic Exegesis

The history of rabbinic exegesis consists of biblical exegesis (as practiced by the rabbis of the Talmud) and talmudic exegesis (the way the rabbis of the Talmud interpreted the Mishnah and other authoritative rabbinic texts). Rabbinic biblical exegesis and talmudic exegesis overlap in time but are distinct in nature, each with its own momentum of change, each with its own course of development. Their constitutive parts display different modes of assumption, different inner creative forces. Yet both, over time, tended toward a greater preference for less interference with the actual wording of the text, a greater preference for peshat.

Biblical Exegesis: Historical Survey

Reading In: From the Bible to the Third Century C.E.

The process of reading in, in the sense of diplacing the content of the simple meaning (the case of "an eye for an eye" serves as a paradigm),[1] has its origin in antiquity. Perhaps even in late biblical times,[2] this way was employed to solve contradictions found, for instance, in 2 Chr. 35:13· "and they cooked the Passover (lamb) with fire." This unusual combination of cooking with fire (cooking is usually done with water) is the result of a harmonization of Exod. 12:9 ("Do not eat it [the Passover] raw or cooked in water") and

23

Deut. 16:17 ("And you shall cook and eat [the Passover]").[3] Other instances of reading in may not be as early as late biblical times, but they are nevertheless quite early, dating back to tannaitic times, and I venture to say early tannaitic. I cannot point to a single case of reading in that can plausibly be attributed to a late *tanna*, let alone to an *amora*. By the third century, during the period of the *amoraim*, reading in was long discontinued in halakha (though the practice has continued in Aggadah to this day).[4] It was a privilege granted in the past that could not be granted in the present.

However, what is unclear is whether reading in of the kind "where the rabbis negate the interpretation of the verse but do not deny the content of that interpretation,"[5] because the content is derived from another source, was also not practiced by rabbis after the third century. (An example of this sort is the verse "Fathers shall not be put to death for the children" [Deut. 24:16], which the rabbis interpret to mean that children shall not testify on behalf of their fathers. The rabbis derive the principle that parents shall not be put to death for their children's sin from the end of the verse: "every man shall be put to death for his own sins." The prohibition against accepting children's testimony on behalf of their fathers changes the exegesis of the first half of the verse, but it does not displace its content.) Specifically, for example, I am not sure at what time the rabbis changed the exegesis of the verse in Lev. 19:14: "You shall not put a stumbling block before a blind person" to mean "You shall not give false advice to a spiritually blind person," negating the interpretation but not the content. For there is another verse, Deut. 27:18, which says "Cursed be he that makes the blind go astray in the way," prohibiting putting a physical stumbling block before a physically blind person.[6] When was the exegetical negation of this verse first expressed? *I do not know.* R. Nathan, a second-century scholar, went beyond the "false advice" interpretation to include also abetting wrongdoing.[7] In his time, it seems, the false advice interpretation was already an accepted interpretation to which he added abetting wrongdoing. Both, however, were probably additions to the text (implying that just as you cannot put a physical stumbling block, so too you cannot put a spiritual stumbling block), not intended to displace the simple meaning even exegetically. When did the exegetical displacement take place? I do not know, but I suspect after the time of R. Nathan.

Textual Implication: The Amoraic Period

In the absence of reading in, the method most employed during the talmudic period after the third century was the *textual implication* method. During that period, virtually all halakhic deductions, as against the tannaitic period where some deductions were based on "reading in," were now made somehow to reside in the text, sometimes based on a supposed textual superfluity. The expositions were relatively simple with the early *amoraim* and became progressively more complicated with the stammaim [427–520]. R. Yochanan, a third-century Palestinian scholar, one of the early *amoraim*, deduces, for instance, from the use of the word "times" in the phrase in Esth. 9:31 ("To confirm these days of Purim in their appointed times") that "they instituted to them many times." Beside the regular reading of the *Megilla* (the scroll of Esther) on the fourteenth of Adar, "The *Megilla* is read also on the eleventh, twelfth, and thirteenth." The exposition is based on the extra letters of *bizmaneihem* instead of *bizmanam*, "times" instead of "time." This is a relatively simple *derasha* (exposition). On the other hand, the *stammaim*, for instance, in *b. Pesach* 41b,[8] went so far as to deduce from the variation of the text *bashel mevushal* (Exod. 12:9)—the usual combination in Hebrew of the verb and its infinitive[9]—two separate expositions: that the Passover lamb that had been boiled in water or other liquids could not be eaten, and that if the flesh was boiled during the day, it was forbidden at night. It should be noted that this discussion is stammaitic, although it incorporates the statement of Rabbi, a *tanna* who lived earlier.[10]

It was during the amoraic period that the notion *ein mikra yotze middei peshuto*, that "no text can be deprived of its peshat," originated. *Peshat* in this phrase does not mean "simple, plain meaning," as was usually assumed during the Middle Ages and thereafter. The phrase is not, as it is so often thought to be, an anti–reading in crusade. That crusade took place only during the Middle Ages. Peshat here means context. This dictum is against reading in only when the context is violated, when no consideration whatsoever is given to the continuation of the verse (as in the case of levirate marriage [Deut. 25:6] quoted in chap. 1 of this essay). It is not against reading in when the context is not violated, when due consideration is given to what was said before and after the verse.[11] Perhaps because of the paucity of cases in talmudic exegesis (the interpretation of Mishnah and other authoritative rabbinic texts) where context is ignored, we have no parallel warning to adhere to context. We do not have a similar phrase *ein mishnah yotzet middei peshutah*, that no Mishnah can be deprived of its peshat, of its context. It was rare— though such cases are not entirely absent from the Talmud—that an *amora* or the *stam* interpreted a Mishnah inordinately against the context. No explicit warning against doing so was necessary.

Halakha in Post-Talmudic Times

It should be noted that in post-talmudic times we hardly come across a new halakha, a new law, derived solely from a biblical exposition.[12] That is probably because the Talmud so preempted the Bible as a source for the halakha that the latter as a source of new law was, as it were, pushed aside, even though the Talmud was, of course, ultimately based on the Bible. Moreover, in early post-talmudic times it looked as if the *posekim*, the scholars who decided practical matters, were oblivious to biblical study and concentrated their scholarly activity almost exclusively on the Talmud.[13] This changed, however, with the rise in the tenth century of R. Saadya Gaon, who excelled in both biblical and talmudic studies. And this versatility continues through the twelfth and thirteenth centuries. Great *posekim* were also biblical commentators. Rashi (eleventh century), Rashbam (twelfth century), and Ramban (thirteenth century) were the most outstanding ones, but not the only ones. Simultaneously, during this period there seems to have arisen a new class of grammarians and biblical commentators like R. Y. ibn Ganach (early eleventh century) and R. A. ibn Ezra (1089–1164),[14] particularly in Spain, who did not excel in talmudic studies, but who saw in the study of Scripture, directly (as commentators) or indirectly (as philologists) their occupation. Eventually the two disciplines became separated, and the evolution of biblical and talmudic exegesis proceeded even more along different paths.

Despite the discontinuation of reading in, the rabbis of the talmudic period did not seriously challenge the right of their predecessors to have used that method. They seem to have granted the right to their predecessors but not to themselves. Their conviction against reading in was not absolute or thorough enough to impel them to criticize their authoritative predecessors. Their aversion, derived from their interpretive state of mind, was sufficiently strong to prevent them from doing it themselves, but not strong enough to question the legitimacy of such an activity when done in earlier times, having become by now a part of tradition. The past thus remained beyond criticism.

In contrast, during the Middle Ages, starting with Saadya Gaon and continuing at least until the thirteenth century, the aversion to reading in was so strong that it was applied retroactively to the past. The interpretive state of mind of the medieval rabbis allowed no exceptions, either of time or personality. They abstained from reading in even in aggada, the nonlegal material in the Bible. Never before or after, with the exception of the modern critical scholars who practice the "direct-textual reference" method, was there such a rigorous standard adopted against reading in, in all its facets. The medieval exegetes felt compelled to deny that the rabbis of the past occasionally read into a text, and as a result they were apologetic about their predecessors' expositions and sometimes even twisted them so that it would appear as if they were not reading in. Reading in in all its forms was absolutely barred.

The Middle Ages: Rashbam and Ibn Ezra

To be sure, the response to the challenge of the past was not uniform. The two greatest "peshatists" of the Middle Ages, the Rashbam and Ibn Ezra (twelfth century), did not embrace the same opinion. The Rashbam was most insistent on the peshat. He was also more accepting of redundancy (of an extra word or letter) as a legitimate source for halakhic expositions. He could afford to adhere strictly to peshat even when it ran counter to practical halakha because the practical halakha rejected by peshat was almost always readmitted via a redundancy. It remained equally binding, equally authoritative. In contrast, Ibn Ezra, because of his reluctance to accept redundancy as a source of halakhic exposition, had to be less insistent on peshat in order to preserve the halakha, especially in those instances where the *derasha* displaced the simple meaning and canceled its content, and thus he could not attribute the *derasha* to an *asmakhta*, a mere biblical support. In his introduction to the second version of his commentary, which deals with methodological problems, Ibn Ezra is ready to compromise peshat (as we understand it) when it contradicts a practical halakha and assume that the rabbis of the Talmud must have known better what constitutes the true peshat. Ibn Ezra insists that we must trust them.[15] Such was Ibn Ezra's commitment to the ultimate value of peshat that he could not conceive of the rabbis' having violated it. Even when it appears that they did violate the peshat, he thought, we must assume, against our better judgment, that such was not the case.[16]

From the Fourteenth to the Eighteenth Century

From the fourteenth to the eighteenth century there is a paucity[17] of creative biblical commentaries. The most significant commentator of the period, R. O. Seforno (1470–1550, a man of the Renaissance), did not live up to the standards of peshat set by the Rashbam and Ibn Ezra. (The commentary of R. I. Abravanel [1437–1508] is in a class by itself. It resembles the pilpulists [the exegetes who indulged in farfetched casuistic deductions] in leaving the substantive meaning intact and concentrating instead on the derivable social, ethical, and political implications. See, for example, his comments on Deut. 17:14–20 on the monarchy.) Yet the period ought not be characterized as a period of retrogression with respect to commitment to peshat, thus challenging our concept of developmental exegesis. The commitment was there, but the talent was not. In fact, during that period a number of commentaries were actually written on Rashi and Ibn Ezra and a few also on Ramban. They survived only in manuscript form (the Rashbam's commentary was not printed until 1705 and was not known during the period under consideration).[18] But the fact that they were written indicates a sympathy for the stance these scholars embody. Also, no sign of condemnation of heresy against the peshatists appears during this period, further indicating that there was no rupture with the peshatist tradition, only a failure of ability. The same Seforno who, for instance, in his commentary on Exod. 21–23 often deviates from the simple meaning (see in particular 23:2), moves much closer to peshat in his commentary on Deut. 24–25 (see in particular 24:16 and 25:6). This inconsistency in the sense of not accepting a uniform exegetical standard is reminiscent of the commentary of R. Jacob Tur (essentially an abridgement of the Ramban) two hundred years earlier (1270–1340). (For inconsistencies in Tur, see, for instance, his comments on Exod. 23:2, where he quotes two interpretations, only the second being in line with the peshat; his comment to Deut. 16:7, however, is totally against peshat). In comparison with the Rashbam and Ibn Ezra, even Rashi (1040–1105)[19] and the Ramban (1194–1274) appear inconsistent. Inconsistency is not a sign of a rupture with the peshatist persuasion. Within the same interpretive state of mind, different levels of compliance may coexist.

In the eighteenth century there arose a greater sense that peshat could not be compromised. Peshat yielded less and less to derash and gradually became the sole exegetical mode of interpretation. Even the Rashbam, the arch-peshatist of the medieval period, compromised with peshat by recognizing through redundancy the exegetical legitimacy of derash. During this period, however, derash was gradually losing its exegetical—though not its practical—grip, to the extent that by the nineteenth and twentieth centuries, derash dissolved into peshat.

The Eighteenth Century: Moses Mendelssohn

It was also during this period that a very significant commentary appeared. Closely following the commentary of Ibn Ezra, the *Biur* of Moses Mendelssohn (1729–1786) and his collaborators, a German translation and commentary on the Bible, is considered by many as the most notable biblical scholarly achievement of the eighteenth century. In the introduction (pp. 26–27) Mendelssohn paraphrases the above-quoted summary of Ibn Ezra's fourth and fifth methods. He says:

> When the peshat is not contrary to the derash [in our terminology, whenever the derash is merely an addition to the peshat] . . . then the peshat will be the main meaning [reflected in the translation] and the derash will be the secondary meaning. . . . When, however, what seems to us to be the peshat is different and contradicts the accepted interpretation [in our terminology, whenever there is a reading in] . . . then it is our duty to follow the derash and translate the text accordingly.[20]

Since the work was also a translation, the omission of the rabbinic additions was all the more glaring and exhibited tangible attachment to peshat. On the other hand, the inclusion of reading in may have been a concession to public piety. Left to himself and his entourage, he may have followed the peshat both where it was and where it was not against halakha. Had Mendelssohn followed the Rashbam, his translation would have been more uniformly in accordance with the peshat. It should also be remembered that the Rashbam's commentary on the Torah was relatively unknown to the public during the time of Mendelssohn,[21] and relying on him in a translation might have caused undue commotion. However, in the introduction, Mendelssohn says of the Rashbam "that his love of peshat has caused him occasionally to deviate from the truth." This statement has the ring of sincerity; Mendelssohn was genuinely uncomfortable with the Rashbam's utter commitment to *peshat*.[22]

Moreover, Mendelssohn most likely would not have accepted redundancy as a legitimate mode of interpretation. He reviewed very positively Robert Lowth's book *De sacra poesi Hebracorum, praelectiones academicae Oxonii habitae* (1753), an appreciation of biblical poetic style.[23] Without the "backup" of redundancy as the source for derash, it would have been theologically almost impossible for Mendelssohn to adopt the Rashbam's stricter commitment to peshat. It would have left him without justification of those practices that were based on derash.

In the eighteenth century, the interpretive state of mind in the direction of greater acceptance of peshat was quite pronounced. The question is however: are Mendelssohn and his entourage good representatives of rabbinic exegesis? They were so influenced by the outside world, by the non-Jewish world, that they may no longer count as a bona fide link in the chain of traditional biblical exegesis. The evolution of non-Jewish biblical scholarship must be traced through a different line. Mendelssohn and his collaborators were recipients of both traditions, the Jewish and the non-Jewish. They were heirs to both evolutions and as such may not reflect genuine rabbinic exegesis—the subject of our essay.

The Gaon of Vilna

A far better representative of rabbinic exegesis in the eighteenth century is the Gaon of Vilna (1720-1797). In his commentary on the Torah, called *Aderet Eliyahu*, he sporadically displays an attachment to peshat surpassing his predecessors. Of interest is his comment at the beginning of *Mishpatim*. There he compares the contradiction between peshat and "tradition" (which we call derash) to a seal. The visible letters are inverted, but the impression they make on the paper is straight. The peshat is like the inverted letters of the seal—that is why one has to study peshat—and the tradition is like the impression the inverted letters make on the paper. As the impession is different from the inverted letters, so too is tradition different from the peshat. How do inverted letters turn into a straight impression? How does peshat turn into tradition? He does not explain, other than saying "that is the greatness of the oral law that was given to Moses on Mount Sinai, that it abolishes the *mikra*," the reading of the peshat, the exegetical meaning of the text.[24] "Tradition," derash, does not claim textual validity. It does what it does because "of the greatness of the oral law." The two are qualitatively different. For practical purposes, we follow the impression, but the inverted letters remain the object of exegesis. In that respect, the Gaon is closer to peshat than Ibn Ezra or Rashbam. Peshat is the sole expression of the text even when it "contradicts the accepted interpretation."

For our purpose of showing the developmental trend toward greater acceptance of peshat, it is enough that in the time of the Gaon the autonomy of peshat was further enhanced. The Gaon's approach represents an advancement over his predecessors. Perhaps it is not out of place to note here that the Gaon supposedly also said "just as there are peshat and derash in the study of the Bible, so are there peshat and derash in the study of Mishnah."[25] That means one has a right to interpret the Mishnah according to peshat even when that interpretation contradicts the Gemara's interpretation. This widening of the sphere of peshat is in line with the Gaon's greater attachment to peshat, of which the above quoted passage from *Mishpatim* is an example.

The Nineteenth and Twentieth Centuries: Meklenburg, Malbim, Netziv, D. Z. Hoffmann, and M. S. Hakohen

More striking as an indication of the latest interpretive state of mind of rabbinic biblical exegesis is the nineteenth-twentieth cen-

tury apologists' school. Prominent among them were J. Z. Meklenburg (1785–1865),[26] the author of the *Ha-ketav veha-Kabbala*, Malbim (1809–1879),[27] Netziv (1817–1893),[28] D. Z. Hoffmann (1843–
1921)[29] and to some degree also R. M. S. Hakohen (1843–1926), the
author of *Meshekh Chokhma*.[30] Rosen and the Netziv differ from
the others in that they were primarily talmudists, not biblical scholars, and treated the Bible as if it were a talmudic text,[31] every word
bearing halakhic import (the Malbim started out as a talmudist but
devoted his later life increasingly to biblical studies). Also, unlike
the others, their major aim was not to counter the critics of rabbinic
exegesis. Their peshat-oriented work seems to have been more
homegrown. But like them, and unlike the Gaon of Vilna, whose
students' students they were, they saw no split between peshat and
derash. Derash is grounded in peshat. It is "peshat-in-depth" and it
is the task of the exegete to bring this out. Their commitment to
peshat was so complete that they saw no legitimacy in derash. Only
peshat has legitimacy (at least in halakhic matters), and for derash
to be seriously considered it has to show that it is merely another
manifestation of peshat. It is true that in the course of defending
peshat, in making all the halakhic *derashot* comply with peshat,
they often end up with interpretations that appear to us to be far
from peshat. This is true not only of the Malbim's mythological 613
rules of grammar[32] (paralleling the 613 commandments of the
Torah) on which the oral law rests and which the rabbis of the
Talmud employed, but also of the most moderate (and most scientific) among them, R. D. Z. Hoffmann, who sometimes goes out on
a limb to anchor a *derasha* in a pseudopeshat even when the
Talmud itself (*Yevam.* 24a) concedes that the Law is against the
peshat (see his comment on Deut. 25:6 in connection with levirate
marriage).[33] Nevertheless, from their perspective the commitment
to *peshat* was unqualified and binding. Their need to burden peshat
so as to make it the exclusive mode of interpretation is testimony to
an increased tenacity to peshat, a clear change in interpretive state
of mind. *Their execution of what constitutes peshat might be faulty,
but their devotion to peshat was complete and consuming.* It is this
devotion rather than their results that sets them apart from their
predecessors. In the past, the devotees of peshat, including the
Rashbam, allowed some measure of legitimacy to derash. Derash
had its place, even when it was not the result of a textual redun-

dancy. In the apologetic school (preceded perhaps by the Maharal [d. 1609][34]) derash had no standing. Peshat was identical with truth. The fact that they were not successful in doing what they wanted to do, to ground all *derashot* in peshat, does not diminish the developmental force operating within them in the direction of closer attachment to peshat. Paradoxically, in order to protect peshat they introduced kinds of interpretations that in the past even scholars moderately committed to peshat would have rejected. However, upon consideration of what *motivated* the members of this school to do what they did, it is evident that the apologists' intention was fully on the side of peshat; thus they represent the latest interpretive state of mind. It should be emphasized again that the trend towards peshat meant not violating the integrity of the text, not necessarily getting closer to authorial intention. With respect to authorial intention, it is true, rabbinic exegesis displays a zigzag pattern of development.

Summary

Let me now briefly restate the different stages of biblical exegesis, and more firmly relate them to the different periods and their nomenclatures. The first period, starting with the late biblical books and continuing not later than the end of the second century (the end of the tannaitic period) was the *period of reading in*. During that period it happened that the simple (or plain) meaning of a biblical text was displaced by read-in meaning, peshat by derash. What the text seems to say was discarded in favor of an interpretation which to us seems to violate the wording of the text. To the rabbis of that period, however, the interpretation apparently was not doing violence to the wording of the text. They did not find compelling what to us appears to be a close reading of the wording of the Bible. Read-in meaning was equally satisfactory.

The second period, starting with the third century (the beginning of the amoraic period) and continuing until the beginning of the sixth century (the end of the period of the *stammaim*) is the *period of textual implication*. A major exegetical activity during that period and beginning much earlier was centered around expositing the full range of the supposed implicit meaning of the text, sometimes through extra phrases, words or even letters. Every halakhic deduction was somehow based on a textual inference. This was not reading in—the process of reading in, in the sense of displacing the simple meaning, was discontinued during that period—but adding to the text. The simple meaning was retained. The new deduction was an addition to, and was not intended to come instead of the simple meaning. The simple meaning and the new deduction did not contradict each other and were not mutually exclusive, as was the case with reading in. Both were retained.

The third period, starting with the posttalmudic period and continuing to the eighteenth century, but with particular forcefulness and clarity during the tenth to the thirteenth centuries, was the period of *the awareness of the value of peshat*. During that period the scholars became aware of the preference of peshat over derash, of plain meaning over read-in meaning, and felt self-conscious about the readings in of previous generations. After the thirteenth century the number of creative biblical commentators who followed the peshat declined. The decline was due not to a devaluation of the exclusive nature of peshat but rather to the impact of the contributions of the giants of peshat, who flourished between the tenth and thirteenth centuries, leaving the later scholars little to add. To this one may also add a decline in exegetical talent of the caliber of the early masters. In principle, however, they were as much committed to peshat as were their immediate pedecessors.

The fourth period, starting in the eighteenth century with the Gaon of Vilna and continuing into our own century is the *period of the uncompromisability of peshat*. (Although the Gaon's idea of the relationship between peshat and what he called tradition [derash] is not identical with the idea of that relationship as it was exposited by his students' students during the nineteenth century and into the twentieth century, the Gaon could still be looked upon as the one who spurred the movement toward peshat in the last three centuries. He placed derash outside the exegetical orbit.) During that period commentaries were written with the assumption that only peshat has a legitimate claim to exegetical truth, so that for derash to be authoritative it has to be grounded in peshat. They accordingly devised means (grammatical and otherwise) for anchoring derash in peshat. The process of such mooring strikes us as being artificial. But that does not detract from their total commitment to peshat—a commitment unparalleled in the past. Previously, allowance was always made for some degree of inherent legitimacy (depending on the period) for derash. In this period, theoretically at least, derash had no rights. The *derashot* of the rabbis of the past were now seen as peshat in disguise ("in depth"). Such a view of peshat is unique and justifies our calling this period the closest to peshat.

Talmudic Exegesis: Historical Survey

As in biblical exegesis, the interpretation of mishnaic and other rabbinic texts was marked by a trend away from interference with the substantive meaning of the text, a trend towards peshat. Talmudic exegesis, from the third century, after the editing of the Mishnah, up to our own times, can be divided into three distinct periods, each period distinguished by its own interpretive state of mind. While within each period there is a movement away from peshat, as a result of the natural tendency to proceed from the simple to the complex (complexity in textual exposition is conducive to distancing from peshat), when the periods are compared historically they confirm the notion of timebound exegesis, showing movement toward a greater acceptance of the substantive meaning of the words of the text which generally (though not, for example, in the case of a metaphor or allegory) is equal to simple meaning. The movement was in the direction of committing less violence to the simple meaning. Each period violated the simple meaning less than its predecessor. Paradoxically, the premodern period, before the scientific critical method, the period of pilpul (in talmudic exegesis and to some extent the apologetic school in biblical exegesis [see above]) strikes many to be least "peshatic," least committed to the simple meaning. Yet it violates the integrity of the text least. Unlike the exegesis of earlier periods, it leaves the text intact and concentrates instead on the text's logical implications. The logic may be incorrect, the implication farfetched; the substance of the text remains, however, unaffected. It teaches how to explore the logical conclusions of a text (whether or not the author intended to imply them) in contrast to the pilpulist's predecessors' exegesis, which taught how to read the words of a text. *Pilpul* violates the peshat less, preserving the integrity of the reading of the text more than the exegesis of the pilpulists' predecessors.

Within the period, however, the scholars who flourished at the beginning were closer to the peshat, violated the simple or plain meaning less than the scholars who lived after them. Early scholars initiating the mode of interpretation characteristic of the period started with expositions implicitly contained in the text, which are usually uncomplicated, suiting the temper of the peshat. In contrast, the scholars who follow them within the same period, operating with the same norms, with the same distinguishing features, and who take for granted the expository contributions of their predecessors as part of tradition, tend to complicate interpretation.[35] They inevitably add expositions that were implicitly deduced (the more obvious ones having been already preempted by their predecessors) the kind which are generally more complex in nature, hence less akin to peshat. The movement within the period thus tends to be from close adherence to less adherence to the peshat, in contrast to the movements from period to period. When the three periods are compared as units, however, they constitute a chronological sequence where the first violates the peshat most, the last, least.

The Nomenclature of the Different Periods

The first period is the period of *setting the text aright*. It covers the talmudic period, from 200 (the editing of the Mishnah) to c. 520 C.E., comprising both the period of the *amoraim* (200 to 427, the death of R. Ashi), and the period of the *stammaim*, the authors of the anonymous sections of the Talmud, 427 to c. 520.[36] Some of the technical terms are *hakhi ke'amar, eima*, etc., expressions that hover between emendation and explanation.[37] The second is the period of *harmonization*. It covers the posttalmudic period, uninterruptedly from the end of the Gemara (poststammaitic) up to, in some circles, our own time. Harmonization is found in the Talmud too, most often as a response to a contradiction between two *baraitot* or between an *amora* and a *beraita* (*lo kashya* is a frequent technical term expressing the beginning of the harmonization). But it is restricted almost always to flagrant contradictions, whereas harmonization, in posttalmudic literature, also includes obliquely inferred contradictions, thus making it a far more frequent occurrence. The third period is the period of *logical implication*. It started in some circles in the sixteenth century with the advent of *pilpul* (generally associated with the sixteenth-century scholar R. Shalom Shachna)[38] and, allowing for the generational modifications, continuing to this day (most notably in the Lithuanian *yeshivot*). These exegetical modes all preceded the modern mode of study, which can be characterized as insisting upon *direct textual inference*. (It is too early to determine whether this trend will indeed emerge as a distinct and separate period of rabbinic exegesis. I therefore hesitate to include it as a fourth period.) As a conscious movement, direct textual inference started in the nineteenth century with the advent of the so-called "scientific critical method" and is being practiced almost exclusively among academic scholars.[39]

The Talmudic Period: Setting the Text Right

I call the period of the Talmud with respect to its interpretation of the Mishnah and *baraita* (tannaitic material that was not included in the Mishnah) the period of *setting the text aright* because the scholars of that time saw as their major concern the establishment of a correct text[40] of the authoritative rabbinic traditions. In the process, the talmudic sages also engaged in *interpreting out*, a mode of interpretation opposite to *adding to*. Interpreting out limits a text, whose embrace seems to be general, to a few specific instances. Sometimes, it was limited to one instance only. The standard (though not the exclusive) Aramaic formula for this process is *hakha bemai askinan*, "we are dealing here with a case of . . . ," meaning that case only. The rest is interpreted out. A typical example is the first *hakha bemai askinan* in the Babylonian Talmud: *Ber.* 20b (there it is an anonymous statement, but it could well have been a statement by an *amora*—the *stam* inherited this formula from the *amoraim*). The reading there is as follows: The *baraita* says that a minor son (one who has not yet reached the age of thirteen) may recite the grace after the meal for his father (who does not know how to read), who listens and responds periodically with the word Amen. Because of a certain difficulty, the Gemara replies: "We are dealing here with a case when the father ate a small piece of bread not more than the size of an olive or the size of an egg where the obligation to recite the blessing is only rabbinically ordained." Had the father eaten a larger piece of bread where the obligation to recite the blessing is scripturally ordained, the rule of the *baraita* that the son could recite the grace for his father would not have applied. The interpretation curtailed the applicability of the *baraita* by excluding (interpreting out) the more standard meaning: any piece of bread. To be sure, the mode of interpreting out is characteristic of the talmudic sages, but it is not exclusively theirs. (This is true also of the traits ascribed to any of the other periods. They are characteristic of, but not exclusive to them.)

In addition to interpreting out, the *stammaim* also engaged in the interpretive mode of textual redundancy. Their exegesis contains interpretation based on supposedly extra phrases, an activity not previously found in the study of Mishnah and other authoritative texts. In the study of Bible, however, redundancy exegesis, by that time, had a long and revered history. The *stammaim* applied the redundancy method to the Mishnah and other authoritative texts as well. They, and not *amoraim*—as is commonly assumed—are responsible for such questions in the Talmud as *"minyana lama li?"* (Why do I need the number; I can figure it out myself?). When the Mishnah, for instance, says in *Shabb.* 7:2: "The main classes of work [on the Sabbath] are forty save one" and proceeds to enumerate them individually, the *stam* in *b. Shabb.* 73b (not R. Yochanan, even though his name is associated with the answer) asks: Is not the collective number (forty save one) superfluous? We will count the main classes of work ourselves and get the number! Why does the Mishnah have to give us the number explicitly? (And the answer is: to tell us "that if one performs them all in one state of unawareness, then he is liable for each one separately." Mentioning the number explicitly tells us that irrespective of how many main classes of work one performed on the Sabbath, one is culpable for each separately. Mentioning the number explicitly gives each main class of work in its own individuality.) The *stammaim* treated the Mishnah, in their time already an established, authoritative text, the way the *amoraim* (and the *tannaim* before them) treated the Bible.[41] They borrowed their exegetical tools from that model, with some differences, of course. For instance, in biblical exegesis the source for an exposition was sometimes not an extra phrase but an extra word and even an extra letter; whereas in talmudic exegesis, it is rare for an extra word or letter to serve as a source for a halakhic deduction. More often than not it is an extra phrase. The *amoraim*, though most likely active practitioners of the redundancy method in their biblical studies, refrained on the whole from doing so in their mishnaic studies, probably because in their time the text of the Mishnah was not yet stable; redundancy of words was not a secure enough source on which to base new *halakhot*.

The Posttalmudic Period of Harmonization

I call the posttalmudic period, from the sixth century through, in some circles, our own time, the period of harmonization, because the scholars of that time were primarily concerned with upholding the unity of the Talmud and reconciling apparent contradictions. Most of the contradictions, however, were not explicit or self-evident, but were based on oblique inferences, the mode of interpretation most characteristic of this period. During this period the redundancy method, applied previously either to the Bible or to the Talmud, had almost disappeared.[42] Instead, most of the deductions (primarily halakhic) bore a resemblance to the type of argument that may be formulated as follows: the author of the text must have been of a certain opinion about a specific subject. Otherwise, he would have contradicted what he himself had said elsewhere. The inference is oblique because what he said elsewhere was not said necessarily in the context of the subject under discussion, nor was it stated explicitly. It was said in the context of a different subject and only through inference do we surmise the author's opinion concerning the subject we are interested in. Again, the oblique method is not exclusive to the posttalmudic period. It is found quite frequently in the Talmud and constitutes an important part of Talmudic reasoning. It usually concludes with the familiar *veim itta* (if it is the fact) and is advanced as a contradiction to what was said before. If it is true that the author is of opinion *x*, then he (or an authority with whom he must agree) would not have said what he said in a different context. What justifies attributing the method of oblique inference to the posttalmudic period is the fact that in the Talmud the oblique method shared exegetical attention with the redundancy method, the latter being more dominant, whereas in the posttalmudic period the redundancy method was almost entirely absent and the oblique method was ubiquitous. The same may almost be said about the "interpreting out" method.

Also, in posttalmudic literature, especially among the tosafists (twelfth- to fourteenth-century French and German Talmud scholars) and among a few selected *acharonim*, such as R. Arye Leib (1695–1785, the author of the book *Sha'aggat Arye*), the oblique method was more elaborate and composite than in the Talmud, although here and there a very complex oblique inference is also found in the Talmud. (A good example is the inference in *b. B. Kam.* 12b–13a.) These qualities made the oblique method the posttalmudic period's most characteristic feature. They certainly distinguished the period from its predecessors. Naturally, because of the nature of the method, any characteristic example taken from the posttalmudic literature will be complicated. The complexity will be increased if the example is compared with an example of textual redundancy of the Bible taken from the Talmud. It will be further compounded if the subject of the example is semiesoteric, allowing greater leeway in argumentation. Such an example will impress the reader with the deep-rootedness of the redundancy method in talmudic biblical exegesis and the complexity of the oblique method in posttalmudic literature. But such an example, I am afraid, may prove too difficult for a reader with no technical talmudic knowledge, and rather than elucidate may obscure the methodological differences between the talmudic and posttalmudic periods. I therefore choose here a simpler example, less telling perhaps but more manageable to the nontechnical reader, and place the more technical example in a note[43] for anyone who wishes to consult it.

The Babylonian Talmud in *Kidd.* 42b concludes that the old mishnaic law (*Ber.* 5:5) that "A man's agent is like himself," acting in his behalf, does not apply to wrongdoings. When a person instructs another person to commit a forbidden act, the doer and not the sender is culpable. The Talmud questions this modification by quoting another Mishnah (*Meil.* 6:1) which states: "If an agent performed his appointed errand (and thereby committed an act of sacrilege, partaking of Temple property), the sender is guilty. If the agent had not performed his appointed errand, it is the agent who is guilty of the sacrilege." Why, asks the Talmud, is the sender guilty of sacrilege when the agent performed his appointed errand? The agent's act is a forbidden one and therefore the law of proxy that a man's agent is like himself should not apply. The Talmud's question is a direct question asking how the Mishnah in *Meila* can be reconciled with the just-concluded modification of the existing law of proxy.

The tosafists basically ask a similar question, but they made it more complicated by resorting to oblique inference. They argue that there is a difference between whether the agent knew that he is committing a forbidden act or not. If he did *not* know, then even if he carried out "his appointed errand" completely, he is not guilty. The agent had no reason to disobey his instructions. Therefore, no punishment is warranted. If, however, he was aware of the wrongfulness of the act, he should have ignored the instructions given to him and "listened to God (who forbids committing such an act) rather than to men." In following his sender in defiance of God, the agent is indeed culpable.

The tosafists infer the distinction between knowing and not knowing whether the act is forbidden from still a third Mishnah— *B. Kam.* 7:6. The Mishnah there states: If a thief who stole an animal gave it to a priest as a redemption for his firstborn son (Exod. 13:13) or gave it to his creditor or to a guardian, and while one of these three was dragging the animal away, it died a natural death while yet in the original owner's domain, the thief is not liable to the owner, for he did not contribute to the animal's death. But if one of these three persons *lifted* the animal or took it outside the owner's domain, and the animal died there, the thief is liable. The priest, creditor, or guardian is considered to have acted on the thief's behalf, and as his agent, when the animal was lifted up or taken outside—both means of acquisition in Jewish law—it is as if the thief himself who had done so, giving him title to the animal, and therefore making him culpable to the owner.

But, inquired the tosafists, why would the priest, creditor, or guardian be considered an agent of the thief, when according to the Talmud's conclusion in *Kiddushin*, the law of proxy does not apply to forbidden acts? The only plausible explanation is that the priest, creditor, or guardian did not know that the animal was stolen, and therefore the modification to the law of proxy does not apply to them. Had they known the act was forbidden (that they were abetting the act of theft), they would not have participated.

Having made this inference, the tosafists challenge the Talmud's question from the Mishnah in *Meila*. The discussion in the Mishnah *Meila* centers around one who had *inadvertently* partaken of

Temple property. For one who deliberately violates Temple property, the punishment is different and more severe. In light of the above inferences, the tosafists conclude, the case in the Mishnah *Meila* is not a proper instance of the modification of the law of proxy. The Talmud was not justified in questioning the modification of the law on the basis of the Mishnah in *Meila*, which deals with cases where the agent did not know that he was committing a forbidden act (he did not know that the property belonged to the Temple), whereas the modification of the law of proxy applies only when the agent is aware that he is committing a forbidden act, mistakenly thinking that acting on someday else's behalf absolves him of any responsibility. The two are not the same.

I hope that the reader has gotten some feeling from this single, simple example of the much greater complexity of posttalmudic literature, and how much more it relies on oblique inference.

Logical Implication or Pilpul:
The Sixteenth Century and Beyond

I call the period starting with the sixteenth century and continuing in some circles to our own day the period of logical implication because the scholars of that time were primarily concerned with exploring the logical possibilities of a given text and showing that the authors of the text were aware of the logical possibilities. During this period a sizeable number of scholars more than ever engaged in *pilpul* (farfetched casuistic deductions). This method almost always ignores the substantive meaning of the text and concentrates instead on its logical implications. It tries to penetrate into the "depth" of the meaning of the text (note the resemblance to the apologists in Biblical exegesis who call derash peshat-in-depth). It goes, as it were, below the surface, while the surface, the simple meaning, remains untouched.[44] *Pilpul* does not read into the text. Nor does it add to the text. It merely "expresses" the hidden logic that underlies the text. One suspects that the dissatisfaction often voiced by the exponents of *pilpul* concerning the scholarship of previous generations stems from the fact that they find that scholarship to be loosely attached to the text—the standard criticism against those who do not follow the peshat. Because the pilpulist shares this sentiment, I feel justified in classifying him exegetically between those who practiced the "oblique inference" method—who emphasize inference but nevertheless have a great stake in the substantive meaning of the text—and those who are committed to the scientific critical method, the product of modern times; between the former, who may on occasion deviate from the peshat, and the latter, who adhere to the substantive meaning of the text, shunning any kind of interpretation that is not directly inferred from the words of the text, including logical implication, unless it is clear from either the words or the context that the author of the text was aware of the implication.

A very popular example of logical implication is the interpretation given of the controversy between R. Judah and the sages in Mishnah *Pesach.* 2:1.[45] R. Judah is of the opinion that *chametz* (leavened bread on Passover) "may be disposed of only by burning," whereas the sages allow any means. "It may be crumbled up and scattered to the wind or thrown into the sea." They disagree—so runs the interpretation—whether the biblical command to remove *chametz* on the first day of Passover (Exod. 12:15) is a positive commandment implying that if one has no *chametz* on that day one is duty-bound to get *chametz* and remove it; or whether the commandment to remove *chametz* is a negative commandment, in order to avoid having *chametz*. By this interpretation, he who has no *chametz* on that day, by simply not having any, has fulfilled the commandment; the sages are understood to have held that the commandment is merely an exhortation to avoid having *chametz*. Any means of removing is therefore acceptable. R. Judah, on the other hand, is of the opinion that the commandment is a positive one. It is not enough not to have *chametz*. One has to remove *chametz* actively and can do so only through burning. Only burning will satisfy the ritual of removing *chametz*. It is a part of the commandment.

Note that the substantive meaning of the text is hardly affected by this interpretation. What sounds so new and radical is the claim that according to R. Judah one who has no *chametz* is obligated to get *chametz* and remove it in order to fulfill the commandment "on the first day remove all leaven out of your houses" (Exod. 12:15). One may reject this interpretation on the grounds that it is almost absurd to require the purchasing of *chametz* before Passover. But it cannot be rejected on the grounds that it violates the integrity of the text. One may object, justifiably, that the statement of R. Judah doesn't necessarily imply this logical deduction. Objectively, what R. Judah is saying is that short of burning one cannot be sure that the *chametz* will not reappear in some form.[46] Crumbling up or scattering to the wind or throwing into the sea is no guarantee that the *chametz* will not reappear. Whereas according to the sages even if the *chametz* reappears, with the crumbling or other means of disposal one has fulfilled the commandment. One cannot, however, challenge this interpretation on the basis of the wording or even context of the text. The interpretation satisfies both. *Pilpul* is not against peshat, the simple meaning of the text.

By way of summary, one may say that during the setting-the-text-aright period, the interpretation impinged directly upon the text; during the harmonization period, the interpretations indirectly affected the text. During the logical implication period, the interpretations hardly touched the text. The latter, therefore, is the closest to peshat in the sense of preserving the integrity of the text. Rabbinic exegesis proceeded along lines that with each period brought it closer to peshat.

Critical Objections to the Traditional Methods

Critical scholars object to the interpreting out method on the grounds that it unduly narrows the meaning of the text. The reading of the text calls for embracing a wider range of meaning, one that will include everything that fits into the words of the text. The assumption of these scholars is that had the author of the text intended to narrow it that much—to limit it only to a few instances, sometimes to one instance only—he would have formulated the statement differently. He would have explicitly made mention of the instances that he is supposed to have referred to exclusively. By formulating the statement in a general manner he implies a larger purport, excluding only those instances which are obviously excluded by the wording or the context of the text. All other cases should be included. The objection to the interpreting out method is thus textually motivated, claiming that it is not according to *peshat*.

The critical scholar objects to the textual redundancy method (both in Bible studies and in talmudic studies) on the grounds that much of what is considered redundant may be a stylistic peculiarity (in the case of the Bible, to say appointed "times" instead of appointed "time" in the example above from the *Megilla* reading)[47] may be purely stylistic. Similarly, in the case of the Mishnah in the example above, it may be for reasons of style that the Mishnah gives the number of the main classes of work even though we can count the individual classes ourselves. No exegetical deductions ought to be drawn from modes of expression that are peculiar to language. Even when there is a seemingly legitimate case of redundancy, for the deduction to be valid it has to emerge from the words or letters of the text and not—as is the case in the majority of instances—be superimposed from the outside. The objection to the redundancy method is also textually motivated but embraces a smaller portion of the text than is the case in the objection to the interpreting out method.

The critical scholar objects to the oblique inference method on the grounds that the method assumes that the author of any text knew all opinions and all possible permutations and combinations resulting from opinions found anywhere in the Talmud (as in the example from the tosafist, *Chul.* 70b quoted in note 43 above). One has no right to attribute a view to the author himself when he has not directly discussed the subject, when we have no record of his having expressed an opinion about it. The entire subject may have escaped his attention when he composed the text. For an inference to be valid, one has to establish afresh from the text that the author was aware of the argument from which the inference is drawn. The objection to the oblique method is not directed as much to the text itself as it is to the author's awareness. Therefore, the method can still be deemed closer to the peshat than the previous methods.

The critical scholar objects to the logical implication method, as we have seen, not on the ground that it is textually assailable but rather (as with the objection to the oblique method) because the implications may be logically correct (which was not the case in the *chametz* example) yet not historically true. They may not have been consciously implied by the author. The author may not have realized the logical consequences of his own statements and, therefore, these should not be attributed to him.[48] The text ought ultimately to express, if not the author's specific intention, at least his general framework. Modern literary critics may object, but they must make adjustments for religious legal texts where the imprint of the author, the conscious knowledge of the author, determines authority.[49] The logical implication method does not always recognize this criterion. The objection to logical implication is even less textual than the objection to the oblique method, and that is why I have been saying that *pilpul* is not anti-peshat.

I hope the reader noticed that only the "textual redundancy" method terminated at a fixed time (the end of the talmudic period). The oblique method, for instance, continues in some circles up to our own time. Many traditional scholars today are practicing the oblique method. The *pilpul* method was never adopted by all scholars, though some mode of logical implication (a subdued form of *pilpul*) is in wide use today and has been so for a long time. In the past, apparently, no period followed one mode of interpretation exclusively, though individual scholars may have done so. Each period contained active and creative scholars of various modes of interpretations. No period was confined to one mode only. Different modes of interpretation intermingled, influenced and fructified each other, yet each period had its own hallmark, its own specialty, its own characteristic feature. It is this hallmark, this specialty, this characteristic feature that enables historians today to classify the periods according to their different modes of exegesis. Analysis of these periods leads to the conclusion that with each new period the reluctance to read in or add to the text increased. This is true of biblical as well as of talmudic exegesis. As one traces their historical development, one discovers that although they did not always proceed in the direction of plain meaning, they gradually shared the propensity to desist from interfering with the integrity of the text. As time went on they came to respect the substantive meaning of the text more and more. Such was the evolution of rabbinic exegesis.

The Evolution of Talmudic and Biblical Exegesis: Summary

Let me restate very briefly the history of talmudic exegesis as sketched above and refer more often, by way of comparison, to biblical exegesis. In the earliest talmudic exegesis in the third century, as in biblical exegesis, reading in was not practiced. But unlike biblical exegetes, the early *amoraim* did not engage in textual redundancy either. Apparently, at that early period talmudic texts (including the Mishnah) were not stable enough to warrant exegesis of the textual redundancy sort. Gradually the *amoraim* engaged in what may be called interpreting out of the text, limiting the content of a text to a minimal number of cases, sometimes to even one case only. It is almost the opposite of adding to the text (found so abundantly in biblical exegesis of that time); it shrinks the text. It makes the text applicable to a particular case only. The same limitation is often suggested when two authoritative texts contradict each other (two *mishnayot*, two *baraitot* or a mishnah and a baraita). One of the texts is confined to a special case, even though linguistically the formulation of the texts is identical, apart from the points of contradiction. You interpret out one text by rejecting its inclusive meaning and reducing it to an individual case.

By the time of the *stammaim* (ca. 427–520), talmudic texts, particularly the Mishnah, began to be treated like the Bible, where supposedly extra phrases (or even words) were made to yield new halakhic deductions and very little was attributed to stylistic peculiarities. This type of activity was greatly diminished after the so-called completion of the Talmud, and although it occasionally appears in posttalmudic literature, it is no longer the mainstay of talmudic exegesis. Its place was gradually taken by what I called oblique inference, a method that leaves the substantive meaning of a text (the meaning that is implied in the wording of the text) more or less intact and concentrates on inferences. The technique is to draw inferences from different places in the Talmud, show their seeming incompatibility and then reinterpret them in such a manner that the incompatibility disappears. This activity is typical of the tosafists but not exclusive to them. Similar approaches can be found among the *geonim* from the tenth century on, and for antecedents one might consult also the Talmud. Their gradual detachment from the substantive meaning of the text demonstrates the continuing tendency toward less interference with the actual words of the text. Their methods of exegesis entail less interference than the methods of their predecessors, but more than those of their successors, the pilpulists.

While it is true that the tosafists, especially R. Jacob Tam (1100–1171), often obviated contradictions through logical distinctions, making the contradictory instances look dissimilar, they differed from their successors, the logical implicationists, in that they saddled the text with those distinctions, thus making the words actually contain them. The logical implicationists, however, did not involve the words of the text much. They concentrated on the implication of the content, which for their purposes might just as well have been paraphrased, summarized. The locus of their discussion was the abstract content, not the concrete formulation. They usually took the simple meaning for granted and proceeded by explicating its logical consequences. They dealt little with the substantive meaning of the text and consequently had less occasion to violate it. They were therefore closer to peshat in the sense of preserving "the tenor of the words and the thrust of the context," not necessarily reflecting the intention of the author. From that perspective, paradoxically enough, the pilpulists were the most advanced peshatists. A similar claim could be made of the apologetic school in biblical exegesis. From the perspective of what the author of the text probably meant, the members of the apologetic school represent a retrogression from the medieval biblical commentaries. But from the perspective of commitment to the peshat, they are second to none. They extended—albeit artificially—the surface of simple text (by creating either peshat-in-depth or new grammatical or syntactical rules) and, as it were, pushed out derash. Every true interpretation, every true exegesis, had to be peshat. Even the Rashbam, the greatest peshatist, had to allow for a dual system of peshat and derash, the latter being derived from textual redundancy (which to our exegetical taste was not always redundant). Even to the Rashbam, peshat was not exclusive. It shared the exegetical limelight with derash. Not so for the apologists. For them there was only peshat. Whatever was not peshat was not legitimate. The *derashot* found in the Talmud were peshat in disguise. Consciously, at least, they lived with the illusion that peshat is and was all-supreme and that they lived according to peshat. The halakhic laws of the past were all motivated by peshat. The integrity of the text was never violated. Such a commitment to peshat was new in the history of rabbinic exegesis.

Fluctuation and Continuity

Viewed that way, I believe, one can discover a linear pattern through the different periods of the history of rabbinic exegesis. Conventionally, rabbinic exegesis is perceived as behaving in a zigzagging manner, of going back and forth, on the extent of commitment to the simple, literal (or plain) meaning of a text (peshat), which scholarly convention tacitly equates with authorial intention. Talmudic interpretation of the Bible is generally considered by modern exegetes to be quite distant from the peshat, out of tune with the "natural" meaning of the biblical text it purports to explain. In contrast, medieval exegesis, especially that of the Rashbam (twelfth century) and Ibn Ezra (1090–1164) is regarded as close to peshat (relatively speaking), in line with accepted standards of explication. Postmedieval exegesis is again unacceptable, harking back to talmudic interpretation of the Bible, which brought external factors to bear on the text. (While allowance is generally made for such interpretation in aggada, the nonlegal sections of the Bible, as part of preacher's license, a stricter standard is demanded in halakha, where the difference of interpretation may result in different practical demands. Our discussion in this essay is almost exclusively confined to halakha. Rules governing interpretation in aggada are generally taken to be lax, and as such are not given to structural, evolutionary models.)[50]

Similar although not parallel zigzagging is observed in the exegesis of the oral law. Talmudic exegesis, which interprets its own authoritative texts, such as the Mishnah, is considered satisfactory by contemporary critics. So are the comments of the *geonim* and *rishonim* (posttalmudic scholars who flourished between the tenth and the fourteenth centuries) but not those of the *acharonim* (the scholars who followed the *rishonim*). The latter, particularly since the sixteenth century, are accused of being pilpulistic, of employing a quasi-casuistic method that alienates one from the spirit and intent of the text. Neither in the history of biblical exegesis nor in the history of Talmudic exegesis is linear development usually seen.

This arbitrary, even chaotic pattern is perceived in the history of rabbinic exegesis (which includes both biblical exegesis and talmudic exegesis) because the historians evaluated it in terms of today's standard of proper interpretation: that of original intent, what the author meant when he wrote the text (a view still regnant despite the serious challenge posed by the new deconstructionist school in literature). Judged by this criterion, the history of rabbinic exegesis indeed displays sharp turns to one side and then to the other. Thus, for instance, modern *pilpul*, used here in the widest possible sense so as to include the biblical interpretations of the modern apologists, is not less removed, and perhaps may be even more distant, from the original intent of the author than talmudic interpretation of the Bible performed two thousand years ago.

Nor would linearity be evident if one chose simple meaning as the historical criterion. (Simple meaning may imply things that the author did not intend to convey.) *Pilpul* would still undermine the notion of linear development. In all its varieties, almost by definition, *pilpul* cannot be equated with simple meaning and cannot therefore be considered a sequel to an earlier period that was close to simple meaning.

I suggest that if one changes the historical criterion from the original intent to integrity of the text, one gets a different perception of the history of rabbinic exegesis. Modern *pilpul* is more respectful of the integrity of the text—by leaving it intact and concentrating on its logical implications—than talmudic exegesis, whose interpretations frequently alter the substantive meaning of the text. It is also more respectful of the text than the interpretation of the *rishonim*, who sometimes saddle the text with distinctions of their own making. Medieval exegesis represents a transition from the bold interference with the plain meaning of a text practiced by the Talmud to the indifference to the plain meaning of the text evidenced by *pilpul*. Seen in this way, rabbinic exegesis forms a linear developmental pattern.

Logic and Textual Integrity

Before I leave the subject of biblical and talmudic exegesis, let me point out an additional difference between the two, not noted before by scholars. Commentators on Scripture generally show a greater sensitivity to problems related to extra words or letters than commentators on Mishnah do, and commentators of Mishnah show a greater concern for logical attractiveness than commentators on Scripture do. It is difficult to say whether that is because each in its own way is attempting to obviate the difficulty of having abandoned the simple, literal meaning, or because somehow the concern for tight expression free of superfluity seems better suited to a divine document like the Bible[51] and the concern for logical smoothness seems better suited to a human document like the Mishnah. In either case, the difference is an old one, reflective of the difference between the *tannaim*, authors of the Mishnah (who flourished before the second century C.E.), expositing Scripture; and the *amoraim* (who flourished between the second and fifth centuries C.E.), explaining the Mishnah (and other authoritative rabbinic texts).[52] The *tannaim* were totally dependent on the Bible for legal guidance, whereas the *amoraim* could draw upon the Mishnah (and other authoritative rabbinic texts) as well. The Bible as a direct source for legal decisions was gradually diminishing during the *amoraic* period and almost disappeared afterwards.[53] The *tannaim* were more occupied with the wording of the text, the *amoraim* with the logic of the content. Posttalmudic commentators justified forced *amoraic* textual interpretations on the grounds that logic of the content takes priority over the integrity of the text. In the words of R. Bezalel Ashkenazi (d. 1592) in his *Kelalei ha-Talmud*,[54] paragraph 56: "It is proper to adhere to a forced interpretation (*dochak*) when reason or logic supports it" (the content of the forced interpretation). A similar sentiment was expressed by R. M. Hameiri (1249–1316) in his *Bet ha-Bechira* on *b. Shabb.*, 62b: "How could we innovate strange things [from the standpoint of content] because of a minor indication of the language?"[55]

One can almost say that the difference between traditional and modern talmudic exegesis is that traditional exegesis insists that the logic of the content shall not be forced, whereas modern exegesis insists that the integrity of the text shall not be forced. To the modern exegete, integrity of the text is a better criterion, a more reliable antidote against subjectivism, than is the logic—or more accurately, the reasonableness—of the reading. Logic or reasonableness tends to be more individualistic, less rooted in objectivity. And when it collides with the integrity of the text, the latter has the right of way.

3

The Meaning and History
of the Noun *Peshat*

I suspect that the notions that exegesis is timebound and that rabbinic exegesis, though it generally did not prefer peshat over derash, did, however, move in the direction of less interference with the substantive meaning of the text, will encounter opposition from some quarters. It will be argued that despite the objections raised by some recent scholars against the traditional understanding of the noun *peshat* when it connotes a mode of interpretation, these scholars' own interpretation of this noun leaves much to be desired. In the absence of a more satisfying substitute meaning, it may be argued, the accepted meaning remains regnant. As such, no theory that ignores it or, what is worse, contradicts it, can claim legitimacy. If the traditional meaning of the noun *peshat* is correct, then, as I have already stated in chapter 1, the dictum "that no text can be deprived of its peshat" is an indication that the rabbis of the Talmud valued the plain, simple meaning over derash (for a text can be, and often is, deprived of its derash).

I believe that there is no genuine reason for opposition to the theses we have proposed so far. I believe that there is, in fact, a convincing and satisfying substitute meaning of the noun *peshat*. Furthermore, it is, in reality, no substitute; it is the standard meaning of the root *p-sh-t* (extension) which, when applied to the noun, carries the additional connotation of "context." This meaning satisfies all the places in talmudic literature where that noun *peshat* appears in the sense of an interpretive mode. Philologically, there is no need to follow the traditional understanding of the noun *peshat*. Indeed, peshat in the sense of plain, simple meaning is entirely the) invention of the medieval exegetes. It has no basis in the Talmud.

The Talmudic Period

"Extension" ("Context") and Proposed Alternatives

There is a considerable literature, mainly of the last century, on the subject of peshat and derash. Numerous articles and several books have appeared; the articles generally deal with the nature of peshat and derash while the books take up some aspect of the history of biblical exegesis as well.[1] On the subject of talmudic exegesis very little has been written. I am singling out two major works: a long article written by R. Loewe entitled "The 'Plain' Meaning of Scripture in Early Jewish Exegesis"[2] and a book in Hebrew by S. Kamin, entitled *Rashi's Exegetical Categorization: With Respect to the Distinction Between Peshat and Derash.*[3] They are both valuable studies. The former is particularly noteworthy for projecting peshat and derash on a larger canvas, bringing to bear also non-Jewish sources and for applying for the first time sound philological criteria to the whole range of peshat in talmudic literature, and not only to a fraction as was done hitherto. The latter excels in the summary of the literature, primary as well as secondary, in the criticism of this literature, and in the categorization and subtle nuancing of the various possible meanings offered for peshat and derash.[4] Moreover, each offers its own explanation of peshat: to the former, peshat is identical with authoritativeness,[5] implying that the *derashot* are not authoritative; to the latter, *peshat* corresponds to either the text itself or to the semantic meaning of the text. When the Talmud asks what is the peshat of the text, it asks what does the text say or what is the meaning of the text. That meaning could be either plain or applied. Thus very little meaning or significance is attached to the word *peshat*.[6] It merely designates what the text means. Both of these scholars, like their predecessors, consider the standard meaning of the root *p-sh-t*—extension or continuation—to be inadequate as a comprehensive explanation of the noun *peshat* when it connotes a mode of exegesis. (The other meaning of the root *p-sh-t*—teaching or explanation—is certainly inadequate to cover all the places in the talmud where *peshat* as a mode of exegesis is employed). Like their modern predecessors, these two authors were constrained to look for alternative meanings.

I am convinced, however, that there is no need for alternative meanings, that the standard meaning of the root *p-sh-t* (extension or continuation) can also be applied to the noun *peshat*. The scholars' assumption to the contrary stems from their seeming lack of rigorous examination of the relevant passages. I believe a close examination of the texts will show that there is no need to burden the noun *peshat*, wherever it appears in the Talmud, with additional meaning other than that which the root carries in its other inflected forms.

I will take up each of the individual passages separately and explain them in conformity with the standard meaning. I will do so by dividing the pasages into two categories. The first category will include those instances in the Talmud where the dictum "no text can be deprived of its peshat" appears and the second category will cover those instances in the Talmud where the Aramaic word *peshatei* (or in the Palestinian Talmud, *peshutei*) with or without the word *dikra* (in the Palestinian Talmud, *dikarta*), appears. In all these places, except perhaps in one—*b. Ketub.* 38b— I can show that the meaning of *peshat* is uniform. Nor does it appear that there is a difference between the Hebrew and Aramaic or between *peshuto* and *peshatei* as some scholars have suggested.[7] In all these places, *peshat* means extension, continuation, and derivatively, context.

"No Text Can Be Deprived of Its Peshat"

b. Yevam. 11b

Of the three places in the Talmud where the dictum "no text can be deprived of its peshat" appears (*b. Shabb.* 63a, *Yevam.* 11b and 24a) the one in which the meaning of *peshat* is clearest is *Yevam.* 11b. The Talmud quotes a dispute between R. Yose the son of Kipper (a mid-second-century Palestinian scholar) and the sages as to what the phrase "after she is defiled" refers to in Deut. 24:4. According to

R. Yose the son of Kipper, *she* refers to a husband's remarriage of his divorced wife, who since the divorce, married a second husband, who in turn subsequently died or divorced her. According to the sages it refers to a *sota*, a woman who remained in private seclusion with a man other than her husband. The question arose what the law would be, according to the sages, concerning the remarried divorced wife's "rival" (the husband's other wife) with respect to levirate marriage. If a man dies without children, biblical law requires that one of the deceased's brothers shall marry the widow. This is called levirate marriage.

If the deceased had several wives and one of them is unqualified to marry the brother—either because she is generally unqualified to marry a Jew (the deceased brother had lived with her illicitly) or because she is related to the living brother through another relative and their union is independently illicit—then all of the "rival" wives are disqualified from marrying the brother and may marry whomever they wish. However, in order to extend this disqualification to all the wives, the prohibition which prevents her from marrying her brother-in-law must be called in Scripture "defilement," or uncleanness. The Gemara queries what was the intention of the sages. If, when the sages claimed that the verse referred to a *sota*, they implied that it does *not* refer to a woman who rejoined her first husband, then the rival of such a woman, another wife would not be disqualified for levirate marriage for this remarried woman is not considered defiled. If, however, the sages only meant that the phrase "after that she is defiled" refers *also* to a woman who rejoined her first husband (after she married another one and he died or divorced her), then the consequence would be that the "rival" of such a woman would also be disqualified for levirate marriage.

To answer this, the Talmud employs the dictum that "no text can be deprived of its peshat," implying that since the context of the passage in Deut. 24 is a woman rejoining her first husband (the matter of *sota* is found in Num. 5) the sages may say that it refers to *sota* also, but they cannot deprive the phrase of its peshat, of its context, claiming that reference to a woman who rejoined her first husband is excluded from the verse. Thus, the word *defiled* necessarily includes such a woman, and her "rival," the other wife, is disqualified from levirate marriage. It should be noted that the

Talmud also quotes another version according to which there is no question that the sages' view is that the "rival" is also unqualified for levirate marriage. "Since the text ('After that she is defiled') has once been torn away" (from the context of a woman who is rejoining her first husband) "it must in all respects so remain." Even according to this version a text cannot normally be deprived of its peshat; but in those few instances where a text is deprived of its peshat (see Rava's statement in the next example), the deprivation is complete. The deprivation cannot be partial.[8]

b. Yevam. 24a

That *peshat* there meant context is indisputable. It is less obvious in the next case, that of *Yevam.* 24a, but not less certain. Deut. 25:5–6 states (again in connection with levirate marriage):

> If brothers dwell together and one of them dies and has no children, the wife of the dead shall not be married abroad . . . her husband's brother shall . . . take her as his wife. . . . And it shall be, that the firstborn that she bears shall succeed in the name of his brother that is dead, that his name be not blotted out of Israel.

Commenting on the last phrase, Rava says: "Although throughout the Torah no text is deprived of its peshat,[9] in this case the *gezera shava*, [the second of the seven hermeneutical principles that Hillel (a first-century Palestinian *tanna*) exposited, as quoted in *t. Sanh.* 7.11] has come and entirely deprived the text of its peshat." What Rava meant was that the interpretation given by the Mishnah and *baraita* to this verse (that "the firstborn that she bears" refers to the eldest brother) violates the context of the verse. Specifically, the verse says "the firstborn that she will bear shall succeed in the name of his brother that is dead," i.e., the child that will be born in the future of the levirate union of the widow and her late husband's brother shall succeed in the name of the deceased person. Instead, the Mishnah and the baraita (found also in *Sifrei Deut.* 289) interpret the verse to say that the firstborn brother (the oldest brother) of the deceased shall succeed in the name of the brother that is dead, that is he should have priority to marry the deceased's wife. As the Mishnah (*Yevam.* 2:8) puts it: "the duty of levirate marriage falls on the eldest (surviving) brother."

This interpretation is not only against the simple, literal meaning of the verse, a deviation which the rabbis of the Talmud would have tolerated, but is also against the context. For in order to uphold this interpretation of the Mishnah and *baraita*, the two Hebrew words in the verse *asher teled* (that she will bear) cannot refer to the oldest brother, who was already born, but must mean that the widow must be capable of bearing children, thus excluding a barren woman. Here is how the *baraita* puts it: "'that she bears' excludes a woman who is incapable of procreation, since she cannot bear children." A woman who cannot bear children is exempt from levirate marriage. According to this *tanna*, the real context of these two words is not, as would appear to us, the words immediately preceding them (the oldest brother, according to this interpretation) nor the words that follow them, but rather the text in the previous verses: "that the wife of the dead shall not be married abroad, to one who is not his kin." The wife has to be one who is capable of giving birth, of bearing children.

It is this contextual incongruity that Rava thought was caused by the *gezera shava*,[10] that prompted him to point out "that although throughout the Torah, no text is deprived of its peshat, here the *gezera shava* has come and deprived (the two words, *asher teled*) of their context." The written context of these two words is verse 6, and the subject is the older brother, whereas the context of the content is verse 5, and the subject is the prohibition of the levirate woman to marry abroad. Throughout the Torah we do not ignore the written context; here we do.[11]

If I may briefly digress, I would like to say that during the Middle Ages, R. Saadya Gaon and Maimonides parted company with the Talmud and interpreted the two words *asher teled* in the past tense rather than in the future tense, thus referring to the mother of the deceased, who gave birth in the past to the oldest remaining brother. They cite several other [rare] instances where the tenses are interchangeable. They were motivated by a desire to avoid having these two words interpreted out of context, which was totally unacceptable to them, though not to Rava. To Rava, interpreting out of context was unusual but clearly not impossible; here and there an exception was made, such as the second version in *Yevam.* 11b, cited above. Maimonides and R. Saadya Gaon, however, tolerated no exceptions.

b. Shabb. 63a

The third instance where the dictum "no text can be deprived of its peshat" appears in the Talmud is *Shabb.* 63a. This case has been least understood by scholars dealing with the subject of peshat and derash, and no connection between peshat and context has been noted. A greater scrutiny of the text, however, will reveal that there, too, *peshat* means context. The subject dealt with is whether or not a man may go out on the Sabbath "with a sword or a bow or a shield or a club or a spear." Since women are allowed to wear jewelry outside and are not considered to be violating the prohibition of carrying, the question arose whether or not a man's weapons were considered at all decorative, and therefore could be carried. R. Eliezer says: "They are his ornaments," that is, they are not dedicated exclusively to war, and are therefore allowed to be worn on the Sabbath and carried outside. The Talmud quotes *amoraim* who said that the reason for R. Eliezer's opinion is the verse in Ps. 45:4: "Gird your sword upon your thigh, O mighty one, your glory and your majesty." The exhortation suggests that girding a sword is an adornment. R. Kahana (a Babylonian scholar of the second half of the fourth century) objected: "But this verse refers to the words of the Torah" (not to an actual physical sword). Mar the son of R. Huna answered: "No text can be deprived of its peshat." Said R. Kahana: "I was eighteen years old and I had already studied the entire Talmud,[12] yet I did not know that a text cannot be deprived of its peshat."

On the surface, the arguments in the Talmud are as follows. R. Kahana thought that the word *sword* ("your sword") in the verse in the Psalms referred exclusively to the words of the Torah, not to an actual sword. He therefore objected to R. Eliezer's proof from the verse that a sword is an adornment. Mar the Son of R. Huna corrected R. Kahana explaining to him that the peshat of the verse must always be retained and that the peshat of the word *sword* in that verse is an actual, physical sword, so that R. Eliezer was justified in deducing from that verse that a sword is an adornment. R. Kahana expressed surprise that he, who had studied the whole Talmud by the time he was only eighteen years old, had never heard of this exegetical principle.

What does peshat mean there? It is generally assumed to mean that a word like *sword*, even when it is a metaphor for the "words of Torah," nevertheless retains the denotation of an actual, physical sword, and that all the attendant inferences can be drawn from it. Peshat there seems to be identical with what we have called all along the simple, literal or plain meaning. Indeed, this passage, more than its parallels, is often quoted as proof of the identity of peshat with simple meaning. And since only peshat, not derash, is always to be retained, the passage further proves that the rabbis of the Talmud, in exegesis, prefered simple meaning over applied meaning.

I disagree. While it is true that the simple meaning of the word *sword* is an actual, physical sword (not the "words of Torah"), it is not true, I believe, that R. Kahana did not know that. It is extremely unlikely that R. Kahana had not heard of the many *derashot* where biblical verses (or words) were metaphorically or allegorically exposited while at the same time retained their simple meaning. The many halakhic texts exposited for aggadic purposes were not transformed, but retained their binding halakhic nature according to the simple meaning. When, for instance, *Lev. Rab.* 13:5 exposited Lev. 11:7—"and the *chazir* (swine) refers to Edom, to Rome"—it certainly did not intend to say that the flesh of a swine was permitted to be eaten.

One may, however, make a distinction and say that in the case of halakhic texts, the halakhic meaning is primary, the aggadic meaning secondary. The latter therefore cannot displace the former. However, in the case before us, the simple meaning of *sword* is empty, devoid of significance, for it is certainly not the purpose of the Psalmist to tell the hero to gird his sword. Some religious and ethical lesson must be contained therein. It takes on significance only when transformed into a metaphor, when it denotes "the words of Torah." Because of that, the former is completely supplanted and the full meaning is carried over to refer to the words of Torah. Granting that, one may still make his aggadic derash of a halakhic text and ask, along with Z. H. Chajes,[13] if R. Kahana did not know that the simple meaning is always retained, how did he know, for instance, that when the Torah says "this shall serve you as a sign on your hand and as a reminder on your forehead" (Exod.

13:9), it does not mean metaphorically only, implying no need to put on actual phylacteries?[14]

R. Kahana most likely knew that with a few exceptions a derash, an exposition, does not displace the peshat (and thus differs from the readings in of the earlier periods). So that even if the word *sword* in the above-quoted verse from Psalms is a metaphor for the words of Torah, the very choice of the word *sword* to convey that metaphor is an indication that a sword shares a common property with Torah, that it too, to the mighty, is glorious and majestic, even as it serves as a metaphor for the words of Torah. R. Kahana's teacher, Rava, knew that[15] when he said (*b. Yevam.* 63b):

> How precious is a good wife, for it is written (Prov. 18:22): "Whoso finds a good wife, finds a great good." If Scripture speaks of the woman herself [simple meaning] then how precious is the good wife whom Scripture praises. If Scripture speaks of the Torah [wife being a metaphor for Torah], then how precious is the good wife with whom the Torah is compared.

R. Kahana should have known—and indeed did know—that if the Torah is compared to a sword with respect to glory and majesty then the sword, too, is glorious and majestic, that it, too, is an adornment.[16] R. Kahana objected to R. Eliezer's reasoning because R. Kahana thought that the verse in Psalms was constituted of two halves. The first half, "Gird your sword upon your thigh," talks about a sword, which serves as a metaphor for the words of Torah; and the second half, "your glory and your majesty" talks about the words of Torah only ("O mighty one!" may refer to the scholar: "Mighty are those who are mighty in Torah").[17] As a whole, the verse reads: "Gird your sword (your knowledge of Torah) upon your thigh (be fluent, have the knowledge ready for decision making),[18] O mighty one (that such readiness will be) your glory and your majesty."[19]

R. Kahana held that mere comparison of Torah to a sword does not make the sword an adornment. The comparison may refer to other properties of the sword, like its being ready for use. If "your glory and your majesty" does not refer to a sword, then the comparison in the first half of the verse of Torah to a sword does not by itself make the latter glorious and majestic. He therefore objected to

R. Eliezer's proof from the second half of the verse that a sword is an adornment. That part of the verse talks about the words of Torah, not about a sword. The words of Torah are glorious and majestic, not the sword. To which Mar the Son of R. Huna replied: "No text can be deprived of its peshat (meaning its context, its connection with what was said before and what was said after). You cannot sever the phrase "your glory and your majesty" from its context, from its connection with the first half of the verse, with the word *sword*.[20]

"Im eino inyan legufo teneiho inyan l'"

In general, it seems to me that the dictum "No text can be deprived of its peshat" is a modification of an earlier and older exegetical principle *im eino inyan legufo teneiho inyan l' . . .* (if it has no bearing on its own subject, apply it elsewhere).[21] Our dictum modifies this principle saying that a phrase or a word can be applied elsewhere only if the content of the phrase or word is retained locally as well. It cannot just leave its home verse. Only when the content is valid in both places, where it is written and to where it is being transferred, can a phrase or a word be relocated. One cannot remove a phrase or a word from one verse to another verse and deny the validity of the content at the place where it was originally written. One cannot transfer a phrase or a word to another place and make it appear as if it were not written where it is written. For no text, no verse, can be deprived of its peshat, of its context. The text remains attached to its context, retaining the validity of the content. Content cannot be removed from its context.

In other words, "No text can be deprived of its peshat" means that the cause for transferring a text cannot be that it does not fit where it is written. It must always fit there. But its formulation may be superfluous either because the content is self-evident or because it has already been stated. In such a case the phrase or word expressing the content is consigned to another verse, to another subject. The other subject shares the content with the old subject. It does not preempt the content of the old subject, a situation that would have arisen had the cause for the transference been incompatibility of the content with the subject. The dictum teaches us that no such incompatibility is possible. The relation between content and context cannot be severed. Basically, the dictum limits the exegetical mode of reading into applications when the content is preserved. It seems to have no objection to reading in of the kind we have in the case of an eye for an eye, where the context is not disturbed. It does, however, object to the kind of reading in where—as in the case of levirate marriage—the context is abandoned. I am inclined therefore to place the origin of the dictum— the formulation is later—sometime between the exegetical practice of reading in in early rabbinic period (if not earlier) and the discontinuation of that practice at about the third century. The dictum reflects a not yet total abandonment of reading in.

Relevant to the old principle, it is noteworthy that there are a few places[22] in rabbinic literature where the principle is applied with the intention of preempting the meaning of the old subject. The most outstanding and perhaps the oldest example (with roots already in the book of Nehemiah)[23] is found both in the *Mekhilta*[24] and in the *Sifrei* to Numbers[25] in connection with the phrase in Num. 18:15: "You shall redeem the firstling of unclean beasts." Says the Midrash:

> I might understand it to mean all unclean beasts [need to be redeemed]. Scripture says [Exod. 13:13] "every firstling of an ass" [only the firstling of an ass need be redeemed, not the firstling of other beasts]. If so, what purpose is there in saying "You shall redeem the firstling of the unclean beasts"? If it has no bearing upon the subject of redeeming the firstling of the unclean beasts, consider it as bearing upon the subject of consecrating unclean beasts for the Temple repair; that one should redeem them if they had been so consecrated.

Using the principle of *im eino inyan* . . . , the Midrash takes the phrase in Num. 18:15 ("You shall redeem the firstling of unclean beasts") and transfers it to another subject: that of consecration for the repair of the Temple, a subject that belongs to Lev. 27:27, which incidentally makes no distinction between firstborn and not firstborn. This is a rare case of depriving a text of its peshat, of its context, an extreme kind of reading in. The reason for doing so was compelling. Among the unclean animals, Exod. 13:13 mentions explicitly only that the firstborn ass needs to be redeemed. There seems to be a contradiction between the two texts. To remove the

contradiction, one of the texts had to yield, and it yields through
being interpreted according to derash.[26] Occasionally, as in the
above case, the derash is such that it deprives the text of its context.
The dictum that no text can be deprived of its context is not
absolute. During the period of reading in, depriving a text of its
context was not condemned. Reading in virtually disappeared later
on, and by the third century, the dictum "No text can be deprived of
its context" had emerged. But it was not foolproof. We have already
mentioned that the second version in *b. Yevam.* 11b does not honor
this dictum. Rava, who quotes the dictum in *Yevam.* 24a and who
was the first to promulgate it,[27] found that the laws of levirate
marriage (which originated centuries before his own time) contradicted the dictum. And, finally, R. Kahana was surprised that
despite his broad knowledge of Talmud, he did not hear of the
dictum till late in life. The dictum was either not too well known or
not honored by all scholars.

"Peshatei *or* Peshutei *Dikra*"

The other category of occurrences where the noun *peshat* carries
the standard meaning of extension, referring to context, is the word
peshatei or *peshutei*. Of the places in the Talmud where the word
peshatei (in the Babylonian Talmud) and *peshutei* (in the Palestinian Talmud), literally meaning "the peshat of," appear, *b. Ketub.*
111b is most clearly a case of context and continuation. It would
therefore serve us well as our first example. The content is not too
complicated, though it is a bit of a strange exposition, not too
common even in aggada. I shall quote it first and then proceed with
the rest of the examples according to the order of the Talmud.

b. Ketub. 111b

The Talmud in *Ketub.* 111b reports that when R. Dimi (a fourth
century scholar) came from Palestine to Babylon, he exposited the
verses in Gen. 49:11–12 imaginatively, in a sense far removed from
the plain meaning. He began asking: "What is meant by 'binding his
foal into the vine'?" and answered "There is not a wine in the land
of Israel that does not require all the inhabitants of one city"
(playing upon the word *'irah* [foal], which can also be read as its *'ir*,
its city) to harvest it. He continues:

> In case you should imagine that it contains no wine, it was explicitly
> stated in Scripture "he washes his garments in wine" . . . and since
> you might say that it is suitable for young people but unsuitable for
> old, it was explicitly stated "and his teeth white with milk" [verse 12].
> Read not "teeth white," but "to him who is advanced in years."

Leven shinayim, which literally means "teeth white," is now being
interpreted through a change of vowels as *leven shanim*—a man of
years, a man of advanced age.

What escaped the scholars dealing with R. Dimi's exposition in
connection with the meaning of peshat, but was noted by the
Maharshah[28] (a sixteenth-century Polish scholar), was that
R. Dimi's exposition stops short of the last word of verse 12. The
word *mechalav* (from milk) at the end of the verse is left unexposited. This word is not consistent with R. Dimi's exposition that the
two words *leven shinayim*, immediately preceeding it, refer to wine.
Indeed some variant readings[29] imported here a new exposition
suitable for the word *Mechalav* found elsewhere. The authors of
these readings were aware of the need to exposit the whole verse,
including the last word. They were not aware, however, that this is
exactly what the Gemara is asking immediately after the completion of R. Dimi's exposition. "What is the meaning of *peshatei
dikra*?" (literally: how is the *peshatei dikra* written?) What is the
exposition of the continuation, of the last word *mechalav*, which
R. Dimi left unexposited? And the Gemara quotes another exposition by R. Dimi which includes the word *mechalav*:

> The Congregation of Israel said to God . . . show us Thy teeth,
> which will be sweeter than milk. . . . "And his teeth white with milk"
> should read not "teeth white," but "showing the teeth."

Clearly the exposition that follows *peshatei dikra* is not much closer
to the simple meaning than the one preceding it. *Peshatei dikra* is
not identical with simple or plain meaning, but with completion,
continuation. By asking what is the *peshatei dikra*, the Gemara is
asking what is the exposition which would include the entire verse,
including the last word? And the Gemara responds by bringing
another exposition by R. Dimi which incorporates the last word as

well. In *Ketub.* 111b, *peshatei* surely means continuation. In the other citations, it is less certain but quite likely that *peshatei* means continuation, referring to context. I will take them up in the order in which they appear in the Talmud.

b. Eruv. 23b

In *Eruv.* 23b, R. Judah (a third-century Babylonian scholar) exposits the verse in Exod. 27:18: "The length of the court [of the Tabernacle] shall be a hundred cubits, and the breadth fifty by fifty" to mean: "take away fifty and surround with them the other fifty." R. Judah was apparently wondering how the breadth, a linear term, could be fifty by fifty, a measure of area, especially since the length is a hundred cubits. He therefore removed the word *bachamishim* (by fifty) from its context and transferred it to another subject, to that of the Sabbath, saying that the word informs us that the measurement of a court (for the purposes of being allowed to carry within its confines on the Sabbath) is the area of one hundred cubits by fifty cubits distributed over a square area, which the Mishnah already calculated as being equivalent to seventy cubits and a fraction by seventy cubits and a fraction. It is as if the word *chamishim* (fifty) were written twice,[30] once describing the measurements of the court of the Tabernacle to yield the measure of the area—five thousand square cubits—and once reading it together with *bachamishim* (*chamishim bachamishim*), giving us the legal definition of the measurement of a court for the purposes of the Sabbath: "fifty surrounded with fifty," which, as already mentioned, is seventy cubits and a fraction by seventy cubits and a fraction, which also adds up to five thousand. The only difference is that in the second reading the measurement is square. Whether or not the court has to be square for a person to be allowed to carry anything within its confines on the Sabbath is a matter of dispute in the Talmud (*Eruv.* 22a: *katin vearih*).[31] On the explanation of R. Judah, the Talmud asks: "What is the *peshatei dikra*" (literally, how is the *peshatei dikra* written) i.e., how does one explain the final verse, especially the word *bachamishim* without depriving it of its context, of its peshat, which is the measurement of the Temple court? And the Gemara quotes Abaye (a fourth century Babylonian scholar), who exposits the whole verse, including the word *bachamishim*, in connection with the measurements of the Temple court. Without actually quoting Abaye's exposition here, let me just say that his exposition, which fully satisfies the context, does not fully accord with our sense of the plain meaning of the verse.[32] He does, however, unlike R. Judah, cover the full verse, thus satisfying the dictum that a text must make sense in its own context, satisfying, in the language of the Gemara, the *peshatei dikra*. This example from *Eruv.* 23b is perhaps the most difficult one in which to see the connection between peshat and context. Not only did the modern scholars who dealt with the problem of peshat and derash misunderstand the explanation of R. Judah, but even some traditional scholars did not fully grasp it. The most accurate interpretation of R. Judah's explanation was given by R. A. C. Shor (d. 1632) in his book *Torat Chaim*, and even his explanation is incomplete.

b. Kidd. 80b

In *b. Kidd. 80b* the word *peshat* clearly refers to context. Had we not known from other places how Rashi understood the noun *peshat*, from his wording at this text we would have concluded that he too identifies peshat with context. The Talmud says: "R. Yochanan in the name of R. Simeon the son of Yehotzadak said: Where is the prohibition against *yichud* (the private mixing of the sexes outside the marital relationship) alluded to in the Torah? It is written (Deut. 13:7): 'If your brother, the son of your mother, entices you.' Can only the son of your mother entice and not the son of your father? It is to teach that only the son may be alone with his mother, but no other man may be alone with women biblically forbidden on account of incest." The context of the verse in Deuteronomy is idolatrous enticement, "to go and serve other gods which neither you nor your father have known." R. Yochanan's exposition that the verse is referring to (or more accurately, alluding to) *yichud* (the mixing of the sexes) is out of context. It more likely belongs to Lev. 18 or 20, where the prohibitions against incest are enumerated. The Gemara, therefore, asks: "What is the *peshatei dikra*?" Rashi comments: "Concerning the peshat (context) of the verse, which talks of enticement—why does the verse mention only 'your mother's son'?" Remember, even R. Yochanan called this exposition a *remez*, a mere allusion.[33] Thereupon the Gemara quotes another explanation, again by Abaya, that the verse mentions "the son of your mother" and not the "son of your father" (your half-brother from the same father) to tell you that you should not listen even to him to whom you are close when he entices you to worship foreign idols. You are close to him both because you have no contention with him, unlike your father's son, concerning matters of inheritance and because you probably live with him in your mother's house. Whether Abaye's explanation is right or wrong, it satisfies the context and it is, therefore, a fitting answer to the question of *"peshatei dikra."*

b. Zevach. 113a

The next example is *b. Zevach.* 113a. In our printed editions of the Talmud the word *dikra* is missing, but it is found in the manuscripts. R. Nachman the son of Yitzchak (a late fourth century Babylonian scholar) explains the controversy between R. Yochanan and Resh Lakish over whether the flood rains during Noah's time had fallen also on the land of Israel. R. Nachman's says that the two are disagreeing over how to understand the verse in Ezek. 22:24: "Son of man, say unto her (the land of Israel) 'You are a land that is not cleansed, nor rained upon in the day of indignation.'" R. Yochanan maintains that Scripture speaks rhetorically: "O *Eretz Yisrael* are you not clean? [You are, for] the rain did not descend upon you in the day of indignation." Resh Lakish insists that one ought to understand the verse in line with the *peshatei dikra*: "O' *Eretz Yisrael* you are not clean! Did not the rain descend upon you in the day of indignation?" The difference between R. Yochanan and Resh Lakish, as already noticed by the Maharasha, is that according to R. Yochanan the first half of the verse is to be read rhetorically, "O *Eretz Yisrael*, are you not clean?" and the second half of the verse is to be read declaratively, "the rain did not descend upon you in the day of indignation"; whereas according to Resh Lakish it is the reverse: the first half of the verse is to be read declaratively, "O *Eretz Yisrael*, you are not clean," and the second half of the verse is to be read rhetorically, "did not the rain descend upon you in the day of indignation?" The difference in the interpretation of the verse reflects their respective opinions whether the flood rains descended upon *Eretz Yisrael* or not. R. Yochanan is of the opinion that they did not, and Resh Lakish is of the opinion that they did. Modern scholars found it puzzling why Resh Lakish's interpretation is closer to *peshatei dikra* than R. Yochanan's. Why is interpreting the first half of the verse rhetorically and the second half declaratively less according to the peshat than doing the reverse? The answer is: it is not the formal structure of the interpretation that makes one closer to the *peshatei dikra* than the other. It is the context that makes the difference. According to R. Yochanan, the verse is talking in favor of the land of Israel, counter to the rest of the chapter which condemns the land of Israel and its inhabitants. Resh Lakish is closer to the peshat because he is closer to the condemnatory tone of the rest of the chapter by accusing the land of being unclean. The accusation fits the context, and that makes Resh Lakish's interpretation *peshatei dikra*, fitting the peshat of the larger text.

b. Chul. 6a

Following the order of the Talmud, the next example is from *Chul.* 6a. The Talmud there reports that R. Meir sent his disciple R. Simeon the son of Eleazar to fetch some wine from the Cutheans (the Samaritans). He was met by a certain old man who said to him: "Put a knife to your throat, if you are a man given to appetite" (Prov. 23:2, meaning if you are an observant Jew, abstain from using non-Jewish, Cuthean wine). Thereupon the Gemara asks: "What is the *peshatei dikra*?" The answer:

> It refers to a pupil sitting before his master. For R. Chiya taught [quoting the whole verse] "When you sit down to eat with a ruler, consider well who is before you and put a knife to your throat if you are a man of appetite." If the pupil knows that the master is capable of answering the question then the student may ask [a question]. Otherwise consider well who is before you and put a knife into your throat . . . and leave him [seek for yourself another teacher and do not put your teacher to shame].

R. Chiya's exposition following the *peshatei dikra* is clearly not closer to the plain meaning of the text than what the older man implied when he quoted the verse before the *peshatei dikra*. If anything, it is less plain. What R. Chiya's exposition has over the old man's implied meaning is that R. Chiya covered the whole verse, not only the part quoted by the old man. Pertaining to the actual meaning of that verse, there is little difference between R. Chiya's exposition and the old man's implied meaning; they can both be read into the verse. Both understood it to mean that you have to restrain yourself, not to eat as in the case of the old man, or not to ask questions as in the case or R. Chiya. In both cases, if it is too difficult, "put a knife to your throat." If R. Chiya nevertheless satisfies the *peshatei dikra* better than the old man, it is only because the old man did not reveal to us how he understands the phrase "When you sit . . ." which precedes the text he quoted. Hence, *peshatei dikra* in this context means the extension of the text, that which was said before the quote.

b. Chul. 133a

The most difficult case of an exposition given after the Gemara invokes a *peshatei dikra* that is actually less in accordance with peshat than the rejected exposition is *Chul.* 133a. It prompted the scholars to offer all sorts of forced explanations. The standard text defies even the meaning of peshat as extension or context. The only solution to this difficult text is to accept the reading of manuscript Rome 2, the Rif, and the Rosh,[34] whose text of the verse, when shown to R. Safra in a dream, contained only the first third of Prov. 25:20: "As one who wears a torn garment in cold weather [or] a decorative garment which is not warm."[35] (The standard translation, however, is "One who takes off a garment in cold weather." I believe that the Talmud understood this phrase to mean when one performs a useless act rather than when one performs a negative act, such as taking off a garment in cold weather. That nuance was reserved for the end of the verse, "he that sings songs to a bad [sinful] heart." The useless act symbolizes R. Joseph's telling a halakha which was misunderstood by Rava.) Following R. Safra's dream and its explanation, Abaye[36] asked "What is the *peshatei dikra*?" What is the meaning of the continuation of the verse, which talks about "singing songs to a bad (sinful) heart?" And R. Dimi or R. Joseph answered him:

> It refers to one who teaches a disciple who is unworthy" [unbelieving or nonobservant]. For R. Judah stated in the name of Rabbi: whosoever teaches a disciple who is unworthy, will fall into Gehinom; as

it is written [Job 20:26], "A fire not blown by man shall consume him that has an unworthy remnant in his tent."

From the answer to Abaye's question one can surmise that Abaye felt that an innocent misunderstanding on the part of the student, the type that Rava was guilty of, does not make the student's heart a sinful one. The end of the verse must be referring to somebody else, and Abaye was told it is referring to one who teaches an unworthy disciple. *Peshatei dikra* there means continuation. I can think of no other criterion by which the derash that the verse is referring to an unworthy disciple is more appropriate to the peshat than the interpretation that it refers to a student who misunderstood his teacher's statement.

b. Arakh. 8b

The next example comes from *b. Arakh.* 8b. The Talmud there quotes R. Pappa as having said: "'Your righteousness is like the mighty mountains' [Ps. 36:7] refers to human leprosy [which could last one week]; 'Your judgments are like the great deep' refers to the leprosy of houses (which may last three weeks)." After which the Gemara asks, "What is the *peshatei dikra*?" and answers, quoting R. Judah,[37] that the *peshatei dikra* is: "Were it not for your righteousness, [as great] as the mighty mountains, who could stand before your judgments, [as profound as] the great deep?" Apparently the Gemara assumed that the word *tzidkatkha* (your righteousness) implies mercy, forgiveness for sins committed, and conversely that the word *mishpateikha* (your judgments) implies judgment for sins committed. The juxtaposition of the two words in the verse implies contrast. It was understood so already by R. Ishmael (a late first century Palestinian scholar) who in *Lev. Rab.* 27:1 (and parallels) is quoted as having said:

> To the righteous who obey the Torah, which was given on the mighty mountains, the Holy One accords love in such an abundance that it towers up like His mighty mountains. Hence Your righteousness is like the mighty mountains. But to the wicked, to those who do not obey the Torah, which was given on the mighty mountains, the Holy One, searching out the very depths of their beings, accords the

strictness of His judgment. Hence, your judgments are like the great deep.

R. Pappa's exposition that the verse refers to human leprosy and to leprosy of the houses respectively does not cover the verse's contrast of *tzidkatkha* and *mishpateikha*. It does not explain the entire verse. One can perhaps view leprosy either as mercy—a shield against greater punishment or a warning to repent—or as a punishment. But one cannot view it as both mercy *and* a punishment. There is no reason why human leprosy should be designated as mercy and the leprosy of the houses as punishment. The relationship between human leprosy and the leprosy of the houses relative to the time one must wait may be compared to the relationship between mighty mountains and the great deep but not to the relationship between mercy and punishment. R. Pappa's exposition ignores the latter relationship, prompting the question "What is the *peshatei dikra*?" What is meant by the difference in designation? The Gemara answered by quoting the exposition of R. Judah and Rabbah, who each, though in different ways, make the verse convey a contrast between God's mercy and God's punishment.

b. Arakh. 32a

We have now come to the last instance of the expression *peshatei dikra*: that of *Arakh.* 32a. It concerns the dispute between R. Judah and R. Simeon in the Mishnah: "If a house is built into the city wall, R. Judah says: it is not accounted as a dwelling house in a walled city [which is subject to certain rules if it is sold]. R. Simeon says: its outer wall is deemed to be the city wall." The Gemara quotes R. Yochanan saying that "both [R. Judah and R. Simeon] expounded the same scriptural verse[38] (Josh. 2:15): 'Her [Rahab's] house was upon the side of the wall and she dwelt upon the wall.' R. Simeon explains it according to *peshatei dikra*, while R. Judah maintains she dwelt upon the wall, but not in a walled city."

Some versions[39] of the Talmud do not include the words *peshatei dikra* and instead have: "R. Simeon holds her house was upon the side of the wall and R. Judah holds she dwelt upon the wall, not in a walled city." For symmetry in style and other reasons, I believe that this is the correct reading. Accordingly, R. Yochanan is saying that

R. Simeon is emphasizing the first half of the verse, "Her house was upon the side of the wall," implying that her house was within the wall; while R. Judah is emphasizing the second half of the verse, "she dwelt upon the wall" to which he added "but not in a walled city."

I would have decided more conclusively in favor of this reading were it not for my inability to account for anyone's motive for adding the words *peshatei dikra* to the text—an addition that was already extant during the Middle Ages (both Rashi and his colleague, R. Elyakim of Speyer quote it).[40] During the Middle Ages[41] (as I will show below), peshat was conceived to be identical with plain meaning. R. Simeon's interpretation is not any closer to the plain meaning than is R. Judah's. Why then, would somebody add these two words to the opinion of R. Simeon?

Be that as it may, whoever added these words to R. Jochanan's statement most likely understood R. Simeon and R. Judah to be differing as well over how much of the verse should be exposited. R. Simeon exposited the whole verse, both the first half "her house was upon the side of the wall" and the second half, "she dwelt upon the wall." The first half tells us where her house was and the second half tells us that she was dwelling within the wall. (Because the house was upon the side of the wall, it was subject to all the obligations and privileges attendant upon inhabitants of a walled city.) Whereas R. Judah exposited only the second half of the verse, from which he deduced that Rahab did not live in a walled city. Using the word *peshatei* in the sense of extension, or, as it were, of spreading out the whole text, not only a part of it, someone after R. Yochanan[42] (possibly still during the talmudic period) added the words "kipeshatei dikra" to the opinion of R. Simeon, indicating that R. Simeon, unlike R. Judah, had made use of the whole verse, the full extension of the text.

P. Sanh., beginning

A conclusive example that *peshateih dekarya* means extension, continuation or the flow of the entire verse is the beginning of the Palestinian Talmud, Tractate *Sanhedrin*. The Talmud there asks why the Mishnah specifically mentions that "cases concerning theft or personal injury" are decided by three judges. It already said at the beginning that cases concerning property are decided by three judges, and property includes theft and personal injury. The Talmud answers: "It [the Mishnah] comes to tell you *kipeshuta dikarya*," the Mishnah follows the order or the flow of the verses in Exod. 21. Verse 1 begins with a general statement of the Mishnah about property and then proceeds to talk about theft and personal injury. Peshat there is clearly continuation.

Similarly, in the other instance in the Palestinian Talmud (*p. Sanh.* 10.2 29b) where *peshutei dikaryei* is mentioned, the expression has a similar connotation. It concerns 2 Sam. 6:1: "And David again gathered together the chosen men of Israel, thirty thousand." R. Berachya in the name of R. Aba the son of Kahana interpreted it to mean that David gathered together ninety thousand chosen men. He deduced this from the first two words of the verse, *vayosef 'od* (gathered again), each word designating a set of thirty thousand and *peshutei dikaryei*, thirty thousand. The first sixty thousand (the two sets of thirty thousand) R. Berachya deduces from the two words of the beginning of the verse whereas the last thirty thousand are given explicitly in the *peshutei dikaryei*, in the continuation of the verse, at the end of the verse. Note he does not quote the language of the end of the verse. He merely says that the continuation of the text mentions a third set of thirty thousand. Had he quoted the end of the verse, he would not have said *peshutei dikaryei*. The straight meaning of a text is not called peshat.

b. Sanh. 100b

The same meaning of *peshat* is evident in *b. Sanh.* 100b, even though the commentators, both traditional and modern, understood it differently. It begins with a statement of R. Joseph (an early fourth century Babylonian scholar) that "it is forbidden to read the book of Ben Sira."

> Abaye said to him: Why so? Is it because it is written in the book: "Do not strip the skin of a fish (some say:[43] of a beast) from its ear so that the skin would not go to waste, but roast it in the fire and eat with it two twisted loaves"? Now, Abaye continues, if you object to it as understood according to the *peshatei*, the Torah too states [Deut. 20:19]. "You shall not destroy the trees thereof." If you object to it as understood according to *midrasha* [derash], this teaches us proper manners, that one should not cohabit unnaturally.

It is generally assumed that the difference between *peshatei* and *midrasha* in that case is similar to what later on during the Middle Ages was called peshat and derash, plain meaning and applied meaning. If this were so, then Abaye (mid-fourth century Babylonian scholar) would have already called plain meaning, or a meaning close to it, peshat.

This view is not correct. *Peshatei* there, as in the examples quoted above, means extension, continuation, the whole verse, and sometimes the larger context. What seems to have escaped the scholars dealing with the relationship between peshat and derash was that the *midrasha* interpretation covers only the first sentence of the verse, namely, "do not strip the skin of a fish from its ear." The *midrasha* interprets "do not waste the skin" metaphorically as meaning not to cohabit unnaturally, not to waste semen. The continuation of the verse, however, does not fit this interpretation. It is extremely difficult, despite the efforts by R. Jacob Emden (1698–1776) in his glossa on the Talmud, to connect the rest of the verse, "roast it in the fire and eat it with two twisted loaves," with wasting semen. The *midrasha*'s interpretation conceives the first sentence as a metaphor for not wasting semen while the rest of the verse is conceived of literally, as a command not to waste the skin of a fish (or a beast) but "eat it with two twisted loaves of bread." (The plausibility that the idea that the latter half of the verse is not connected with the first sentence is strengthened by the reading of the *Yalkut Shimoni*, a twelfth-century collection of commentaries on the Bible, in a manuscript quoted by R. R. Rabbinovicz in *Dikdukei Sofrim* (*Sanh.* p. 303, n. 30) *velo* [the conjunctive] instead of *delo*, allowing for a new independent sentence.)[44] The interpretation that makes the fish sentence refer to skin is therefore called the *peshatei* interpretation because its illustration is the same as the continuation of the verse, not to waste skin. The verse thus forms a unit. In contrast, the *midrasha*'s interpretation separates the first sentence from the rest of the verse. The topic is the same, not to waste, but the illustration is different: the illustration of the first sentence is semen; that of the rest of the verse, skin. There is nothing unusual here about the use of *peshatei*. What is unique here is the use of *midrasha* as counter to *peshatei*. In the talmudic literature this is the only place where the two are mentioned together as opposites.

b. Ketub. 38b

A somewhat problematic example is to be found in the *b. Ketub.* 38b. There R. Akiva in the *baraita* ignores the three words *asher lo orasa* (Exod. 22:15; Deut. 22:28—"that is not betrothed") which imply that a woman who was betrothed and divorced and then seduced is not entitled to the fine the Bible imposes on a seducer. R. Akiva is of the opinion that she is entitled to the fine. These three words in both places, in Exodus and in Deuteronomy, according to R. Akiva, do not have meaning of their own but serve merely as a *gezera shava*—a hermeneutic principle which makes two disparate subjects share similar characteristics by virtue of their having similar words. In this instance the two subjects are seduction and violation (rape), and the similar characteristic is that they both pay the same fine. The Talmud is surprised that R. Akiva would allow a *gezera shava* to deprive a text of its peshat. There *peshat* could easily mean plain meaning. However, it does not have to mean that. The surprise of the Talmud was not that R. Akiva abandoned the peshat in favor of a derash, a plain meaning in favor of an applied meaning—this is not uncommon—but that he abandoned the peshat without replacing it with a derash. He merely cited a *gezera shava*, which by nature contains no new *derasha*, no new meaning, only a linking together of two different subjects. A *gezera shava* cannot substitute for the text or for the meaning. The text remains and still needs to be explained—in our case, the words *asher lo orasa* still need to be explained even after the *gezera shava*—and R. Akiva does not explain it. The surprise is that R. Akiva could on the basis of a *gezera shava*, which by nature cannot change a text nor modify it,[45] ignore the text altogether. Had he offered an alternative meaning in the form of a derash, the *gezera shava* could then have served as a support for the *derasha*. But without an alternative meaning, how can the peshat of the words *asher lo orasa*" (which implies that a woman who was betrothed, divorced, and then seduced or violated is not entitled to the biblical fine) be suppressed? Peshat, therefore, in this case, does not refer to the plain meaning in contrast to applied meaning, but to the meaning of the text. *Peshatei* there has the other connotation of the root *p-sh-t* in rabbinic literature (given by the dictionaries) that of explanation, teaching.[46] The question was how can a *gezera shava* do away with the teaching of the text? To which R. Nachman the son of Yitzchak replied: "Read in the text 'that is not a betrothed maiden.'" His reply was misunderstood by the commentators. Elsewhere[47] I explained that R. Nachman suggested changing the vocalization of *orasa* to *arusa*, which if taken in the posttalmudic sense would be a passive participle: one who is not presently betrothed, and not one who formerly was betrothed and divorced, the subject of R. Akiva.[48]

The Meaning of "Vadai" in Talmudic Literature

Before I leave the talmudic period[49] and proceed to the Middle Ages, let me correct an erroneous impression that may have arisen from the above analysis, namely, that the rabbis of the Talmud were not aware of the difference between peshat and derash, between the plain and the applied meaning of a text. This is not true. Modern scholars have already pointed to several terms in rabbinic literature that connote the type of meaning one obtains with initial reading, akin to what we call plain meaning. They are *vadai, mamash*, and *kemishmao* (or *kishemuo*). Of these terms, *vadai* is most consistent, which is why it was singled out in the earlier part of this essay. When used as an exegetical term, it always means something close to what we call today peshat, or a variation thereof. The other terms do not always mean that. That *kemishmao* sometimes means "plain meaning" is clear when one compares the statement in *m. Sota* 8:5, which has *kemishmao*, with the same statement in *t. Sota* 7.22 which has *vadai*. On the other hand, that *mishmao* does not always mean plain meaning can be seen, for instance, from the *Pesach.* 2.1, p. 28c, which states that from Lev. 7:23—"You shall eat no fat of ox or sheep or goat"—we can learn *mimashma* the following verse— that "the fat of that which died by itself and the fat of that which is torn of beasts may be used for any other service" other than eating. Plain meaning does not compel us to assume—which this *mimashma* takes for granted—that whenever the Bible says not to eat something, that something is permitted for other usages. For our purpose, however, to show that the rabbis of the Talmud were aware of the difference between plain and applied meaning, it is enough that *vadai* consistently signifies something resembling peshat. For that, the reader could consult the literature in the secondary sources.[50] They collected the examples and generally interpreted them correctly. I will nevertheless, quote one example, the oldest example of *vadai* from the *Mekhilta, Yithro*, tractate *Amalek*:[51] "'Zipporah and her two sons in a strange land.' [Exod. 18:3] R. Joshua (a late first century Palestinian scholar) says: 'It was a land strange to him, *vadai*'. R. Eliezar of Modi'im says: 'In a strange land—where God was like a stranger.'" R. Eliezar of Modi'im's exposition is derash. The plain meaning of the phrase "in a strange land" is as R. Joshua said. The strange land is Midian, where Moses sojourned, married Zipporah, and had a son whom he named Gershom because "he said: I have been a stranger in a strange land." R. Joshua calls his interpetation *vadai*. *Vadai*, when used as an exegetical term, has the connotation of plain or a cognate meaning. R. Joshua and all those after him who used the word *vadai* in the same sense that he used it were aware of the difference between plain and nonplain meaning. He used a special term to designate this difference, and there is no reason to doubt that the other rabbis of the Talmud were equally aware of this difference. What I am arguing for is not that the rabbis did not know this difference but that they did not consider peshat as being inherently superior to derash to the extent that, like a modern exegete, they would not abandon the peshat unless it were hopelessly unintelligible. To the rabbis of the Talmud, the slightest impetus or provocation, even a light textual or logical difficulty, was sufficient to prompt them to embrace an applied meaning. A typical *derasha* will begin with the applied meaning and rhetorically ask: "You said A or perhaps it is B" (B will be the plain meaning). "It cannot be B because of. . . ." The A often does not meet the standards a modern exegete will consider sufficient to warrant changing the plain meaning, which, by the way, may or may not be identical with the reading obtained at first reading. *Vadai* almost always describes a meaning which is both plain and obtained at first reading.

The Rabbis' Sense of Plain Meaning

Moreover, there is good evidence that the rabbis' sense of plain meaning (more accurately stated, their sense of what is not derash) does not correspond to ours. As mentioned earlier in the essay,[52] they often attributed to the Samaritans (and the Sadducees) halakhic expositions that are far from the plain meaning of the text while claiming all along that the Samaritans and the Sadducees considered obligatory only those laws that were written explicitly in the Torah. Laws that are not written explicitly in the Torah, that are obtained through interpretation, are not obligatory (see, for example, *b. Sanh.* 32b). Yet the rabbis assumed that the Samaritans (and the Sadducees) observed certain laws that to our understanding are not written in the Torah at all (see, for example, *b. Hor.* 4a). Often in the recorded debates in the Talmud between the Pharisees and the Sadducees, expositions are exchanged between the two groups that bear little resemblance to the written text (see, for example, *b. Menach.* 65a–66a).[53] An interesting example in this regard can be quoted from Rashi's commentary on Lev. 16:2. The verse states: "for I appear in the cloud upon the ark cover"; upon which Rashi comments: "For I [God] always appear there (in the Holy of Holies) in the cloud . . . make sure that you (the high priest) do not frequent there. This is the peshat. But our teachers have exposited it to mean the cloud of the incense burned on Yom Kippur" (see verse 13). The interpretation which Rashi calls derash in contrast to peshat, that the phrase refers to the incense burned on Yom Kippur, is also the interpretation of the Sadducees.[54] Apparently, the rabbis of the Talmud did not consider this interpretation derash. But it was derash to Rashi, living as he did in a different period with its own sense of peshat.

The Meaning of "Beferush" in Amoraic Literature

Let me also note that several times in the Talmud an *amora* uses the word *beferush*, which generally means "explicit" (often in contrast to *mihlala*; "through deduction") or "expressly" in connection with an exposition that to our taste is far from being explicit or expressly stated. *B. Ketub.* 32b is a good example: "R. Elai said: the Torah has expressly stated that the *zommemim* [false witnesses] have to pay money." The anonymous *stam* inquires:

Where has the Torah stated thus? Consider it is written [Deut. 19:19] "You shall do to him what he has done to his brother." Why is it written further "hand for hand"? that means a thing that is given from hand to hand, and that is money. And the same appears to be the case of a person who injures another person. It is written [Lev.

24:19], "As he has done, so shall be done to him." Why is it written further "so shall it be rendered to him"? That means a thing that can be rendered, and that is money."

None of these expositions appears to us to be "expressly" stated in the Torah. But they did appear so to the rabbis of the Talmud. Similarly, *b. B. Kam.* 78a states: "If with respect to sacrifices, is it not explicitly (*be hadya*) stated: 'A bullock or a sheep' (Lev. 22: 27) which excepts a hybrid?" To us, the phrase "a bullock or a sheep" does not explicitly except a hybrid. The difference between the rabbis of the Talmud and us is not only that they were more receptive to applied meaning but also that their notion of what constitutes applied meaning seems to be narrower than ours. That, too, is part of their particular exegetical state of mind.

The Medieval Period

Shemuel ben Chofni: Peshat Alone

The picture during the Middle Ages was quite different. The interpretive state of mind of medieval rabbis embodied a belief in the superiority of peshat over derash, which around the tenth century was projected back into the talmudic period. The impetus came from the Arabs.[55] Some of the rabbinic terminology of the period distinguishing peshat from derash (and extolling the former) was taken from the Arabs. But the receptivity was their own. They were ready for that awareness by virtue of their state of mind. Their interpretive state of mind was such that interference with the substantive meaning of a text was less and less tolerated. They accordingly responded to their environment and chose among the ideas extant those that were in sympathy with their inclination. In an earlier period the choice would have been different.

The first rabbi to ascertain the superiority of peshat over derash was R. Saadya Gaon (882–942), who says in several places, most notably in his magnum opus, the *Book of Beliefs and Opinions*, at the beginning of chapter seven, that "everything that is found in the Bible has to be understood according to peshat except when the peshat is against the senses, or against reason, or if it contradicts

another verse in the Bible, or if it opposes tradition." In the exceptional cases, one has to interpret the text according to derash.
R. Saadya does not explicitly state, though he tacitly assumes, that
the rabbis of the Talmud shared his conviction. He has not yet
connected the inviolability of peshat (except for the cases mentioned above) with the dictum in the Talmud (profusely quoted
later on) "No text can be deprived of its peshat." That was left for
a much younger contemporary of his (who was also the head of
the academy in Sura, Babylon), R. Shemuel ben Chofni (d. 1013).[56]
R. Shemuel ben Chofni was the first one, according to the extant,
literature, to interpret the word peshuto in the celebrated dictum to
mean simple or plain meaning and to make the dictum imply the
invincibility of peshat. R. Shemuel's interpretation spread rapidly
throughout the Jewish world. In less than a few decades after
R. Shemuel's death, a younger contemporary of his, in Spain, R. J.
ibn Ganach (died c. 1040)[57] quoted the dictum already. R. Tuvia the
son of Eliezer, the author of *Lekach Tov*, who lived in Bulgaria
around 1100, quoted it.[58] Both Rashi (d. 1105 in France)[59] and
R. A. Ibn Ezra (who was born in Spain and died somewhere else in
1164)[60] quote it a few times. And it has since been repeated numerous times until challenged by modern scholars.[61] There is, however,
an interesting difference between R. Shemuel ben Chofni and the
others with regard to the full significance of the dictum of the
Talmud, which R. Shemuel connected with plain meaning. R. Shemuel, who took the idea of the invincibility of peshat from
R. Saadya and who in turn most likely took it from the Arabs,[62]
both sources of which give, if not an overwhelming endorsement of
peshat (with exceptions), at least a very strong preference for peshat
over derash, understood the dictum in the Talmud, as did Maimonides in his *Book of Commandments*, root 2, to mean that no text
can be deprived of being interpreted exclusively according to peshat. The derash has to be rejected. In contrast, R. J. ibn Ganach,
Rashi, Ibn Ezra, and others understood the talmudic statement to
mean that peshat and derash coexist. The derash is not to be
rejected. Paradoxically, R. Shemuel's interpretation of the talmudic
dictum, even if one grants that peshat there means plain meaning, is
in itself against the peshat of the dictum. The plain meaning of the
dictum, as already argued by the Ramban in his criticism of Maimonides' *Book of Commandments*, is not that the peshat is the only

correct meaning, for then the dictum should have read "A text has
only its peshat." By saying "A text cannot be deprived of its
peshat," the rule implies that the derash remains but is never
exclusive. It always shares the text with peshat, while the peshat
may or may not be exclusive (depending on whether or not there
is a bona fide derash). Such was R. Shemuel's reliance on Arabic
sources (and that of Maimonides afterwards) that he refracted
the dictum in the Talmud in a way that would make it comply
with what he derived from these sources. The claim was made
there that in general peshat ought to be the exclusive meaning of a
text, and the dictum in the Talmud was made to fit that claim.
Ibn Ganach and the others had no such reliance and, guided by
the words of the dictum, understood them to mean that a bona
fide derash has a legitimate claim, so that while a text can never
be deprived of its peshat, neither can the peshat deprive the text
of its legitimate derash. There is room for derash alongside of
peshat.[63]

Rashbam and Ibn Ezra: Balancing Peshat and Derash

How did the rabbis of the Middle Ages, those who were committed
to peshat, cope with the historic problem that the rabbis of the
Talmud did not always adhere to peshat, that many a derasha in the
Talmud (including *derashot* on which laws, demanding compliance,
are based) are offensive to peshat? I have already mentioned that
the two greatest advocates of peshat in the Middle Ages, the Rashbam (d. 1160)[64] and Ibn Ezra, did not offer a common solution.[65]
Ibn Ezra considered the offensive expositions as *Asmakhtot*, the
biblical text serving only as a mnemonic device to ease recall or to
tint the content with biblical authority, not as a source of the law.
The source of the law is either a rabbinic ordinance or a tradition.
Ibn Ezra had to concede in those instances where the exposition
negates the content of the plain meaning, when the two meanings
are mutually exclusive, that the derash is the true meaning of the
text. The rabbis, says Ibn Ezra, would not have based a law on a
text against its peshat. In those few instances where it appears to us
that they did, we have to have confidence in them that they knew
better what constitutes peshat.[66] Being primarily a philologist, he
had little use for seeming redundancies that could easily be attrib-

uted to stylistic peculiarities. One cannot escape the impression that Ibn Ezra wrestled mightily with the problem of peshat and derash, yet did not fully overcome the tension generated by that problem. The Rashbam, however, was not willing to concede that derash is the meaning of the text, even in those instances where the exposition, followed by practical halakhah, negates the content of the simple meaning. In his commentary on the Torah, he always follows what he considers to be peshat, but makes room for the halakha through the many seeming redundancies one encounters in the biblical text. In his commentary he makes no mention of *Asmakhtot*. Peshat and derash are two distinct levels of interpretation. You follow the peshat when you are interpreting the meaning of the text, and you deduce the *derasha* from "redundancy of the verses, or from peculiarities of language in which the plain meaning is written. It is written in such a way that we can learn from it the binding nature of the *derasha*."[67] When peshat and derash contradict, one teaches the peshat but behaves according to derash. It is as if the purpose of the redundancy is to tell the Jew how to behave, what interpretation to follow in matters of practical halakha. In this sense, derash is more important. The Rashbam calls derash *ikar*, more essential than peshat. When the two are incompatible, one lives by derash. One gets the impression from the two places (on Gen. 1:1; 37:1) where the Rashbam quotes the dictum *ein mikra yotze middei peshuto* that he understood it to mean—and he is not alone in this— "No text should be deprived of being interpreted according to peshat." Even when the peshat is not followed practically, one still has to study the text according to peshat. The theoretical value of peshat ought never to be ignored. This is not the sense in which the dictum is quoted by Ibn Ezra (and by the Rambam and others for that matter). To them the dictum indicates equality of peshat and derash, which they found difficult to reconcile with the prevalent halakha. Perhaps because of this understanding, despite his enormous halakhic expertise on the one hand and his critical acumen on the other, the Rashbam, unlike Ibn Ezra, does not display tension when dealing with the problem of peshat and derash. To him, the dictum did not generate halakhic problems. It was intended only for exegetical purposes.

Maimonides and Divrei Sofrim: Safeguarding Peshat

What I have said about the difference between the Rashbam and Ibn Ezra is known. I repeated it mainly to contrast their positions with that of Maimonides, which has escaped scholarly notice, probably because what he had to say on the matter was not explicitly stated but rather needs to be inferred from the way he occasionally changes or modifies the *derasha* of the Talmud. It is my contention that Maimonides was even less accepting of derash than was the Rashbam or Ibn Ezra. He was not ready to readmit the derash via redundancy as the Rashbam did nor was he willing to concede to the rabbis of the Talmud a better grasp of what constitutes peshat, as Ibn Ezra did.

His position can be summarized as follows. Whenever there is no contradiction between the plain meaning and the exposition, and the former does not support the latter, Maimonides attributes the exposition to a source outside of the text, what he called "according to tradition"—*Mipi kabbala* or *Mipi hashmu'a*"[68] (akin to Ibn Ezra's *asmakhta*). He in fact created a new concept, *divrei soferim* to account for a number of *derashot* in the Talmud. What exactly the concept is, is not clear. In terms of its binding nature, it is less binding than a biblical law but more binding than a rabbinic ordinance. It is neither biblical nor rabbinic. This concept of Maimonides has been the subject of many comments since. Indeed, a whole book has been written containing primarily the summary of the comments, Jacob Neubauer's insightful study *Ha-Rambam al Divrei Sofrim*.[69] Yet the concept remains elusive. Whatever the concept is, it is an attempt to avoid grounding some expositions in the text. To Maimonides, the text doesn't always support the exposition.[70] The exposition derives its "sustenance" as it were from elsewhere. In this, Maimonides is not alone. Other scholars during the Middle Ages shared this view. What is unique to Maimonides is that sometimes when there is a contradiction between the exposition and the plain meaning—a decided minority of cases—he will change the nature of the exposition of the Talmud or subtly modify it in a manner that will reduce the flagrancy with which it is superimposed on the text. I will cite three examples:

1. I already quoted Rava's statement in *b. Yevam.* 24a that Deut.

25:6 in connection with levirate marriage was deprived of its peshat. The peshat of the verse says "the first born that she bears shall succeed in the name of his brother that is dead." The first child of the levirate union shall succeed in the name of his uncle. In contrast, the rabbis interpreted the verse to mean not the firstborn that *will be born* but the first born *that was already born*, the deceased's eldest brother "shall succeed in the name of his brother that is dead." Maimonides ignores Rava's acknowledgement that this is an instance where the text is deprived of its peshat and instead says (in *Mishnah Torah*, "Laws of Levirate Marriage" and *Chalitzah* 2.6):

> *Mipi hashmua* (from tradition) we know that the reference is to the oldest brother, that he should marry his brother's widow. As to the words *asher teled*, that she bears, the verb should not be taken in the future tense (that the widow will bear) but in the past tense (what the mother of the deceased bore already). The oldest that the mother bore shall succeed in the name of his brother."

In his commentary on *m. Yevam.* 2:8, Maimonides adds that "the Hebrew language uses sometimes the future tense in the sense of the past." Maimonides' exposition of the verse is against Rava's statement. The author of the book *Tosafot Yom Tov* and others tried hard to reconcile Maimonides' interpretation with the Talmud. Clearly Maimonides could not tolerate deprivation of the peshat even when done rarely. He changed the derash so that it would not imply such a deprivation. He deviated from the Talmud;[71] he had no other choice. His exegetical conscience did not allow him to violate the peshat so grossly.[72]

2. I already mentioned that according to the sages who disagreed with R. Yose ben Kipper in *b. Yevam.* 11b and parallels, the phrase in Deut. 24:4 "after that she is defiled" does not refer to the subject of the passage, that of remarrying a former husband, but to a *sota*, a woman who secluded herself with a man. The Gemara explicitly calls this interpretation a deprivation of peshat, a deprivation of context. In contrast, Maimonides ("Laws of Divorce" 11.12) quotes the view of the sages but subtly modifies their exposition. They are not saying that the verse "after that she is defiled" does not belong where it is written; that would be, for Maimonides, an unallowable supposition. Rather, they are comparing a *sota*, a woman who

secluded herself with a man, to a woman who remarried her former husband. Both are now labeled defiled, with the same consequences as those attendant upon any woman who is called defiled. "Included in this prohibition," says Maimonides, "is also a woman who was (or is suspected of being) unfaithful to her husband . . . that she cannot rejoin him, as it is written 'after she is defiled'—and she is defiled." The verse remains in its context of a woman who is remarrying her former husband. What the sages are saying, according to Maimonides, is that *a fortiori*,[73] one can deduce the case of a *sota* (who committed or is suspected of committing a greater sin) from the case of a woman who is remarrying her former husband, that like the latter, the former too is called "defiled." There is no interference with the text itself. The text remains in exclusive reference to a woman who is remarrying her former husband. Only by analogy is the text made to include a *sota* as well. But that is not what the Gemara is saying. To the Gemara, the sages "tore out" the phrase from where it was written and attached it elsewhere (possibly to Num. 5, where the subject of *sota* is taken up). Maimonides could not accept deprivation of peshat and substituted a different version of the sages.[74]

3. The following example is most subtle. The Babylonian Talmud in *B. Kam.* 82b–83a and parallels (both in the halakhic *midrashim* and in the Palestinian Talmud) utilizes the seeming difficulty, indeed the nigh impossibility, of measuring out an eye for an eye in the literal sense of calculating and inflicting equivalent physical losses in order to prove that when the Torah said "an eye for an eye," it did not mean a physical eye for an eye but monetary compensation. The clear implication of the Talmud is that the wording "an eye for an eye," despite its plain meaning to the contrary, was intended from the very beginning to be understood as monetary compensation. But according to Maimonides[75] in *The Guide of the Perplexed* (3.41), the wording of the Torah conveys physical punishment. The rabbis changed that to monetary compensation, following the Torah "whoever destroyed a human limb, similar punishment shall be meted out to him." However, since this is a practical impossibility—no two people are alike and similar bodily punishment is just not feasible—the rabbis decreed a substitute: monetary compensation. When one studies the verse, one has to interpret it to mean physical punishment. Similarly, when one

gives reason for the laws of the Torah, one has to give a reason commensurable with the sense of physical punishment. God, the author of the Torah, could be exact in meting out physical punishment measure for measure. Man cannot do that. He has to follow the oral law which decreed "incidents caused by humans which cannot be exactly retaliated, shall be compensated monetarily." The difference between the Talmud and Maimonides is clear. The Talmud saw no inconsistency between the wording of the text and the administering of the law. Both affirm the same principle, that of monetary compensation. In contrast, Maimonides saw in this law an inconsistency between the wording of the Torah and the way the rabbis interpreted it. He, therefore, assigned the wording of the Torah to what the perpetrator deserves and the interpretation of the rabbis to what he actually gets. He deserves physical punishment but receives monetary punishment. For the Talmud there is no discrepancy between the plain meaning of the text and its rabbinic interpretation; for Maimonides there is a discrepancy between the two. He mitigates it somewhat by saying that the Torah expresses the ideal, as it were, and the interpretation of the rabbis the viable. To men physical bodily punishment is not a viable alternative. Again, Maimonides cannot accept incongruity between peshat and derash.

In *Mishnah Torah*, however ("Laws of Wounding and Damages" 1.6), Maimonides retreats somewhat from this stance. He says: "even though these laws [pertaining to monetary compensation] appear to be a matter of [rooted in] the written Law, they were all made clear to us by Moses our teacher from Mount Sinai."[76] However, it only "appears" to be a matter of the written Law. It is not written explicitly in the Torah.[77] It is difficult to know whether there is here a change of mind or perhaps, in *Mishnah Torah*, written in Hebrew and intended for a different audience, he did not dare say that the intention of the Torah was physical punishment, and he hid behind an ambiguity.[78]

Also, of the two instances mentioned above where the Talmud says "the Torah expressly said that they have to pay money," the first instance is not quoted by Maimonides at all (in the "Laws of Witnesses" 18.1). The second instance, that of a person injuring another person, is quoted by him ("Laws of Wounding and Damages" 3.9; see also 1.3), but he omits the Gemara's exposition and substitutes another. Instead of quoting the Gemara's exposition that a person who had injured another person pays money (even though he also receives forty stripes for having violated the divine injunction not to injure a human being) because of the redundancy of the phrase (in Lev. 24:19) "so shall it be rendered to him," Maimonides quotes another verse, Exod. 21:19: "he shall pay for the loss of his time and shall cause him to be thoroughly healed." Maimonides clearly was not satisfied with the Gemara's expositions. They were not close enough to peshat. He omitted one and substituted another verse for the other.

For some reason that I cannot explain, Maimonides was less willing to follow the peshat when it came to counting the number of the commandments. He counts for instance among the negative commandments (no. 282) not to convict a person on the basis of a majority of one. He cites Exod. 23:2: "You shall not follow the multitude to do evil." That verse plainly understood hardly supports the notion that a majority of at least two witnesses is required in capital cases. Similarly, in negative commandment no. 287, he counts among the commandments not to accept the testimony of a relative. The verse he cites is Deut. 24:16: "Fathers shall not be put to death because of their children and children shall not be put to death because of their fathers." Again, the simple meaning of the verse is not testimony. He is, however, following the principle he set up in the first part of the work, called *Shorashim* (roots), in root two. No exposition, no *derasha*, shall be included among the commandments (they are considered *asmakhtot*)[79] unless the sages themselves indicated that this particular exposition is part of "the basic laws of the Torah or that it is scriptural. Then it is worthy to be counted among the commandments, since those who received it said that it was like scripture."

In the two examples mentioned above, Maimonides conceived of the sages of the Talmud as having thought of them as being "part of the basic laws of the Torah." He almost tells us that, perhaps apologetically, in no. 287. After stating the commandment and the verse, he says "the received interpretation is found in the *Sifrei* that parents shall not be put to death by the testimony of their children and children shall not be put to death by the testimony of their parents." He needs the support of the *Sifrei* to show that this interpretation was considered by the sages as the scriptural meaning of the commandment. On his own, he might not have said so. What still remains puzzling is his assertion in negative commandment no. 299 that the simple meaning of Lev. 19:14 "You shall not put a stumbling block before the blind" is not to give false advice to an ignorant person. Here it seems Maimonides sincerely believed that this is the plain meaning of the text, and, unlike no. 287, in which he may have had a different feeling but bowed to the *Sifrei*, to the "received interpretation," here he added his own explanation, that not giving wrong advice is the plain meaning of the text.[80]

One is inclined to conclude that when Maimonides wrote the *Book of Commandments*, he was less attracted to peshat than when he wrote the *Guide of the Perplexed* and the *Mishnah Torah*. Perhaps in the *Book of Commandments* he wanted to sound less radical than in the other books (the commandments are recited with different poetical embellishments in some synagogues as part of the prayer ritual). Surprising, of course, is his revolutionary attitude to derash and peshat in *Mishnah Torah* and in the *Guide of the Perplexed* rather than his traditional attitude in the *Book of Commandments*. The latter needs no explanation, the former does. One can safely assume that Maimonides would not have abandoned the exposition of the Talmud without having what may be called "meta-halakhic" reasons. He considered the relationship between peshat and derash as a nonhalakhic matter, a matter of thought, thus not subordinate to the Gemara.[81] Just as in matters of thought, in contradistinction to practice, he often deviates from the Gemara, so did he in matters belonging to the relationship of peshat and derash. The Gemara's halakha he always accepted, the exposition supporting the halakha he sometimes either modified or ignored. The exposition of halakha belongs in the realm of thought. And just as he attempted to reconcile the conflict between revelation and reason in a way that favors reason, so did he try to reconcile the conflict between peshat and derash in a way favoring peshat. Unlike the Rashbam, he could not, as it were, stand the tension between peshat and derash and hold on to both. He was compelled to choose between the two and he occasionally chose the peshat—the more reasonable.

II

ON MATTERS
OF THEOLOGY

Introduction to Part II: A Comment on Methodology

Any attempt to outline precisely and systematically the governing principles of rabbinic theology must confront the reality of rabbinic texts which lend themselves neither to theological precision nor systematization. Though the rabbis of the Talmudic era did engage in theological speculation about such classical religious issues as the nature of God and the dynamic of revelation, and about such eminently Jewish concerns as the chosenness of the Jewish people and the essence of Torah, such speculation seems to be haphazardly sprinkled throughout rabbinic literature. Rabbinic theology is not categorical nor easily categorized, and is more prone to homiletical discourse than to carefully groomed, neatly disciplined speculation. Rabbinic theology is often packaged and shrouded in aggada, within a folkloric context, functioning more as hortatory and pedagogic than as speculative literature. The rabbis of the Talmud were sophisticated legalists but not systematic theologians, and their attempts at theology were often quite expressive and intuitive but rarely methodical. These characteristics of rabbinic theological sources—the proliferation of theological viewpoints and their disorderly arrangement within rabbinic literature—can impede the construction of a modern Jewish theology that seeks to build upon the foundations of rabbinic thought. The challenge for modern

Jewish theology that aspires to be the legitimate heir of rabbinic thought remains: how to be both traditional and systematic?

That challenge represents our assignment and aspiration, in modest proportions, in the next two chapters. Though the labyrinthine nature of rabbinic theological literature can frustrate an attempt to formulate modern theological ideas in the spirit of the original sources, we hope to demonstrate that such a goal is not unachievable. The haphazard presentation and multiform content of rabbinic theology do not preclude the viability of a modern Jewish theology that is initiated through a survey of and inquiry into classical rabbinic theological sources. Rabbinic theological ruminations *can* be subjected to scrutiny and analysis despite the resistance occasioned by their nature. Statements of theological nuance found in rabbinic literature can be amplified to generate a contemporary brand of traditional Jewish theology, which we hope to exhibit through the remainder of the book.

Inference and Analogy as Means of Extracting Rabbinic Theology

The systematic mining of rabbinic theological sources can be fulfilled through two different methodologies. The first is to draw appropriate inferences and implications from rabbinic passages of theological significance for issues of contemporary relevance, in our case the interrelationship of peshat and derash. Rabbinic theological statements can in this way serve as the building blocks of a modern Jewish theological edifice. Just as an art critic may gain insight into (and from) a work of art that the artist himself never consciously recognized or intended, so may an interpreter of rabbinic theology explore and embrace the implications of the theology never explicitly projected by the original thinker himself. The interior and latent dimensions of art—and theology—represent fertile grounds for continual reinterpretation and fresh exposition.

This first method of theological extrapolation, of drawing justifiable, if perhaps unanticipated, inferences from rabbinic sources, will be reflected most prominently in the next chapter in our discussion of the famous talmudic story of R. Eliezer and R. Joshua and the latter's celebrated exclamation, *lo bashamayim hi*! ("It is not in

relation of these two methods to the practice of derash?

heaven!").[1] In that story, in which R. Joshua and his colleagues, constituting a majority, reject the opinion of R. Eliezer despite the fact that a heavenly voice has attested to its correctness, the rights—and sometimes the truthfulness—of minority opinions are championed. From this dramatic account of the collision of majority and minority (even though divine) halakhic positions, we will draw and defend the inference that underlying this rabbinic source is the concept of the dichotomy between practical halakha and intellectual study. This theological claim that the realms of practice and intellect do not necessarily converge is, admittedly, not expressly stated in the story of R. Eliezer and R. Joshua. Our theological assertion is *inferred* from the story following a careful analysis of its literary structure. Though the rabbis do not consciously or explicitly express the claim that we make, our theological conclusion is, nonetheless, defensible and warranted.

The second method of extracting systematic theology from otherwise unyielding rabbinic sources is through the use of analogy. A rabbinic source can serve as an explanatory paradigm that sheds light on an issue not directly discussed. The theological paradigm suggested by one or more rabbinic passages, when refracted through the prism of reasoning by analogy, can be transferred to a new, though related, theological context. This method will be employed in the concluding chapter of the book, as we address the issue of the occasional discrepancy between scriptural peshat and rabbinic derash. One rabbinic source which discusses changes in the script and language of the Torah will be conjoined to another which describes Ezra's role in emending the pentateuchal text. This confluence of contexts will yield theological benefits for our attempt to resolve the conflict of peshat and derash.

These two strategies of fashioning theological claims, which allow us to address contemporary concerns while not straying from rabbinic theological premises, may strike the critical reader as unsanctioned by scholarly standards. In such efforts at a modern recasting of rabbinic theology, the authorial intention of the original passages may occasionally be neglected or sidestepped—which violates a fundamental scholarly commitment. A dedication to the authorial intention of a text is usually considered the sine qua non of critical scholarship (see Appendix II). Theology via inference or analogy may be forced to sever the scholarly attachment to authorial intention in its pursuit of contemporary relevance and may consequently face the charge of "unscientific" method. The price of such theological extrapolation is that we cannot rightfully claim that the rabbis explicitly "said" or "intended" what we, in fact, assert. This price is one we must pay, however, if our theology is to be both traditional and contemporary.

The Multifariousness of the Sources

We have just conceded that the theological implications we draw from relevant rabbinic materials may transcend the explicit denotations, or authorial intentions, of the original sources. Our theologizing, however, will *not* violate another of scholarship's cardinal commitments: the integrity of mutually exclusive sources. That is, it will reject the tendency of certain brands of theology to harmonize conflicting passages. The reconciliation of theological passages that reflect divergent perspectives will be shunned. The multiplicity of rabbinic theological standpoints must be respected and affirmed. A fully consistent and comprehensive theological system can be gleaned from rabbinic sources only at the expense of the genuine multifariousness of the materials. Our theological project, limited in scope, will avoid abusing or compromising the rabbinic sources it handles by eschewing the facile harmonization of irreconcilable sources.[2]

Dogmatists have traditionally attempted to muzzle speculative diversity within Judaism. Theological variety has been increasingly perceived as particularly dangerous and potently corruptive. Theological options have been narrowed and limited through subjective, and selective, readings of previous rabbinic views. While halakhic variability over time is rationalized and explained away, intellectual dogmatists often try to place constraints upon speculative options, especially by tampering with the peshat of theological statements. For this reason the critical scholar, with an allegiance to the dictates of objective truth and accuracy—indeed, to peshat—must play the role of foil to proponents of speculative conformity. Critical scholarship, which repudiates the method of reading in, can serve to discern and isolate the divergent strands of Jewish thought. The genuine modern Jewish theologian must emulate the ways of the critical scholar, rejecting harmonization which serves to blur the distinctiveness of conflicting views. Speculative unanimity and uniformity must not be created artificially out of diversity. An honest reading of rabbinic theology must abstain from positing congruity and compatibility between intellectual positions where such does not exist. Theological latitude must be preserved.

We have so far touched on the variegated character of rabbinic theological stances and have asserted that though they elude transparent categorization and systematization, they are nevertheless susceptible to inference and analogy. Our task now is to explore the disparate modes and processes of *halakha* and *hashkafa*, of Jewish legal decision making and Jewish speculation. The theological claim that a dichotomy between practice and study is sometimes — necessary will be a byproduct of our discussion of the decided contrast between the respective traits of halakha and hashkafa.

The Difference between Jewish Theology and Jewish Law

As we have stated, diversity, and not unanimity, has been the distinguishing hallmark of rabbinic theology. In this respect, Jewish theology differs in its very essence from Jewish law. In the realm of halakha, the theoretical goals of the system, because of the demands and considerations of communal practice, are the determination of consensus and the development of uniformity. Halakhic opinions once branded as minority positions are dismissed as inoperative, unless resurrected later as majority views. The quest for halakhic unanimity and consistency may indeed interfere with and hamper critical scrupulousness and objectivity. Logical truth does not always determine the "correctness" of halakhic decisions. In other words, systemic halakhic guidelines may safeguard halakhic correctness, but not necessarily guarantee objective truth.[3] In the pursuit of the understanding of objective reality, however, truth and logic cannot be compromised. Speculative differences need not be suppressed or stifled, for the demands of halakhic uniformity are not relevant in the realm of the intellect. Only the protection of the full range of speculative options (within recognized systemic boundaries which serve to distinguish classical rabbinic Judaism from Jewish sects and from other religions) can ensure the vitality and future prosperity of the intellectual quest.

The spirit of the halakhic process is contrary to the spirit of Jewish theology described above. While rabbinic theology is presented in neither systematic nor uniform fashion, halakha strives to be decisive, precise and orderly, as well as systematic and uniform. However, the respective semblances of theology and halakha belie their true character. Ironically, the tendency towards multiplicity and untidiness within Jewish theology does not accord with the very nature of intellectual speculation, that is, with thought that seeks to ascertain, through the objective methods of science and logic, the facts of external reality. The halakhic propensity toward uniformity and constancy, on the other hand, does not conform to the very contours of its historical process—one that is, by its very nature, characterized by variability and mutability. Indeed, as we shall see, the halakhic process, which aspires towards precision and systematization, is often quite idiosyncratic and subjective, precisely because it is propelled by human initiative.[4] Jewish theology, which theoretically seeks to capture a reality that is objective and static, is irrepressibly—almost systemically—individualistic; halakha, with pretensions to systemic stability and perpetuity, is actually contingent upon the passing of time, the conditions of the environment, and the standards of the majority. In sum, though Jewish theology appears disorderly, its prescribed and intrinsic task is to relay the orderliness of truth; halakha, though abstractly constant and uniform, is in reality the function of a process that is, concretely, both conditional and provisional.[5]

The Realms of Halakha and Hashkafa

The dichotomy between the spheres of practice and intellect, between the realms of halakha and *hashkafa*—philosophy, science, and theology—is most clearly evident when one realizes that halakhic determinations evolve through a process that must bear the burdens of time and space, while matters of *hashkafa* exist, theoretically at least, above and beyond the flux of time and the shifting of space. That is, practical halakha is shaped by human beings within the workings of historical time and must therefore bear the imprint of temporal and material conditions. In this way halakha is unavoidably ideological and tinged by subjective human decision making.[6] Issues of doctrine, in contrast, cannot be definitively settled merely through the consensus suggested by a vote of the majority nor by the judgment rendered by the passage of history.

Scientific or theological dilemmas are not ultimately resolved on the basis of discretionary adjudication. The logical mode does not suffer the caprices and tastes of popular opinion. While halakha functions on the plane of "correctness," for halakhic practice is often adjusted to conform with some standard or required condition, science grapples with questions of truth and falsity and need not succumb to the dictates of tradition.[7] Scientific truth is true for all times and places; halakha, that is, individual *halakhot*, may be correct for only a generation at a time.

The contingency and provisionality of halakha—its rootedness in consensus and history—do not make it inferior to science, but simply dissimilar. Halakha disguises its historical stratification in that the latest stratum of halakhic practice is retroactively determinative. The present reviews and rationalizes the past through the perspective of its own halakhic sensibilities. A prominent example of halakhic arbitration that develops through the passing of time and the emergence of consensus is that of the fate of R. Yose Haglili's advocacy of the kashrut of the eating of poultry and milk together. In his own day, R. Yose's position represented a viable and legitimate halakhic stance. However, with the passage of a couple of generations, halakhic judgment was rendered and R. Yose's position dismissed and branded as halakhically illegitimate, never to be resuscitated. Were R. Yose, a great *tanna*, alive today, the maintenance of such a halakhic position would obviously not be countenanced. If R. Yose were today to *act* on his halakhic opinion—a sanctioned and authoritative, though minority, position in his own day—he would be considered ineligible to give legal testimony in a Jewish court. With the passing of time and the judgment of history and tradition, the original legitimacy and viability of R. Yose's halakhic opinion have evaporated.[8]

Such temporal reassessment of halakhic opinions can have no parallel in the realm of speculation. The question of the eternality of the universe, for example, cannot be resolved satisfactorily through the halakhic channels of legal referendum. Maimonides, Jewish theologian, scientist and halakhist par excellence, explicitly segregated speculative matters from the determination through majority consensus that marks halakhic debate.[9] Quantitative superiority can play no determinative role in the qualitative realm of speculation. Although matters of science, logic, and theology—of objective reality—can be debated, they cannot ultimately be settled in the chambers of the Sanhedrin.

Additionally, a theological doctrine that was once considered legitimate cannot simply be branded heretical through the mere passing of time, for historical, and thus contingent, factors have no role to play in the resolution of purely intellectual matters. If an authoritative figure of the Jewish past maintained a certain speculative standpoint, the truth or falsity of such cannot be determined by tradition or consensus, and thus its legitimacy cannot be judged by the systemic principles which govern the halakhic process. Avenues of intellectual speculation once considered theologically sound cannot be thwarted merely because they are no longer popular. The famous passage in *b. Sanh.* 99a that discusses the dating of the messianic era illustrates the continued viability, despite unpopularity, of minority theological positions. It states: "R. Hillel said: There shall be no Messiah for Israel, because they have already enjoyed him in the days of Hezekiah. R. Joseph said: May God forgive him [for saying so]." The fact that R. Hillel's opinion was recorded and transmitted in the Talmud despite its obvious unpopularity exhibits the multifariousness and license of rabbinic theology, and preserves this speculative viewpoint as a viable one within the spectrum of traditional Jewish thought.[10] One would have expected, not unreasonably, that such a controversial theological claim would be purposefully excluded from the purview of rabbinic literature. So too with the provocative statement of R. Yose in *b. Sukk.* 5a: "Neither did the Shekhina (the divine presence) ever descend to earth, nor did Moses or Elijah ever ascend to heaven . . ." This audacious theological claim—though apparently in conflict with the peshat of several biblical verses—can never be branded heretical, for it has been preserved in a canonical rabbinic document. Unconventional or heterodox theological opinions that rest upon the precedent of views already canonized and thus legitimated cannot in and of themselves disqualify one from testimony, i.e., from full participation in the Jewish legal system.

Halakhic Process and Intellectual Pursuit

The distinctness of the halakhic process from the intellectual pursuit of objective truth and the divergent methods employed in each are captured dramatically in the "intermediate" rabbinic conception of the revelation of the oral Torah. A nonmaximalist (here, the "intermediate") position is clearly articulated within rabbinic sources and is thus theologically defensible and welcome within the parameters of classical Jewish thought.[11] The intermediate position is expressed quite forcefully in the following rabbinic midrash: "R. Yannai said: The words of the Torah were not given as clear-cut decisions. For with every word which the Holy One, blessed be He, spoke to Moses, He offered him forty-nine arguments by which a thing may be proved clean, and forty-nine other arguments by which it may be proved unclean. When Moses asked, 'Master of the Universe, in what way shall we know the true sense of a law?' God replied, 'The majority is to be followed (*acharei rabim le-hatot*)—when a majority says it is unclean, it is unclean; when a majority says it is clean, it is clean.'"[12] Contradictions are thus woven into the fabric of revelation. No legitimate halakhic argument or solution can be in conflict with the divine halakhic standpoint, for all such arguments and solutions constitute legitimate elements of God's revelation. This midrash also forwards the notion that God's revelation permits, even requires, human augmentation and adaptation, and is thus not definitive or exhaustive. It embodies a vivid portrayal of man's decisive input into the process of implementing God's word. The Torah is not absolutely self-sufficient. Man's participation is not only permissible and legitimate but compulsory. Human autonomy in the halakhic process itself falls under the rubric of the divine mandate. Man must rely upon himself, and not upon God, to fashion a halakhic system that is conclusive and categorical from a revelation that was purposefully inconclusive and indeterminate. The governing systemic principle of *acharei rabim le-hatot*, of following majority opinion in matters of dispute, reflects the divinely sanctioned human factor in halakhic decision making. Man is thereby empowered and commissioned by God to consummate the process of revelation, to make tangible and exact what had been revealed only in outline. Because of God's purposeful withdrawal (*'tzimtzum*) from the final arbitration of halakhic issues, man can capitalize on the privilege of halakhic autonomy.

Yet with human autonomy and halakhic license comes the potential for halakhic variability over time. The halakhic determinations of a later majority may displace and supersede the halakhic precedents of a previous majority.[13] Not only is practical halakha potentially mutable depending on changes in consensus, but the very essence of revelation is fraught with antinomies. Halakhic "truth" is imprecise and nonobjective from its very inception and can never, therefore, approach the exactitude of scientific truth. Scientific truth is unyielding, unchanging, coherent. Halakhic decision making, in following the lead of the majority, struggles toward creating human clarity out of divine ambiguity. The details and particularities of halakha are therefore, from the *divine* perspective, not intrinsically valuable or inherently compelling. This notion of the ultimate dispensability of halakhic particulars (as opposed to other, conflicting particulars) in the eyes of God is expressed in a passage in Midrash Rabbah: "Rav said: The precepts were given only in order that man might be refined by them. For what does the Holy One, blessed be He, care whether a man kills an animal by the throat or by the nape of its neck? Hence its purpose is to refine [or "try"] man."[14] The details of the halakhic system are ultimately human—and thus subjective and variable—artifacts. The "forty-nine arguments by which a thing may be proved clean, and forty-nine other arguments by which it may be proved unclean," which symbolically represent the legitimate exposition of the oral law within the realm of practical halakha, cannot, of course, be simultaneously applied to issues of science and logic without ignoring the law of contradiction. There simply are not forty-nine legitimate arguments in defense of both sides of a logical or scientific issue. The truth about objective reality is a demandingly one-sided affair.

The Difference between the Role of the Historian and the Jurist

Practical halakha is thus governed by subjective and historical factors that help shape its development. In fact, halakha not only exists within history, but it has created its own systemic temporal framework through which facts can be harnessed and manipulated.[15] The dichotomy between the realms of halakha and *hashkafa*, of practice and intellect, should thus by now be clear. Halakha and speculation are impelled by divergent motivations, considerations and methodologies. A spectrum of critical meticulousness can be applied to the range of traditional rabbinic materials. Aggadic discourse is only loosely tied to a text, stimulated by, rather than subjugated to, a scriptural text. Despite ambitious attempts by certain scholars to capture descriptively the method of aggada, its spirit yet remains elusive. Textual commentary that is more integrally dependent on a text becomes exegesis and leaves the plateau of discursive aggada. Halakhic argumentation is more rigorous and meticulous than aggadic discourse, yet, as we have seen, it is molded by changing material conditions and affiliated with shifting standards of behavior. Only intellectual speculation is, in theory, scrupulous in its attachment to logic, truth, and objective reality. Critical scholarship, as the epitome of rigorous intellectual speculation, is—or should be—constrained by the determinism of peshat. Halakhic discourse, by contrast, is more pliable and fluid, able to assert its autonomy and confront the sovereignty of Scripture through the devices of derash. The roles of historian and jurist must be differentiated. The historian seeks to register and unravel the objective data of history by searching for the origins of society and culture. The jurist, by contrast, seeks to regulate his data by adjusting and accommodating them to create equity. Truth and justice do not always converge. Scholarship and piety can thus function comfortably on different planes. Each can reign supreme in its own domain. The modern Jew who is committed to both objective truth and religious practice must recognize the imperative to view the same religious document (such as the Talmud) from the dual perspectives of reason and revelation, each in its own time and space. The equilibrium of such a scholarly approach to religious documents maintains the distinction between textual interpretation engaged in for the purpose of critical study and that for the demands of practical behavior. Because the affairs of praxis and intellect are propelled by different considerations and inspired by different motivations, their disparate realms must not be confounded nor intertwined, for in so doing the integrity of each is compromised.[16]

4

Contradictory Yet Complementary: The Dichotomy between Practice and Intellect

Two-Tiered Verity

One may be tempted to deduce from the thesis of a historically developing exegesis—the underlying theme of this essay—that Jewish normative law, which derives from exegesis of the Bible, must also change. If exegesis is timebound, so should behavior be subject to the vicissitudes of time. Each generation should have its own halakha as it has its own mode of interpretation.

This conclusion is based on the assumption that behavior and intellect must be in harmony. A counter possibility is to argue that even though each period has its own mode of interpretation, the interpretation expounded by those who received the initial revelation has priority.[1] God spoke to them in their language, according to their mode of interpretation, giving their exposition a divine dimension not enjoyed by any other human interpretation. Pertaining to observance, one has to follow the interpretation of those to whom the initial revelation was given, just as Maimonides accepted the halakhic decisions of the Talmud, although he at times resisted the exegetical justification offered in the Gemara.[2] Pertaining to exegesis, one remains a child of one's own age, following the standards of one's own time.

Since behavior in Judaism is the way by which man most effectively achieves closeness to God (who is identified with absolute truth), it follows that any dichotomy between practice and exegesis of the divine Torah necessarily leads to a double standard of religious verity or to a double-tiered religious verity, one pertaining to behavior and one pertaining to the activities of the mind. This position seems to contradict the traditional rabbinic stance. The rabbis never affirmed a double-verity theory. The rabbis never sanctioned the notion that contradictory interpretations have respective truth values, one for practice and one for study. They never divorced study from practice. Most likely, the rabbis would have at all costs looked for harmony between the mode of interpretation employed in the intellectual exercise of study and the mode of interpretation employed as the basis for practical behavior. They would have used all their interpretive ingenuity to prove, and to believe, that there is only one true mode of interpretation and the interpretation is always consistent with practice. They would have instinctively recoiled from any kind of dichotomy that divides truth into two realms, study and practice, which bear an anomalous relationship to each other, contradictory yet complementary.

Nevertheless, it seems that the rabbis too resorted, on occasion, at least by implication, to the dichotomy between study and practice, that they too would not have been in principle averse to following the interpretive mode of their predecessors with regard to practice and engaging in intellectual study in line with the interpretive mode of their times. I base my opinion on the few instances where the rabbis both in halakha and in aggada hint at a conflict between the law as it was in practice and the law which should have been, had the free intellect prevailed; specifically, the conflict between the law as it was decided by majority rule and the logical appeal that a minority opinion sometimes had. The rabbis were also concerned with the behavior of the author of the minority opinion vis-à-vis the majority decision. They insisted in most cases that the author of the minority opinion should in practice, at least publicly, behave according to the majority opinion.[3] But may he persist in advocating his contrary opinion? If the answer is yes—and the rabbis seem to have favored that—how will he theologically justify to himself, and to others who watch him, staunchly defending a position which he himself flaunts in practice? How can his opinion be wrong to practice but right to advocate? What kind of truth is it that does not extend beyond advocacy, that turns into falsity when translated into action? The rabbis struggled with this and similar questions and tacitly conceded that it can only be resolved even in part if one admits to some kind of a double standard of religious verity or, if you prefer, to a double-tiered religious verity; specifically, allowing for a verity which lies outside the realm of practice, in the realm of intellect, that can be pursued only if it is not translated into behavior—an abstract verity which remains forever abstract, which can never be concretized. This verity sometimes collides with the verity that reigns in the realm of practice (like majority rule). When that happens, the abstract verity does not disappear entirely. Sophisticated interpreters avail themselves of it and use it as a means of fulfilling the commandment to study Torah. They are studying *Torah Lishmah*, purely for its own sake. In a previous work[4] I singled out the commentary of the Rashbam (d. 1174) on the Torah as an example of the highest genre of *Torah Lishmah*; the Rashbam, one of the greatest *posekim* (adjudicators) of his time, often explained the text against practical halakha to which he strictly adhered. He saw in this type of commentary, free of the restraints of practical halakha, the epitome of the fulfillment of the study of Torah, which in rabbinic law is a commandment by itself and therefore ought not be reduced to a means of making possible the fulfillment of other commandments. For the command to study Torah to be wholly independent, it has to be divorced from practice. It has to be an end in itself. It has to have a verity of its own. The dichotomy between practice and intellect is built in in the *Torah Lishmah* commentaries. Analogously, I believe that the rabbis in principle would not have opposed making a distinction between practice and intellect with respect to following the mode of interpretation of their predecessors in matters of practice (the more important of the two, the more uncompromisable of the two) and their own mode of interpretation in matters of intellect.[5]

The resolution of this issue has significance beyond the mere contrast between the rabbinic mode of interpretation and modern rules of exegesis. It accredits critical textual scholarship both of the Bible and the Talmud as a bona fide religious activity, the practi-

tioner of which fulfills the commandment to study Torah (by critical study, I mean here interpreting an authoritative text in a manner
different from the interpretation which is endorsed by an earlier
authority or upon which a practical law is based). Its verity belongs
to the realm of intellect, not to the realm of practice. To practice
according to critical norms is strictly forbidden, but to study critically as a religious activity, as part of the fulfillment of the commandment to study Torah, though presently not particularly en-
couraged and not very popular, is nevertheless a legitimate
historical aspect of religious learning and one that requires the
recitation of the blessing reserved for the commencement of Torah
study. Indeed, it could be argued, as I have done elsewhere,[6] "that
when one studies the Bible critically, i.e., according to the Peshat,
with no intention of changing practical Halakha, one is fulfilling
the commandment to study Torah to a higher degree than when one
is studying the same law according to traditional interpretation.
This is especially true if the peshat proves to be in contrast with
traditional interpretation (as, for instance, interpreting 'an eye for
an eye' literally, as opposed to monetary compesation). This learning is fuller, purer, having no vested interest other than the welfare
of learning."[7]

   It is noteworthy that the standard verse cited by the rabbis of the
Talmud on behalf of majority rule is Exodus 23:2 which they
interpret to mean: "after the majority one must incline." This interpretation, which makes the verse refer to the judges and the verb
"incline" an intransitive verb, is against the simple, literal meaning.
As indicated by the preceding clause in the verse, "you shall not give
perverse testimony in a dispute," the verse clearly refers to the
witnesses and the verb *incline* is transitive. Instead of a positive
commandment to follow the majority, the verse contains a negative
commandment not to incline after a majority for the purpose of
perverting justice.[8] It says nothing about majority rule. The rabbis,
by citing this verse as the source for majority rule, deviated from the
simple, literal meaning.

   One can safely assume, since no explicit contrary voice is heard in
the Talmud, that this interpretation (like so many other deviating
interpretations) is reflective of their exegetical state of mind, which
they most likely inherited from their predecessors. It is also a fair
assumption[9] that whenever a dissenter pursued his view aggres-

sively (as in the story of R. Eliezer, quoted below), refusing to submit to majority will and actually instructing followers to behave according to his opinion, the author of the minority opinion must have defended himself against the charge made by the majority that the Bible had invested them with authority by virtue of the above verse. Freedom of dissent was not then a given right, as it is in the modern period, and had to be justified on a case-by-case basis. He could have defended himself either ad hoc, showing that the law in that verse did not apply to his particular case[10] or he could have defended himself generally, denying the very principle that the majority had a verity claim over the minority. The possibility exists that some defenders of minority right took refuge in the simple, literal meaning of the verse. When that happened and the majority rejected the simple, literal meaning vis-à-vis practice but allowed the minority to continue advocating its position as part of the intellectual activity of studying Torah, there arose a confrontation between two modes of interpretation. The majority insisted on the mode of interpretation sanctioned by their predecessors (the interpretation that today looks like, though is not quite, "reading in") while the minority defended the right to follow their new mode of interpretation (the simple, literal meaning). The conflict between peshat and derash may well have been at the base of the conflict between majority and minority opinion.

Talmudic Examples

It is now appropriate to discuss the few instances in the Talmud which display a dichotomy between practice and intellect. The clearest and most decisive is the law pertaining to the *zaken mamreh*—"the elder that rebels against the decision of the court." The *m. Sanh.* 11:2 states: "If the elder has returned to his city" (after a visit to the [highest] court, situated in the Chamber of Hewn Stone, in the Temple in Jerusalem, where he heard a decision against his opinion) "and again taught as he was wont to teach, he is not yet culpable; but if he gave a (practical) decision (*pesak*) concerning what should be done, he is culpable." I take that to mean that "the elder that rebels against the decision of the court" even after his visit to Jerusalem, could continue to teach very much the same way as he was wont to. When the Mishnah says "he is not culpable," it does not mean that he is only capitally not culpable, that he would not be guilty of a capital crime. It means also that he is not liable to censure, that he can freely advocate his position.[11] What he cannot do, however, is to behave according to his position, and more importantly, he can not instruct others to follow him. It should be remembered that the view of "the elder that rebels against the decision of the court" was at odds not only with the view of the majority of his colleagues, but also with the view of the judges of the highest court, situated in the Temple, "whence the law goes forth to all Israel, as it is written [Deut. 17:10]: From that place which the Lord shall choose" (*m. Sanh.* 11:2). Yet he was not muzzled. He could freely express his opinion.

That was true also of Akabya ben Mahalel. The Mishnah in Ed. 5:7 records that "in the hour that he (Akabya) died he said to his son: My son, retract the four opinions which I gave (against the majority of my colleagues). The son inquired: Why do you not retract? Akabya said to him: I heard them (the opinions) from a majority, and they (my colleagues) also heard their opinions from a majority. I continued steadfast to the tradition that I had heard and they continued steadfast to the decision that they had heard. But you have heard (a decision) from the mouth of an individual and a contrary decision from the mouth of a majority. It is better to leave the opinion of the individual and to hold to the opinion of the majority."

Why is it incumbent upon the son only to follow the opinion of the majority? Why did not Akabya himself follow the majority, instead of continuing to hold steadfast to the tradition he had heard? The law in the Bible to incline after the majority applies also when either or both parties evoke earlier traditions. Having a tradition is no excuse to flaunt majority opinion.[12] Why did not Akabya respect that law? He did respect it, for the law applies only to practical decisions, not to theoretical learning. Akabya was continuing steadfast to the tradition he had heard only with respect to teachings. With respect to tendering practical decisions, he, too, followed the majority. What he told his son was—as already correctly interpreted by R. Israel Lipschutz (1782–1860) in his famous commentary on the Mishnah, *Tiferet Yisrael*—that after his death, the son should desist from even theoretically advocating Akabya's positions. The son apparently possessed no inner convictions about the subjects under discussion. He followed his father's stance theoretically, that is, more out of filial piety than out of conviction. Akabya instructed his son that after his father's death, he should join the ranks of the majority and discontinue teaching his father's ideas even theoretically.

In the celebrated case mentioned in *m. Rosh Hash.* 2:8-9, even after R. Joshua celebrated the holy days according to the calendar reckoning of his opponent, R. Gamaliel, he was still insisting on the correctness of his position. He did not change his mind, as can be inferred from his encounter with R. Akiba. He merely followed R. Gamaliel's reckoning in practice. In theory he remained opposed to R. Gamaliel's reckoning—a clear case of the dichotomy between practice and theory. In matters of calendar reckoning, the insistence on uniform behavior was especially emphasized, because celebrating two different holy dates would create a new sect, something the rabbis opposed with all their strength.[13]

Less explicit, though more dramatic, is the source pertaining to the dispute between R. Eliezer and R. Joshua[14] (recorded in the *b. B. Metz.* 59b, and in a substantially similar form at the beginning of the third chapter of *p. Moed Katan*). In that story, R. Eliezer defied majority opinion and was excommunicated. "They took a vote and excommunicated him," which seems proper under the circumstances. Had he lived during Temple times he may have been capitally indicted (as we have seen from the Mishnah in *Sanhedrin*). Yet the Talmud reports that when R. Eliezer was notified of the excommunication: "Tears streamed from his eyes. The world was then smitten, a third of the olive crop, a third of the wheat, and a third of the barley crop. Some say, even the dough in women's hands swelled up. A *tanna* taught: great was the calamity that befell that day, for everything at which R. Eliezer cast his eyes was burned up." Why was such a severe wrath unleashed? Why was the world punished for an act (excommunication) which is halakhically mandatory and practically necessary to prevent further schisms? The condemnation of R. Eliezer seems to have had divine sanction. God agreed, not without, as it were, a change of mind, that "my sons" (the majority) "have defeated me, my sons have defeated me." Why then that ire, that stern anger that ultimately—according to the story—claimed the life of R. Eliezer's own brother-in-law, the

patriarch R. Gamaliel, who may have been one of the more prominent leaders in the opposition to R. Eliezer? It seems to me that the
most plausible explanation is to pay attention to the order of the
story, which suggests a close connection between the excommunication and the wrath. Immediately preceding the excommunication
the story tells us "on that day all objects which R. Eliezer had
declared clean were brought and burnt in fire." Could it be that the
burning of all the objects that R. Eliezer declared clean, successfully
brought an end to R. Eliezer's decision-making capacities, that he
no longer had the chance—or desire—to continue to render practical decisions (relevant to this controversy), so that the purpose of
the excommunication was to deprive him of listeners, of an opportunity to advocate his position intellectually? Could it be that the
wrath was directed against the majority for having muzzled him, for
having prevented him from intellectually continuing to defend his
position—which was his right? Even "the elder that rebels against
the court," as we have seen, was allowed to teach "as he was wont to
teach." That privilege was taken away from R. Eliezer when he was
excommunicated. He became unable to communicate with his students, and the perpetrators were punished.[15]

Logic versus Consensus

But the story of R. Eliezer and R. Joshua goes further than any of
the above-quoted instances in proving what I called the dichotomy
between practical halakha and study, made necessary by the conflict across periods as to what constitutes peshat and derash, whose
history we have been tracing in the preceding pages. This story not
only tolerates minority opinion, as one may tolerate something that
is not true, but it even attributes to it divine sanction. A heavenly
voice called out: "Why do you dispute with R. Eliezer, seeing that in
all matters the halakha agrees with him?" Although later on the
prophet Elijah met with R. Nathan and informed him that God had
changed his mind, as it were, and agreed with the majority, R.
Joshua and his colleagues had no way of knowing that. Yet they
ignored the opinion of R. Eliezer even after a heavenly voice
vouched for its veracity. R. Joshua and his colleagues most likely
postulated that the truth delivered from heaven refers to a realm

other than that of the practical sphere. Minority opinion may have verity in the realm of intellect, in the realm of logic, but not in the realm of everyday behavior. In the realm of practical decision, the majority rules. That is why we occasionally encounter a final decision in favor of an opinion which is not the most logical. For example, in *b. Shabb.* 60b, it is quoted that R. Matnah said that the law is not like R. Elazar the son of R. Shimon. The Gemara, that is the anonymous author, asked: "Why does R. Matnah have to tell us that? Is it not obvious, since the view of R. Elazar the son of R. Shimon is a minority view?" And the Gemara answered: "R. Matnah tells us that the law is not like R. Elazar the son of R. Shimon *even though* his view is logical." Logicality does not always determine the practical outcome of a law, a halakha.[16] A striking example is R. Ashi's statement in *b. Yevam.* 67a: "Does it read 'and they accepted it'? It was only said 'and they agreed' [which may only mean] that this view is logical (but not that it was accepted)."[17] In fact, most controversies in the Talmud are determined by comprehensive rules, such as "the law is always (almost always)[18] like the Hillelites against the Shammaites." It is unlikely that the Shammaites were *always* wrong in terms of logic. In a similar case pertaining to the controversies between Abaye and Rava (fourth century Babylonian scholars), where the law is almost always like Rava, it is stated that this rule applies only to controversies in matters of practical law. In matters, for instance, of giving reasons for existing laws, the more logical reason is to be followed.[19] The implication is that in matters of practical law, one does not always follow the more logical. Similarly, whenever there is a controversy between the Babylonian and the Palestinian Talmud, the law is like the Babylonian Talmud. Yet in matters of correct reading of the text, says an eighteenth-century scholar,[20] one may follow the Palestinian Talmud whenever logic dictates. Again, the implication is that in practical law one follows the Babylonian Talmud even when logic does not dictate. The decisions of the Palestinian Talmud are, therefore, wrong for practical purposes even when they are right logically. Indeed, a case could be made that Rabbi, the anthologizer of the Mishnah, by recording dissenting views affirmed the right of the minority view to be heard, and of the author of that view to freely advocate that opinion. The Gemara frequently asks "*mai ta'ama de-rabbi ploni*", what is the reason of the author of the minority view, thus adding respect and breadth to the view that in practice cannot be followed.[21] There is a double standard of religious verity or, if you prefer, doubled-tiered religious verity, one prevailing in the world of behavior and one in the world of the intellect. Minority opinion is wrong in the world of behavior but could be right in the world of intellect.

Nowhere is this dichotomy more pronounced than in that bizarre story told in *b. B. Metz.* 86b that there was a dispute in heaven concerning a question pertaining to the laws of purity, between the Holy One, blessed be He, who ruled that the individual in question was clean and the entire Heavenly Academy, the majority, which ruled that the individual in question was unclean. The final law as codified in the Mishnah at the end of the fourth chapter of Negaim,[22] is like the Heavenly Academy. God's opinion cannot be conceived of as untrue. "His stamp is truth."[23] His truth in this instance must be assigned to another realm—a realm that does not include the practical arena, a realm that is entirely intellectual.

Moreover, both of these stories—that of R. Eliezer and R. Joshua and that of the dispute between God and the Heavenly Academy—indicate, it seems to me, that the Ramban's (1194–1270) and the Kuzari's (twelfth century) explanation of the famous statement in the *Sifrei* to Deuteronomy is not correct. The *Sifrei* interprets Deut. 17:11, "You must not deviate from the verdict that they announce to you either to the right or to the left" to mean "One has to obey the decision of the majority (of the High Court in Jerusalem) even if he (the judge) tells you of the right that it is left or of the left that it is right." According to the Ramban,[24] one has to obey the majority because the majority is always right, for they are preserved forever from error and stumbling. The Torah was given "subject to their (majority) judgment. Even if that judgment appears to you to exchange right for left," you are wrong.[25] A similar sentiment is expressed in the book of the Kusari (III, 41): "For they have divine assistance and would never, on account of their large number, concur in any thing that contradicts the law. There was much less likelihood of erroneous views. . . ."[26] In the above two stories, the defender or the holder of the minority view was none other than God Almighty Himself, who is always right and whose opponents—even if they are a majority—are always wrong. The reason for following the majority view, therefore, is not a matter of right and wrong, or of truth and falsity. Even when a minority view is right and true, it may still not be followed practically.

Similarly, in the conflict across periods as to what constitutes peshat and derash, even though one is convinced of the correctness of his or her interpretation on the basis of one's contemporary mode of interpretation, it doesn't necessarily mean that one has to act upon it practically. While exegetical truth, perforce, must be derived through the contemporary rules of exegesis, practice may follow an independent course. Contemporary exegesis, like the minority view at the time of the Talmud, may be right and true, yet not be followed practically.

Practical Truth and Heavenly Truth in the Talmud

Before we proceed fruther, I believe it would be helpful to summarize briefly what we have said thus far in this chapter. We began stating that a timebound view of rabbinic exegesis—the theme of our essay—does not preclude a normative Jewish religious behavior. Different modes of interpretation do not necessarily entail different modes of behavior. One can posit a double-verity theory which dichotomizes between practice and intellect—in our case, exegesis—allowing for practice to remain relatively constant while the exegesis is subject to the changing states of mind of the respective periods. We further claimed that such a division is not unrabbinic. It was indirectly implied by the rabbis of the Talmud in their treatment of the majority-minority controversy, particularly in the two stories of R. Eliezer and R. Joshua and the dispute between God and the Heavenly Academy, and by the Medieval *Torah Lishmah* commentators whenever they explained a biblical text against practical halakha.

This is not to say that the rabbis consciously assented to different types of truth along different time periods, that each generation has its own system, and hence its own truth of exegesis, a system derived not from particular social conditions (acquired characteristics) but from irreversible inner dictates. The rabbis of the Talmud were not aware of what we called "timebound interpretive states of mind." Time, as an active agent determining events, is rather a modern idea.[27] The rabbis did not subscribe to such a view. To them, and to the ancients in general, time was a sort of "container" through which events move. It does not cause them.

What we are claiming is that the rabbis occasionally hinted at a double-verity theory, operating at the same time and in the same world. I added "in the same world" to emphasize my disagreement with the sixteenth-century Rabbi Moses Bonmash,[28] who, on the basis of the above stories and several other obscure sources, concluded that the rabbis of the Talmud distinguished between a this-worldly truth and a heavenly truth. To him, majority rule was more than a necessary convenience to avoid tearing the community apart. It was a part of the divine truth incorporated in Exod. 23:21: "After the majority one must incline." Yet majority rule is puissant only on this earth. In heaven, the truth of an argument is judged by its logicality, not by the number of advocates. The case of the *zaken mamrei* ("the elder that rebels against the court") and a few more that we touched upon above, however, do not seem to support this neat distinction. Somehow, even in this world, the rabbis seem to imply the existence of more than one verity.

To be sure, nowhere do the rabbis explicitly state, let alone explicitly justify, the double-verity theory.[29] Yet there are too many instances in the Talmud that hint at a conflict between practical behavior and theoretical study that can be resolved only by positing the existence of a double-verity.[30] It is a necessary implication of what they said and thought.

To say, however, that the double-verity theory is not unrabbinic does not mean that it is unanimous, that every rabbi accepted it. The authors of the two stories subscribed to it—and so did, to a lesser extent, some other sources. But a very popular notion of the nature of revelation seems to be against it. To accept the idea of a double verity, one has to follow an alternative notion of the nature of revelation. So we turn now to a brief discussion[31] of the various notions of the nature of revelation found in rabbinic literature and their effect on the double-verity theory.

The Nature of Revelation: Various Positions

The two stories are either opposed to, or imply that we should not take literally, the statement in *b. Meg.* 19b that "the Holy One, blessed be He, showed Moses the minutiae of the Torah";[32] or, as it is stated in *p. Pea* 17a, Moses received the whole Torah from God, including "the comments" and even the questions that an astute student will someday make in the presence of his teacher.[33] A similar view was expressed by Maimonides in the very beginning of his *Mishnah Torah*, which, undoubtedly, is responsible for its popularity today. If all the laws and their explanations were dictated by God to Moses on Sinai, however, how could there have been a dispute generations later between God and his human majority or between God and His Heavenly Academy? God's word to Moses should have determined the law for all posterity. Any disagreement would have constituted a deviation from revelation.[34]

These two stories, it seems, subscribe to a nonmaximalistic view of revelation, perhaps that of Midrash Tanchuma Tisah 16 "that principles were given to Moses on Sinai" (referring to the oral tradition), not detailed laws or explanations. Detailed laws or explanations were worked out, on the basis of the principles, by men. The case of the mid-festival days (*chol hamoed*) may serve as a concrete example. From the Bible itself it is not clear which day is a festival day proper and which only a mid-festival day. "Scripture left it to the sages to tell on which day work is forbidden [a festival day proper] and which day it is permitted [mid-festival day]; which manner of work is forbidden and which is permitted" (*b. Chag.* 18a and parallels). The principle (not necessarily an exegetical principle) is that there are days of festival proper and days of mid-festival. When exactly they happen to fall and how one celebrates the mid-festivals was left for men to work out.[35] Among men, disputes inevitably arose (some of which they resolved through majority rule) and in a few instances concomitant disputes either arose in heaven or reached heaven.

A more radical position in the form of a parable can be found in the *Tana* debei Eliyahu Zuta, (whose authorship is not later than the twelfth century, possibly earlier)[36] chapter 2, that God gave man "a *kab* of wheat (from which to produce fine flour) and a bundle of flax (from which to produce cloth)." Man is doing the weaving, man is doing the baking. Not every law was determined for man beforehand. Some laws (and many explanations) he had to determine for himself. Man is more than a passive receiver. He is an active creator.[37] This is perhaps a third position.

These various positions can be seen as interconnected with respect to the views on double verity whose existence we posited in order to account for the behavior of rabbis who clung to derash while intellectually advocating peshat, a frequent incongruity observed in the history of rabbinic exegesis. For those who follow a maximalistic view of revelation and interpret literally the statement that God revealed to Moses all the comments an astute student will ever make, who say that every law with its explanation was given to Moses on Mount Sinai, there can be no double truths. There is a single Truth, determined by its conformity to God's Word to Moses on Sinai. There can be no conflicting verity claims made by both the majority and minority. Only one of them is True. Since the law is like the majority, only its view conforms to God's Word to Moses, by virtue of which the minority view must necessarily be wrong. Those who follow a nonmaximalistic view of revelation and who either oppose the statement about the "astute student" or interpret it nonliterally say that not all laws and certainly not all explanations were given to Moses on Mount Sinai. Many a determination of law and explanation was left for man to work out, in the process of which he utilizes majority rule, but only for practical purposes. Intellectually, however, a minority opinion may conform to God's opinion. When that happens there is a double verity, a practical and an intellectual verity. Both the majority and the minority make legitimate verity claims, one on the practical realm, the other in the intellectual realm.

It should be noted that the maximalistic position leaves itself vulnerable to the questions of how after such a detailed and all-inclusive revelation, there arose later so many controversies, and why we should not consider deviations from the revelation as mistakes and those (among later sages) who advocated and practiced these deviations as sinners—inadvertent and unknowing sinners, but sinners nevertheless.

These questions and their supposed "solutions" were taken up at length by a sixteenth-century kabbalist, R. Meir Ben Gabbai (b. 1480) and by a seventeenth-century kabbalist, R. Isaiah Horovitz (c. 1565–1630).[38] It was natural for the kabbalists to adopt the maximalistic position. It suited their temper. To it they added that revelation included not only "all the laws and the hedges around the laws, the degrees and the regulations . . . as well as everything new, that may ever be said in any future about the decisions, laws, and comments" but also "all the hidden meanings of the Torah and the reasons for the commandments and their secrets" (Ben Gabbai). "The master of the universe revealed all this to Moses his prophet. May he rest in peace." The Kabbala, too, was revealed in all its entirety to Moses on Mount Sinai. As to the controversies which are mutually exclusive, the kabbalist insists that they are all equally divine, citing statements from the Talmud which in their original context expressed different and opposing positions concerning the nature of the revelation of the oral law. (This is not unique to kabbalists. Even seasoned talmudists discuss the talmudic view of revelation as if it were homogeneous). They admit, however, that logically it is inconceivable that contradictory views should both be true, for this would violate the law of contradiction. But that is only because "we are unable to penetrate to those points where the contradictions are resolved. And it is only because we are unable to maintain two contradictory teachings at the same time" (Ben Gabbai). In the higher realm where revelation took place, the law of the excluded middle is not operative. "This seems to be very alien to human understanding, and man's nature would be unable to grasp it were it not for the help given to him by the prepared way of God, the pathway upon which dwells the light of the Kabbala" (Horovitz). The maximalistic position of divine revelation can be maintained only through a leap of mystical faith, waiving the conventional logical requirement.

An intermediate position is the statement attributed to R. Yannai (a third-century Palestinian scholar), found both in the *p. Sanh.* 22a and in *Midr. Pss.* 12:4, that the words of the Torah (referring to the oral tradition) "were not given as a clear-cut decision" but for every word God spoke to Moses "He offered him forty-nine other arguments by which a thing may be proved unclean and forty-nine arguments by which a thing may be proved clean." When Moses asked: "Master of the Universe, how will I know the true sense of the laws? God replied: incline after the majority."[39] This position accepts the view that God literally revealed to Moses the whole Torah complete with the arguments pro and con, minus, however, the final decisions. The final decisions were left to the scholars of each generation to decide according to majority rule. The advantage of this position is that it accounts for, indeed sanctions, subsequent disputes. The many disputes we encounter in the Talmud among the *tannaim* and *amoraim* are actual replications of the divine presentation to Moses—including the arguments that were advanced on behalf of the rejected opinion. Prior to the majority decision, both sides of the arguments were equally representative of revelation, equally divine. From the standpoint of the divine, the final decision could have gone either way. Either decision would have been accepted. It was man who put an end to this ambiguity and declared the minority opinion "undivine," as it were, unsuitable for behavior.

This position is explicitly stated in Palestinian sources and is indirectly implied in several places in the Babylonian Talmud (by Palestinian sages). The commonly quoted phrase, found in both Talmuds in reference to scholarly disputes that "these and those are the words of the living God," reflects this position. The opinions of the contenders, though contradictory, "are the words of the living God" because according to this position, God does not decide and, hence, does not declare any opinion as false. They are all potentially true. God merely enumerates the arguments (all of them, symbolized by the number forty-nine) pro and con and leaves it to man to make the final decision. Whatever decision man makes meets with His approval and eventually becomes a part of "the words of the living God."

Thus, *b. Gitt* 6b relates that Elijah the prophet informed R. Abiathar (a third century Palestinian scholar) that God had quoted his (R. Abiathar's) opinion together with the opinion of his adversary R. Jonathan without deciding between them. R. Abiathar expressed surprise: "Is it possible for God to have doubts?" Elijah answered: "These and those are the words of the living God." God does not take part in the resolution of controversies. He merely presents them objectively and completely. Man offers the solution. However, since both opinions reflected historical reality, in order for both opinions to be true, they needed to be arranged in a consecutive sequence. "He found a fly and excused it; he (afterwards) found a hair and did not excuse it."

Likewise, *b. Eruv.* 13b wonders how a heavenly voice could have announced both that "These (the Shammaites) and those (the Hillelites) are the words of the living God" and that "the law is like the Hillelites."[40] If, the Talmud asks, the opinion of the Shammaites is also the word of the living God, why then was the law declared like the Hillelites? Because, the Talmud answers, "The Hillelites were kindly and modest." But, queried the famous R. Joseph Karo (1488–1575),[41] kindness and modesty are not legal considerations, and nonlegal entities should not decisively determine the outcome of a legal dispute. What the Talmud is saying is that since God, so to speak, is strictly neutral as to the outcome of the legal dispute— any outcome is satisfactory to Him—a nonlegal consideration may sometimes tilt the balance in favor of one opinion over another. Man may occasionally avail himself of nonlegal entities in deciding a controversy in which, from the standpoint of the divine, both sides are equally valid. When both contentions are valid, even an extraneous factor may have a cutting edge—and decide the issue.

A similar idea lies behind the statement in *b. Chag.* 3a (quoted with embellishments from *t. Sota* 7.12); "Masters of assemblies [Eccl. 12:11]—this refers to the scholars who sit in the assemblies and who occupy themselves with Torah. Some declare a matter unclean, and others declare it clean; some prohibit, some permit; some declare it unusable and others declare it usable. Should a man say: If this so, how can I study the Law? Therefore, Scripture continues: they are given by one Shepherd; one God gave them; one spokesman (Moses) utters them from the mouth of the Lord." God revealed to Moses all possible arguments that can be raised on each issue both pro and con but did not reveal to him which arguments were correct and which arguments were incorrect. That was left for subsequent scholars to determine. To determine properly, the rabbis advised, "Turn your ear into a funnel and fashion yourself a perceptive heart to understand the words of those who declare as unclean, and the words of those who declare as clean, the words of those who prohibit and the words of those who permit, the words of those who declare as unusable and the words of those who declare as usable" (Ibid.). All their arguments are legitimate: "Learn and know the words of them all and then you will know enough to determine the right opinion, to declare the law like it." The arguments were given by God, but the decision is made by men.

This is an attractive position because it allows maximum freedom of argumentation and endows human exegetical activity with divine sanction. Some fourteenth-century scholars[42] arrived at this position on their own without the explicit knowledge of the above quoted Palestinian Talmud and the *Midrash* to Psalms. They were apparently attracted by this position and afterwards read it into the more famous passage in the Babylonian Talmud, including these two stories. It seems to me, however, that these two stories—the story of R. Eliezer and R. Joshua, and the dispute between God and his Heavenly Academy—clearly reject this position. In both stories, God Himself makes the final decision. He is not merely presenting possible arguments pro and con. He takes a definite stand, a stand which is against the majority. In the position of the Palestinian Talmud and the *Midrash* to Psalms, God remains neutral, refraining from making any decision. Decisions are left entirely to men, to the scholars of each generation. In these two stories, however, God takes a clear and succinct stance against the majority. He does not abide by majority rule. If anything, the main purpose of the stories seems to be antimajority, a plea for the rights of and respect for the minority opinion and a protest against the tyranny of the majority. The minority opinion was put in the mouth of God Almighty, whose credibility cannot be gainsaid,[43] whose credibility, moreover, must surpass anybody and everybody else's credibility, both individual and group. His truth must be somehow "truer" than that of the opposite majority opinion. But only intellectually. Practically, the authors of these stories undoubtedly believed that one is to follow majority rule, that the meaning of Exod. 23:2 is to incline after the majority, so that it is divinely commanded to follow the opinion of the many. Indeed, R. Jeremiah (a fourth-century scholar) interprets R. Joshua's rejection of a heavenly voice on the grounds that "the Torah is not in heaven" to mean that the Torah that was given to us on earth contains the command to incline after the majority. Practically, the Torah rejected minority opinion. Its verity is only intellectual. These stories affirm the dichotomy between practice and intellect, between behavior and study, anticipated by peshat and derash; and they indirectly imply two standards of religious verity, each effective in its own realm.[44]

Before I leave the subject, I would like to add the observation that the literature on the subject tends to blur the distinctions between the different positions. Authors dealing with the subject tend to lump together the relevant quotations from the Talmud without noting their mutually exclusive character. There seems to be a reluctance on the part of the posttalmudic scholars to admit to divisive opinions on such a sensitive issue as the nature of revelation. Understandably, they prefer a single position, which more and more seems to mean an extreme maximalistic position. Its attraction may be due to this position's staccato-like, explicit formulation, whereas the other two positions need to be extrapolated from ambiguous statements (see Appendix III).

Divine *Tzimtzum*

But how can both be true? How can God's position be true only intellectually? What value is there to a verity that does not emanate from God? What kind of verity claim does it make? One is forced to acknowledge a divine truth and a human truth. Divine truth stems from the objective nature of things, the way God created them, whereas human truth is derived from tzimtzum,[45] withdrawal. God relinquished some of this power to man, as it were, in a relinquishment similar to that associated with free will, with the profound difference that with respect to free will relinquishment is a means of enabling man to make his own decision of right and wrong, whereas with respect to human truth relinquishment is a means of enabling man to set down his own pattern of religious standards with God's endorsement. The Talmud summarizes free will with the following phrase: "everything is in the hands of heaven except fear of heaven."[46] This means not only that man is free not to fear heaven, to defy Him, but that God created man with the potential not to fear Him, to defy Him. God, as it were, relinquished His power to control man's attitude towards Him. Man is left to himself to determine the kind of attitude he shall adopt towards God. God could have created a different kind of man but chose not to. Similarly, God created man with the potential to make his own Torah. He relinquished His power, as it were, to fully instruct man. He left man to instruct himself. Revelation was not complete. Man had to supplement and complete it, making new laws and finding explanations for old ones. God could have made revelation complete, but chose not to. Man had to do it. In the process, controversies emerged that were resolved in a human way by a majority decision. Majority decision is one of the most effective tools man uses to instruct himself. It is necessary practically and it is divinely sanctioned. It is as if God wants man to make his own decision; He wants him to make his own Torah, even when the outcome is against His own Truth. God's approval endows majority rule—irrespective of its objective quality—with an element of derivative divine Truth, confined, however, to the practical realm, the human realm. Intellectual verity is determined by objective criteria (not a majority) which God did not relinquish to man. Man's verity is confined to practice. Practice is flexible, changeable, readily accommodating man's free exercise of will. God's truth is fixed, permanent. Because it is objective it is unchangeable, intellectually unswayable.

When man exercises his free will to defy God's explicit instruction, that is, when man sins, his freedom is temporary. Ultimately, he will have to give an account of his defiance. His acts of defiance are merely tolerated for a while. Judgment is merely postponed. In the end, such acts will be condemned and punished. When, however, man exercises his religious potential to fill in instructions not given by revelation, the practical results are approved and accepted—provided they were sincerely thought to have emanated from the given instruction—even when they are objectively wrong, even when they say "of the right that it is left or of the left that it is right." The verity, then, is a nonobjective verity. It is a creative human verity, sanctioned by the divine.

The Limits of Majority Rule

Of some relevance to our discussion of dual religious verity may also be the famous controversy between the Shammaites and Hillelites. I already mentioned that this protracted controversy was decisively concluded (about the first half of the second century) in favor of the Hillelites. A late Babylonian talmudic tradition (*Yevam.* 14a) whose source is unknown to me has it that the Shammaites were "keener of intellect" than the Hillelites, but the law was decided like the Hillelites because they were the majority. Do we have here a repetition of the classical conflict between intellectual truth and practical necessity, between the logical superiority of the minority and the prevalence of the majority? Some mystics claimed that "in the days to come" (presumably Messianic days) the law will be like the Shammaites.[47] The reason for their claim is not clear, probably because they felt it inappropriate to confer complete Torah status on the teaching of the Shammaites, who constitute a legitimate part of Talmudic studies, without giving Shammaite views some modicum of relevance. They deferred the relevance to the "days to come."[48] It is also possible that the mystics sensed that majority verity corresponds to human verity and as such it ought not to prevail "in the days to come." In the days to come divine Truth will prevail, and the law will follow the minority, the Shammaites. However, the law should not always follow the minority even in the days to come, as could be inferred from the mystics' vague declaration. The law should cut across majority and minority opinion, depending on the merits of each case. Just as the minority is not always wrong, so certainly the majority should not always be considered wrong even in the days to come. Divine Truth is above the majority and minority opinion. It stems solely from objective criteria. It knows no majority or minority.

Let me add that because majority rule is a human verity, a practical verity, it is an uncertain verity, subject to limitations. In the sphere of belief, says Maimonides[49]—who otherwise follows a strict maximalistic view of revelation—one is not bound by the standard decision-making apparatus of halakha, including majority rule. One may choose the opinion of the minority if that opinion is more appealing. Majority decision does not make its rule inherently true. It is merely a practical necessity, so that whenever feasible, plurality *is* preferable. This applies to almost everything other than practice. Variety of practice was anathema to the rabbis. It was simply inconceivable to them to allow diversity in behavior. Behavior had to be uniform—and majority rule is the most effective way to enforce uniformity.

The limitation of majority determination, however, is felt also in practical halakha, except that there majority is not majority rule but evidence culled from a majority of cases. An authoritative opinion in the Talmud claims that "one does not follow the majority in matters (disputes) of money."[50] Medieval commentators were hard-pressed to explain why a person may be executed on the basis of a majority (of judges) opinion but a money problem may not be solved on the basis of evidence obtained from a majority of cases. It seems that the time-honored principle that the burden of proof falls on the claimant—that the one who holds the object is presumed to be the owner of the object—is stronger than the evidence obtained from a majority of preceding cases. The evidence obtained from this type of majority is uncertain evidence and as such could not withstand the common sense of the above principle. Another instance of uncertainty in evidence obtained from a majority is the celebrated rabbinic law that "with regard to saving life, one does not follow the majority."[51] When a person's life is in danger, minority possibilities must be equally taken into consideration—and whenever necessary, the law be broken accordingly. R. Isaac, the famous Tosafist (thirteenth century)[52] connects this rule with the talmudic exposition of Lev. 18:5: " 'He shall live by them' (the commandments) but not die because of them." Commandments in no way ought to cause death, even when the possibility of death is remote. In matters of life and death one has to reckon with all possibilities, not just majority and minority advocacy. A person has to violate the law in order to save a life. He has to do so even when the saving is not probable, even when it is not based on the evidence of a majority of earlier cases. Majority evidence is not certain enough to risk a life. Stronger evidence is needed.

The idea of uncertainty of majority evidence is best expressed in the following statement by R. Yochanan (a third-century Palestinian scholar) in *b. Nid.* 18a: "In three instances did the sages follow the majority of preceding cases and treat them as certainties. . . ." In all other instances majority evidence was treated as uncertain evidence, with the result that as a precautionary measure the minority evidence was adhered to as well. This was so, especially when the evidence of the minority entailed greater stringency, in line with the notion that "when in doubt, follow the more stringent." In R. Yochanan's enumerated three instances, the majority evidence was followed exclusively, and the minority evidence was ignored completely even when it tended to be more stringent.

"Initial Revelation"

Let me also add that because majority rule is a human verity, a product of divine relinquishment, it is reversible (see *m. Ed.* 1:3).[53] A majority view of one generation may turn into a minority view of the next generation and under certain conditions may change halakhically. Man is temporary and his verity is temporary. In this regard the dichotomy between practice and intellect with respect to majority and minority decision differs from dichotomy between practice and intellect with respect to the different chronological modes of interpretation. The former is a result of the concession to the practical need of human beings, the latter a part of God's choice of a particular time for His revelation. Human practical needs change, and with them the law that was based on those needs, whereas the divine choice remains an irreversible, historical fact. The former is changeable, the latter is unchangeable. The criterion for behavior will always remain the understanding of the text of those to whom the initial revelation was given ("an eye for an eye" will never mean literally, a physical eye for an eye).[54] Its truth is divine Truth made manifest by God's choice to reveal Himself to that generation, with that mode of understanding— and as such, it is eternal.

This subject of divine Truth made manifest by God's choice, of time as an active factor in revelation, deserves a separate treatment, to which the author hopes to return in a future work. Suffice it here to summarize and say that "initial revelation" does not refer to the initial *reception* of the Torah but to the unqualified *acceptance* of the Torah, free of idolatrous syncretism, which took place during the time of Ezra.[55] This religious metamorphosis is expressed in the public confession recorded in Neh. 9, and which coincides with the first mention of Midrash in the later Rabbinic sense as attested to by the phrase in Ezra 7:10: "To seek—*lidrosh*—the Torah of the Lord." "*Derash* in the Bible does not, as a rule, mean exegesis, exposition of a text. Rather, it means seeking information, theological or otherwise, without reference to a text. However, the combination of *derash* and *Torah* connotes an exegetical activity similar to that engaged in by the Rabbis of the Talmud."[56] The genesis of rabbinic exegesis, including instances of reading in, especially those that serve to harmonize seemingly contradictory sources, enabling the sources to be included in the canonical text, dates back to the time shortly after the conclusion of the final phase of the full acceptance of the Torah as the sole religious authority on the part of the people. The confession of chapter 9 of Nehemiah resulted in the faith covenant (*amanah*) of chapter 10 ("For all this, we make a faith covenant"—10:1) which contains ordinances, exegetically derived. In a sense the whole period between Moses and Ezra can be viewed as the period between the receiving and the accepting of the Torah by the masses. They received it during the time of Moses but did not give their unqualified acceptance until the time of Ezra. The genesis of rabbinic exegesis, coming so soon after Ezra, constitutes a part of the Torah's revelatory process—of the acceptance phase, in contradistinction to definition and the like, which constitutes a part of the revelatory process of the receiving phase (they had to know what the law meant as soon as they heard it).

"The great divide in Jewish history according to R. Zadok Hako-hen [a nineteenth–century Polish rabbi] occurred not with the destruction of either Temple [as traditionally assumed] but with the cessation of prophecy,"[57] which inaugurated "the beginning of the Oral Torah or the establishment of the Oral Torah"[58]—the midrash.[59] More specifically, I would say that "the great divide" occurred with the assembly convened by Ezra for expiation and repentance (as described in Neh. 9), which put an end to syncretistic tendencies that prevailed among the masses until then (we hear no more of them) and which declared the books of Moses to be the sole religious guide to the exclusion of any other source. This exclusive-ness demanded that the Torah, now governing every aspect of life, be interpreted not only explicitly (a hermeneutic that would limit the scope of the Torah), but also implicitly—through midrash.

Bracketing of the Period between Moses and Ezra

With respect to halakha, the period between Moses and Ezra, that is, the period of the prophets, is bracketed, as it were—suspended between the receiving and the accepting of the Torah, without much halakhic force of its own. "The law was known from before, from Moses; the prophets merely gave it a scriptural basis."[60] Two basic religious institutions during that period were either not observed at all (the making of the *Sukka*—Neh 8:17) or not observed properly (the preparation of the paschal lamb—2 Kgs. 23:22). When Ama-ziah the son of Joash complied with a law of the Torah, he was singled out for praise: "And he did that which was right in the eyes of the Lord . . . the children of the murderers he put not to death, according to that which is written in the book of the Law of Moses, as the Lord commanded: that fathers shall not be put to death for the children, nor the children be put to death for the fathers." (2 Kgs. 14:6) Not many people of his time emulated his compliance with the law. At best, the law was kept by a few, by an elite.[61]

With respect to exegesis as well, that period is bracketed. The meaning of the Bible is to be perceived according to the understanding of those who lived subsequent to the completion of revelation. Their meaning may appear to us as forced, as read in, or as a reconciliation between contradictory sources, reflecting divergent behavior of preceding generations. Yet our awareness that it may be forced should have no decisive influence. What has happened to the text and its meaning in the period prior to the unqualified allegiance to the exclusivity of the Law of Moses is of little relevance (or at least of no more relevance than the history of many a biblical law or language prior to Mosaic revelation). What counts is the postrevelatory inspiration that infused its recipients with a sense of harmony. Being the first people to accept fully the Torah, their understanding concurred with the divine will, and as such cannot be compared to human verity as manifested by majority rule. The two are different in their very essence and therefore ought not be treated analogously.

5

"Chate'u Yisrael"
("Israel Sinned"):
A Proposed Resolution
to the Conflict
of Peshat and Derash

The Nature of the Conflict

In the previous chapter, we documented the rabbinic evidence in
favor of a dichotomy between practical halakha and intellectual
pursuit, observance and study. This differentiation of the spheres
of normative behavior and critical exegesis was inspired by the instances in rabbinic literature of conflict between majority and minority positions, in which the former systemically holds sway in the
realm of behavior while the latter may yet be granted a certain
status of truth in the realm of the intellect. The lines of demarcation
drawn between a majority view that is halakhically binding and a
minority opinion that is intellectually sovereign served to delineate
and illuminate the dichotomy between praxis and scholarship.

We now come to a different conflict of interests—that which
sometimes unfolds between scriptural peshat and rabbinic derash—
which demands a different illustrative paradigm. The tension that
may develop between peshat and derash is rooted in the theory of
timebound exegesis that we have employed throughout the course

of the book to explain the changing exegetical orientations towards peshat through time. As exegetical sensibilities change and vary with the passing of history, a chasm may develop, in the mind of the contemporary reader of Scripture, between what is perceived as the plain meaning of the Bible (peshat) and its rabbinic interpretation (derash). This opposition of peshat and derash (when the two are mutually exclusive) is not mitigated by reference to the two-tiered truth system of majority and minority views which is occasionally reflected in rabbinic thought and which results, by necessity, in the dichotomy between halakha and exegesis. Such conflicts of peshat and derash on the one hand and majority and minority opinions on the other are not coterminous nor even analogous. In a novel halakhic dispute involving majority opinion and minority dissent, there exists no previous legal record with which to contend. Each position, initially, is enabled to compete within the guidelines of halakhic discourse in the quest for consensus. The position embraced by the majority is delegated normative status while the minority position may, in rare instances, be accorded the stature of logical supremacy. A similar division may be obtained vis-à-vis peshat and derash whenever they are merely divergent and not contradictory. In an instance of absolute disparity between peshat and derash, however, the contemporary critic of the rabbinic exegesis of a particular scriptural verse must, if committed to the authority of rabbinic interpretation, grapple with the tradition of that exegesis. Because a body of authoritative tradition is at stake in the conflict of peshat and derash, the paradigm of majority–minority opposition—in which a tradition of exegesis is not a factor—is no longer serviceable. Because a *contradiction* between peshat and derash is involved, and not a mere multiplicity of valid interpretations that can naturally coexist, the religious primacy of initial revelation does not apply. We must search elsewhere for a paradigm that will allow us to develop a theory to resolve the conflict between peshat and derash.

We have at this point, in a sense, come full circle in our discussion of peshat and derash. Objective analysis of the relevant materials of rabbinic literature has been followed by explanation of their theological implications. We now offer a theological resolution to the problem that has agitated beneath the surface of our discussion for almost its duration. As we noted at the beginning of the book, a well documented, and often scrutinized, feature of rabbinic exegesis is its occasional deviation from the peshat, or *sensus litteralis*, of a scriptural phrase or verse, in favor of more creative and unrestrained interpretation, or derash. The peshat, or the strict philological and syntactical meaning of a verse, is in certain instances forsaken by the rabbis in their attempt to tighten the link between practical halakha and its scriptural foundation. This discrepancy between peshat and derash, between the plain meaning of a verse that is dictated by content and context and rabbinic exegesis that sometimes seems only loosely connected to the text, has been troubling to readers within and without the tradition. This problematic phenomenon of rabbinic literature has itself generated a steady stream of commentary of different sorts—critical, apologetic, and scholarly.[1]

This sometime idiosyncratic nature of rabbinic exegesis is, for the halakhically committed Jew, no mere trivial or scholastic issue, for it impinges on the basic question of the validity and authority of tradition as forged and formulated through rabbinic midrash. The issue of the dichotomy of peshat and derash is particularly relevant to the modern reader of the Bible. The modern exegetical sensibility has embraced the primacy of peshat over derash. Midrashic interpretation that seems unfettered by the plain, straightforward meaning of Scripture can be judged exegetically capricious and textually groundless. Needless to say, such a judgment of rabbinic exegesis must be theologically unsettling to the Jew committed to the authority of traditional halakhic interpretation. An attempt must therefore be made to defuse the religious tension that is produced by the awareness of the occasional discrepancy between scriptural peshat and rabbinic derash.

Mutual Exclusivity of Peshat and Derash

The reconciliation of peshat and derash, free from the uncritical and apologetic defense of traditional interpretation, is not a simple matter, however, particularly when one confronts the reality of instances of rabbinic derash that seem to digress absolutely from the scriptural peshat. In these instances, several of which will be enumerated below, the incongruity of peshat and derash seems patent and irresoluble. It must be emphasized that we are dealing here only with instances in which peshat and derash are mutually exclusive and contradictory (that is, the halakhic prescriptions flowing from peshat and derash cannot be fulfilled concurrently), and not with the broad category of examples in which rabbinic derash supplements or complements, but does not flatly contradict, the scriptural peshat. The latter category can be subsumed under the canopy of multiple interpretation and sanctioned by initial revelation. In the spotlight here are examples of peshat and derash that cannot be harmonized or reconciled without doing exegetical damage to the genuine character of each. The conclusions to be drawn from these types of confrontations and contradictions of peshat and derash are unsavory: either the divine text of the Torah is somehow deficient and thus in need of rabbinic "repair" by means of midrash, or else the rabbinic exegesis is objectionable and un-satisfactory, for it has strayed too far from the divine authorial intention. In either scenario, the authority of halakha, grounded upon the propriety and correctness of rabbinic interpretation, lies prone to challenge and criticism. The fundamental query that can-not be evaded is the following: if the derash really represents the meaning of the scriptural verse, why was the Torah phrased so awkwardly and unfelicitously that peshat and derash seem incom-patible? In fact, given the precedence of peshat, why must Scripture ever be subjected to the "corrective" procedure of derash? The problem of the occasional disparity between peshat and derash thus constitutes a weighty theological issue, for it creates avenues for imputing either imperfection to the divine text or illegitimacy to traditional interpretation.

The paramount concern of Jews dedicated to the rule of halakha is that their behavior accord with the dictates of the divine will. They must be assured that the halakhic regulations that guide their lives, which are the produce of rabbinic exegesis, faithfully and precisely capture the design of the Torah. In other words, the legitimacy of rabbinic derash in the arena of practical halakha must be upheld for that assurance to be maintained. The resolution of the peshat/derash tension may thus yield dividends for the religious consciousness of the halakhically committed Jew, promoting confidence that his religious behavior is, indeed, divinely sanctioned. The resolution to be offered here, though rooted in theological considerations, will be substantiated through reference to rabbinic texts. In this way, the problem of peshat versus derash can be addressed within the framework of rabbinic theology, and its solution, though fueled by modern concerns, can be formulated in the vocabulary of authoritative rabbinic literature.

Let us first sketch briefly a few examples of the discrepancy between scriptural peshat and rabbinic derash and describe the rabbis' own strategy for resolving textual conflicts. The clash between peshat and derash falls under two categories: either a rabbinic interpretation is at odds with the peshat of an individual scriptural verse, or two or more scriptural verses are at odds with each other and must be reconciled through reference to a third verse. Prominent examples of the first category include the rabbinic interpretation of the phrase "an eye for an eye" in Exod. 21:24 to mean monetary compensation, when the simple, literal meaning of the phrase "ayin tachat ayin" is, most likely, physical retribution. This example may serve as the paradigmatic instance of a rabbinic interpretation displacing the peshat of a verse and replacing it with a wholly different, and contrary, meaning.[2]

A second example in which the divergence between peshat and derash is equally stark involves levirate marriage (Deut. 25:5–6), in which the biblical law enjoins a woman whose husband has died without children to marry one of the deceased husband's brothers, prescribing that "the first son whom she bears shall succeed to the name of his brother who is dead, that his name may not be blotted out of Israel." The straightforward meaning of the verse indicates that the living brother is to become a surrogate father for the deceased brother, who is considered the "real," if not natural, father of the firstborn offspring of the levirate marriage. The rabbis altered the meaning of the verse by claiming that the phrase *asher teled* refers not to the firstborn child, as the peshat suggests, but to the firstborn brother, that is, the oldest brother of the deceased, who shall perform the levirate marriage. By interpreting the phrase *asher teled* in the past tense (in the sense of *asher nolad*), and thereby abandoning its peshat, the rabbis modified the halakhic composition of the verse.[3]

The second category of confrontations between peshat and de-rash comprises two subcategories. In the first, two verses contradict each other and one of them is stripped of its peshat, that is, interpreted contrary to its peshat, to "resolve" the contradiction. An example of this subcategory is the contradiction between Exod. 12:9, which states, "Do not eat it (the paschal lamb) raw or cooked in water, but roasted . . . over the fire," and Deut. 16:17, which states, "You shall cook [i.e., with water] and eat it." An attempt to reconcile these two verses is already evidenced by 2 Chr. 35:13, "and they cooked the passover (sacrifice) with fire."[4] In the second subcategory, contradictions between verses are resolved through the aid of a third verse. In these instances, the weight of the third verse tips the exegetical balance in favor of the peshat of one of the original two verses, creating a two against one situation. Though the matter of the correct practical halakha is settled through this accounting of verses, the peshat of the minority verse is virtually annulled in the process, for it is assigned an exclusively derash meaning. This hermeneutic method is embodied in the last of Rabbi Ishmael's thirteen exegetical principles: "If two biblical passages contradict each other, they can be determined only by a third passage."[5] An example of this type of interpretive methodology, in which rabbinic derash overrides and dislodges scriptural peshat while effectively mediating between conflicting verses, is the resolu-tion offered to the contradiction between Exod. 12:5, "you may take it (the Passover offering) from the sheep or from the goats" and Deut. 16:2, "you shall slaughter the passover sacrifice for the Lord your God, from the flock and the herd." A third verse, Exod. 12:21, "pick out lambs for your families, and slaughter the Passover offering," is brought as the deciding factor in this halakhic contro-versy, with the rabbis determining that the Passover sacrifice must come from the flock only and not from the herd. The word "herd" is designated for the *chagiga* offering, even though the context clearly involves the paschal sacrifice, and thus is also plainly interpreted contrary to its peshat.[6] The peshat of one verse is here ultimately abandoned in the cause of textual reconciliation or, rather, halak-hic compromise. This solution is already implied in 2 Chr. 35:7–9. In fact, we have seen that the solutions to both contradictions of the second category—in which one verse is delegated a midrashic interpretation which negates its peshat—are already outlined in 2 Chronicles, a late biblical text attributed by tradition to Ezra the Scribe.[7] The antiquity of this type of midrashic resolution—the resort to derash in the face of problematic peshat—is thus well established.

The two categories of exposition outlined above, in which rabbinic derash displaces and supersedes the peshat of a scriptural verse, adumbrate the theological issue discussed above, namely, why is derash needed to "amend" peshat that is either inherently problematic or that contradicts a scriptural prescription found elsewhere? Why are there ever instances in the Torah wherein the peshat of a verse is either unreliable or misleading? Because the conception of the Torah as the embodiment of God's will is vital to the guarantee that the halakha corresponds to God's bidding, one is led to wonder why the divine text, on occasion, employs other than the most straightforward and unambiguous language with which to communicate its directives. In other words, it is an enigmatic datum of the Torah that, in the example of levirate marriage discussed above, the words *asher teled* are used instead of *asher nolad* when the latter is actually, upon rabbinic interpretation, the intended meaning of the verse. The need on the part of the rabbis to resort to derash because the peshat of a scriptural verse is, in a sense, deceiving, must be theologically puzzling to the reader imbued with the belief that the Torah is divine and in no need of human "emendation." In sum, why would the Torah say peshat when it really meant to imply derash?

Proposed Solution: "Chate'u Yisrael"

We propose here a theory to explain the occasional discrepancy between scriptural peshat and rabbinic derash, thereby solving the theological puzzle of why the Torah is sometimes in need of midrashic revision. In essence, we suggest that in cases where derash seems to depart radically from peshat, an act of restoration, and not revision, has taken place. That is, rabbinic derash actually restores the original meaning of the scriptural verse, recovering its divine authorial intention, in places where the text itself had become corrupted through the historical process of *chate'u Yisrael* ("the people of Israel sinned"), the sinning of the Jews through idol worship and their consequent neglect of the biblical text during much of the post-Mosaic and First Temple periods. Those occasions when rabbinic derash supplants the peshat of a verse signify that the current text of the verse is faulty and that, in fact, the derash was originally the peshat of the verse. In these cases, the peshat *is* actually misleading precisely because it is the result of textual corruption. The derash recaptures the textual sense of the original revelation that had existed before the process of *chate'u Yisrael* set in. What this theory implies is that, in these instances, the uncorrupted Torah actually originally *did* say derash, and that the peshat of our current text is fallacious, a reality which necessarily prompted the corrective, but essentially restorative, activity of midrash.

A consequence of this process of sinning and correlative neglect of the text of the Torah, therefore, was the phenomenon of a divine text whose peshat in some places had become corrupt and thus in need of midrashic emendation. Rabbinic derash restores the "genuine" peshat of these problematic verses, displacing the current peshat which, through the corrosive process of *chate'u Yisrael*, had become textually entrenched. These instances of problematic peshat, however, were not allowed to become exegetically canonized, primarily because of the restorative efforts of Ezra in the early Second Temple period. Ezra impelled the process of the "rehabilitation" of the text of the Torah, partly through a system of markers flagging certain words as spurious, but more comprehensively through restorative oral midrashic exposition. Despite the historical process of *chate'u Yisrael*, which had created a faulty text, Ezra possessed sufficient authority to render the potentially misleading peshat of certain Torah passages harmless by reinstituting their correct meaning, but he did not possess sufficient authority to actually emend the faulty text in most instances. Thus the religious Jew is left with a scriptural text whose peshat is not always authoritative or decisive, yet he does possess a tradition of midrashic interpretation that is authoritative. And therein lies the religious Jew's guarantee that, though the Torah is, in places, textually blemished, his *halakha lema'ase does* correspond with and express the divine will as embodied in the original revelation. Halakha is codified according to rabbinic derash because derash, and not peshat, always conforms to the dictates of the Sinaitic revelation. The upshot of our theory is that derash is always halakhically trustworthy and definitive, while peshat sometimes is not.

Ezra and the Restoration of Monotheism

The historical core of this theory about the text of the Torah is bound up with the historical personality of Ezra and his role in revivifying and stabilizing the monotheistic foundations of Judaism, a role unique to Ezra over all other prophets that puts him in the category of Moses. As we noted at the conclusion of the previous chapter, the unqualified acceptance of the Torah, free of idolatrous syncretism, took place during the reign of leadership of Ezra and Nehemiah in the fifth century B.C.E. This communal regeneration and faith covenant (*amana*, described in the book of Nehemiah, chapters 9 and 10), represents the conclusion to a period of halakhic delinquency and the paving of the halakhic path which leads to rabbinic Judaism and beyond. The historical period between Moses and Ezra must, in terms of halakhic force, be bracketed, suspended between the receiving and the acceptance of the Torah. The period of the prophets was characterized by halakhic inconstancy and instability, summed up in the phrase *chate'u Yisrael*. Two basic religious institutions during that period—the making of the *sukka* and the preparation of the paschal lamb—were either not observed at all or not observed properly.[8] As we shall see, the syncretistic proclivity of the Jews during the prophetic period led not only to sins of omission and commission in the realm of practical halakha, but also to the debasement and corruption of the scriptural text itself.

It was Ezra who arrested this syncretistic backsliding and inaugurated the process of disseminating the proper text of the Torah and its authentic interpretation. It is not coincidental that the first mention of midrash in the later rabbinic sense is attested to by the phrase in Ezra 7:10: "For Ezra had dedicated himself to seek (*lidrosh*) the Torah of the Lord so as to observe it, and to teach laws and rules to Israel." The Torah came to be accepted by the people as the sole textual source of religious authority and had to be interpreted not only explicitly, but also implicitly through midrash halakha, so that its scope could be broadened organically. Ezra was thus the principal architect of the oral law (excluding fundamental meanings of scriptural verses requisite for a basic understanding of the *mitzvot*) and its method of exposition. The process of the development of the oral law was thereby launched with the efforts of Ezra and his generation, and the authority of derash was then constituted and confirmed. The genesis of rabbinic exegesis at the time of Ezra thus represents a great watershed in Jewish history.[9]

The Neglect of the Scriptural Text
during the First Temple Period

The neglect of the scriptural text during the long historical period of halakhic laxity—highlighted by the account of the "rediscovery" of a scroll of the Torah during the reign of King Josiah—is implied by Nehemiah 9:34: *ve-et melakheinu, sareinu, kohaneinu, va-avoteinu lo asu toratekha . . .* ("Our kings, officers, priests, and fathers did not follow Your teaching"). The word "kohaneinu" in this context should be understood as the priests in their role as teachers or guardians of the Torah.[10] These guardians of the scriptures are implicitly held culpable for negligence in their duty of preserving the text of the Torah. Further logical evidence for the neglect of the scriptural text is implied by Neh. 8 which relates Ezra's reading of the Torah before the people, suggesting that such public reading from the Torah represented a social and religious innovation. The implied lack of such official public instruction in the centuries preceding Ezra[11] suggests a general inattention to the sacred writ that could very well have directly resulted in the neglect and abuse of its text. The absence of public, communal reading of the Torah meant that it was in the possession and guardianship of various "private" parties, a situation which may have fostered textual multiplicity and adulteration. Ezra's efforts were thus aimed at communal, and scriptural, consolidation and uniformity.

It should also be noted that the cessation of prophecy, which is traditionally attributed to the time of Ezra (specifically to the death of the prophet Malachi), put an end to direct divine communication. The religious community became entirely dependent on the textual legacy inherited from past generations. This dependence on text stimulated, in turn, greater care and concern for the text and its protection against corruption. During the First Temple period, in contrast, the text of the past was dispensable, or replaceable, for there existed the alternative divine channel of prophecy. The religious community during the First Temple period, in contrast to the post-Ezra period, devoted less attention to the preservation of the text, thereby making it more vulnerable to corruption. Thus, those who were steeped in idolatry or syncretism neglected the text transmitted from the past because it did not serve as their unchallenged source of religious guidance. And those who were attached to the prophetic circles, and thus had access to a direct revelatory source, neglected the text (of course, to a much lesser degree) in favor of a living and contemporaneous religious reality. Only when prophecy "dried up" and disappeared as a ready, available source of enlightenment and instruction did the reliance on text become a religious necessity. Only with the cessation of prophecy did the text become indispensable and, therefore, textual solicitude imperative and urgent. Canonization and midrash were the natural and efficacious byproducts of the expiration of prophetic revelation. Textual interpretation, or midrash, became the primary instrument of postprophetic, or rabbinic, Judaism. Midrash replaced, or substituted for, prophecy as the prime carrier of God's revelation. The midrashic enterprise was largely initiated by Ezra, whose first concern, however, was to consolidate and correct the text of Scripture itself.

"Chate'u Yisrael" in Rabbinic Literature

This historical sequence of, first, sinning by the Jews during the prophetic period (*chate'u Yisrael*), the consequent neglect of the scriptural text on the part of the *kohanim*, and the subsequent restorative and reconstructive activities of Ezra, is alluded to in several passages in rabbinic literature. We will now catalog several of these references which intimate the contours of this historical sequence before focusing our attention in greater depth on a midrashic passage that explicitly mentions Ezra's effort at restoring the text of the Torah to its unadulterated, pre-*chate'u Yisrael* form. We shall then posit that even Ezra, though unique in his authority to modify the scriptural text then in vogue, could not fully extirpate the corruptions that had crept into the text. He could, however, solidify the authority of the traditional interpretations of these tainted passages, thereby reinforcing the prestige of derash. The textual curiosities of the Torah, that is, the instances of manifest contrariness between peshat and derash, will then have been accounted for and explained.

The concept of *chate'u Yisrael* is alluded to directly in *b. Ned.* 22b ("had not Israel sinned, only the Pentateuch and the book of Joshua would have been given to them") and indirectly in *m. Para* 3:5, which states: "Moses prepared the first *para aduma*, [red heifer], and Ezra prepared the second, and five [were prepared] after Ezra, [according to] the view of R. Meir; but the sages say, seven [were prepared] after Ezra." According to this historical calculation, no red heifers were prepared between the careers of Moses and Ezra—the period which we have claimed must be bracketed in terms of halakhic authority and enforcement. This Mishnah thus subtly lends further credence to the conception of this historical epoch as one of ritual carelessness and impurity, and support for the claim that Ezra initiated a process of halakhic reform and renewal.

The notion of *chate'u Yisrael* can be correlated with the idea that certain ritual practices and halakhic regulations—whose origins are disputed—fell into disuse for a time because of neglect and were subsequently reinstated into the religious life of the community. This idea is advanced in regard to a disagreement about the historical roots of the rite of the willow branch on Hoshanah Rabbah, about whether this law was given to Moses on Mount Sinai or was, rather, an institution of the prophets. R. Abahu concludes that this law of the willow branch was forgotten but was reinstituted by the prophets at the divine command.[12] This episode of the forgetting and consequent restoration of the willow-branch ritual, and parallel examples, fit into the larger recurring historical pattern of halakhic negligence and recovery, which comes to its finale in the time of Ezra.

The most explicit correspondence between sinning on the part of the Jews and changes effected in the text of the Torah during the time of Ezra is claimed in *b. Sanh.* 21b–22a, the locus of the axial concept of *chate'u Yisrael*. The fascinating text there reads:

Mar Zutra or, as some say, Mar 'Ukba said: Originally the Torah was given to Israel[13] in Hebrew characters and in the sacred [Hebrew] language; later, in the times of Ezra, the Torah was given in Ashurith script and Aramaic language. [Finally], they selected for Israel the Ashurith script and Hebrew language. . . .

It has been taught: R. Yose said: Had Moses not preceded him, Ezra would have been worthy of receiving the Torah for Israel. Of Moses it is written, 'And Moses went up unto God' (Exod. 19:3), and of Ezra it is written, 'He, Ezra, went up from Babylon' (Ezra 7:6). As the going up of the former refers to the [receiving of the] Law, so does the going up of the latter. . . . And even though the Torah was not given through him [Ezra], its writing was changed through him. . . .[14]

It has been taught: Rabbi said: The Torah was originally given to Israel in this [Ashurith] writing. *When they* [Israel] *sinned* [*she-chate'u*],[15] it was changed into Ro'atz. But when they repented, the [Assyrian characters] were *re*-introduced. . . .

R. Simeon b. Eliezer said on the authority of R. Eliezer b. Parta, who spoke on the authority of R. Eleazar of Modi'im: This writing [of the law] was never changed. . . .[16]

This talmudic passage posits a series of provocative historical-theological claims. The first, though disputed, is that the script (*ketav*) and language (*lashon*) of the Torah underwent changes and reversals through history, the period of Ezra being particularly significant and dynamic. The second claim is that Ezra possesses a stature and status vis-à-vis revelation equivalent to that of Moses,[17] demonstrating that the process of revelation was historically protracted. The third claim, brought in the name of Rabbi, and the one most crucially relevant to our discussion, causally links the historical data of Israel's sinning and repentance to alterations made in the script of the Torah. The correlation between halakhic allegiance and scriptural guardianship is here explicitly articulated. A process of textual loss and recovery is bound up with a cycle of halakhic degeneration and regeneration.

The Ten *Puncta Extraordinaria*

But this paradigm offered by Rabbi is not adequate to our theoretical needs because the claim in *Sanhedrin* is advanced only in regard to the script and language of the Torah, and not to its actual phraseology. We must look elsewhere in rabbinic literature for an even more germane and illuminating theological prototype for our modern resolution to the problem of the occasional discrepancy between peshat and derash. This paradigm is to be found in *Bemidbar Rabbah* III, 13 (and parallels)[18] in a passage that enumerates and explains the presence of the ten *puncta extraordinaria*, or *eser nekudot*, in the Pentateuch. The text begins:

There is point on the vav of *ve-Aharon* (Num. 3:39) to indicate that he was not one of the number. A similar example is, "The Lord decide between me and you" (Gen. 16:5). The (second) letter yod of *beineikha* is dotted to teach that Sarah's complaint was only concerning Hagar alone; some say, concerning those that sowed dissension between him and her. Another instance: "And they said unto him (*eilav*), Where is Sarah?" (Gen. 18:9). There are points over the aleph, yod, and vav of *eilav* to indicate that they knew where she was, yet made inquiries about her. Another instance: "And he knew not when she lay down, nor when she arose—*u-vekumah*" (Gen. 19:33). There is a point over the middle vav of *u-vekumah* used of Lot's elder daughter to indicate that he knew not when she lay down but he knew when she arose. Another instance: "And he kissed him"—*va-yishakehu* (Gen. 33:4). There are points over the whole word to indicate that he (Esau) did not kiss him (Jacob) with all his heart. Another example: "And his brethren went to feed their father's flock" (Gen. 37:12). Why are there points over *et*? It teaches that they did not go to feed the flock but to eat and to drink and to yield to temptation. Another example: "Or be in a journey afar off"—*rechoka* (Num. 9:10). This teaches that it was considered a distant journey even if it was only without the threshold of the Temple courtyard. Some say that even if a person was already near and was unclean he could not participate in the Passover sacrifice. Another instance: "And we have laid waste even unto Nophah, which reaches unto Medeba" (Num. 21:30). There is a point over the resh of *asher* to indicate that there was the same desolation beyond. Some say it teaches that they did not destroy the peoples but the countries. Another instance: "And a tenth (*issaron*), a tenth part you shall offer" (Num. 29:15). There is a point over the first *issaron* that is used in connection with the first day of the festival. It teaches that there was one tenth only. Another instance: "The secret things belong unto the Lord our God; but the things that are revealed belong unto us (*lanu*) and to our children (*u-levaneinu*) for (*ad*) ever" (Deut. 29:28).

> Why are there points over *lanu, ulevaneinu*, and over the ayin of *ad*?
> God said unto them: "You have performed the precepts that have
> been revealed, and I, on My part, will make known to you the things
> which are secret."[19]

After exhausting the list of ten dotted passages and interpreting the
significance of each, the text concludes with this crucial addendum:

> Some give another reason why the dots are inserted (*ve-yesh omrim*).
> Ezra reasoned thus: If Elijah comes and asks: "Why have you written
> these words?" [i.e., Why have you included these suspect passages?].
> I shall answer: "That is why I dotted these passages." And if he says
> to me: "You have done well in having written them," I shall erase the
> dots over them.

From the presence of the phrase *ve-yesh omrim* ("Some give
another reason . . ."),[20] it is clear that we are dealing with two
distinct and disparate opinions in this passage. The two opinions,
though dissimilar, share the common denominator of implying that
the peshat of the Torah in these ten instances is, at the very least,
misleading. What the list of dotted words implies, despite the
variety of textual modifications it embodies, is that, minimally, the
peshat of these dotted passages must be supplanted and superseded
by derash, if not deleted outright.[21] In brief, the dots indicate that
the words must not be understood according to their peshat meanings.[22] The first opinion suggests that the dots indicate that the
words must either be deleted or that unusual or unexpected interpretations be given to them, interpretations that would otherwise be
camouflaged. The list of the ten dotted passages, according to the
first view, encompasses a diversity of textual "modifications," rang-
ing from commonplace homiletical exposition, to derash that
clearly deviates from the peshat, to interpretation that effectively
deletes the word, thus bordering on the purport of the second
view.[23] However, the first opinion does not grant Ezra the authority
to delete a word deemed spurious (he could only place a dot over
such words), implying that his textual license was limited.

The second opinion encapsulates the essence of our historical
theory that Ezra was qualified and allowed actually to "correct"
scriptural phrases which he deemed faulty. This opinion more

boldly admits the possibility of the spuriousness of certain scriptural phrases; from this perspective, the peshat may not merely be deceptive, but may possibly be corrupt and may need to be excised. The second opinion implies that Ezra had the right to delete a word if he was sure of its spuriousness. In these ten instances, he happened to be uncertain of the reliability of the text and therefore resorted to dots, but Elijah's question to Ezra, "Why have you written these words?" implies that Ezra possessed the power of textual emendation.

Misgivings about Ezra's Role

This rabbinic assertion of Ezra's exegetical and textual license has indeed provoked misgiving and irritation on the part of some readers. In the sixteenth century, Azariah de Rossi (1511–78), in his *Meor Einayim*, concluded that this text must have been written by a deviant student without his teacher's knowledge and therefore possesses no authority or credibility.[24] DeRossi could not fathom how the rabbis could have ascribed such powers of scriptural emendation even to as great a figure as Ezra. More recently, Rabbi Moshe Feinstein has been even more unequivocal in his declaration that this rabbinic passage represents unadulterated heresy in attributing to Ezra such excessive leeway with the text of the Torah, and thus it must certainly be excised. He perceives the theological daring reflected in this Rabbinic passage as being theologically scandalous.[25]

The Prophet's Volition versus Divine Command

However, despite objections raised against the credibility of this rabbinic passage about the ten dotted passages in the Torah, its authenticity is beyond reproach, for it is found in several locations throughout rabbinic literature.[26] One may safely assume that the many commentators who have passed over the passage in *Bemidbar Rabbah* (and its parallels) without protestation have not been troubled by it and have seen in it no theological impropriety. In fact, Rabbi Y. F. Lisser, the author of *Binyan Yehoshua*, the standard commentary on *Avot de-Rabbi Nathan*, explicitly endorses the authenticity of the passage and its theological connotations. In his commentary on the *Avot de-Rabbi Nathan* source of the passage, he states categorically, *Ezra ha-Sofer tikken ha-Torah be-tikkun soferim kefi ha-tzorekh* ("Ezra the Scribe corrected the Torah, in the manner of scribal correction, as needed").[27] The claim that the passage is theologically heretical and falls under the category of "he has despised the word of the Lord" (Num. 15:31; *b. Sanh.* 99a and parallels) has also been addressed and repudiated by R. Meir Ish Shalom (1831–1908) in *Beit Talmud*, where a distinction is drawn between the heretical belief that a verse in the Torah was written by Moses (or by any human being) independently of divine revelation or recommendation, and the theologically acceptable notion that God occasionally either instructs the prophet to add words to the scriptural text or approves of such an addition.[28] Only if one believes that a scriptural verse was composed by *Moshe mipi atzmo* (by Moses of his own volition)—and the emphasis is on *mipi atzmo*[29]—would the charge of heresy be legitimate. As long as the belief remains that any human intervention in the scriptural text is not autonomous, heresy is not an issue.[30]

Such a conception of human participation *mipi ha-Gevurah*" (by the divine command) validates the hints of R. Abraham Ibn Ezra and even of R. Judah the Hasid about the non-Mosaic elements of the Pentateuch.[31] R. Joseph b. Eliezer Tob Elem (Bonfils) of the fourteenth century (v. 1335), writing in defense of Ibn Ezra's hint that certain verses in the Torah were authored after Moses' death, vindicates it on theological grounds.

> As he [Ibn Ezra] shows, Moses did not write this word, but Joshua or one of the other prophets wrote it. And since we must believe in the words of tradition and prophecy, what difference does it make whether Moses or some other prophet wrote it, since the words of all of them are truth and given through prophecy (i.e., divine revelation). . . . The Torah warned "You should not add to it" (*Bal tosif*) only in regard to the number of commandments and their fundamental principles, but not in regard to words.[32]

Another medieval scholar, Moses Alashkar (1466–1552), reiterated and corroborated the theological proposition that Ezra's scriptural role must be endowed with the same revelatory stature as that of Moses. In addressing the matter of whether a change in the script of the Torah was introduced by Ezra, and, if so, whether *derashot* can legitimately be made on the basis of a script that is not the original one, Alashkar writes, "It makes no difference whether the Torah was given via Moses or via Ezra in terms of whether sages can exposit upon it."[33] In our passage, the "corrections" made by Ezra in the Torah should then be seen to have been instituted with the consent and approval of its divine author. Imbued with the spirit of prophecy and invested with the status of revelation, the authority of Ezra's involvement with the scriptural text is unimpeachable.[34] Only if one were to believe that Ezra acted capriciously or uninhibitedly would the specter of heresy arise.

The charges of inauthenticity and heresy leveled against the *Bemidbar Rabbah* passage having been addressed and refuted, this rabbinic text about the dotted passages of the Torah, and its depiction of Ezra's function as a divinely ordained "emender" of the text, can serve as the paradigm for our conjecture about the emergence of the discrepancy between peshat and derash. The corruptions of the scriptural text, though implicitly acknowledged by the first view of the passage and virtually explicitly acknowledged in the second, are nevertheless not explained, that is, their origins are not accounted for, in the *Bemidbar Rabbah* text. We must therefore supplement this text with that found in *Sanh.* 22a (Rabbi's opinion) and formulate a theory that couples *chate'u Yisrael* with changes effected in the text of the Torah. It must be emphasized, however, that the rabbinic texts that we have cited have not constituted definitive proof for our proposed solution to the textual conflict of peshat and derash, but have rather offered an explanatory paradigm. Our proposed resolution to the occasional discrepancy between scriptural peshat and rabbinic derash is grounded upon the theological premises of these rabbinic texts, but must ultimately expand upon and broaden the explanatory paradigm that these texts suggest. In other words, the *Bemidbar Rabbah* passage does not explicitly or exclusively address the conflict of peshat and derash that we have outlined, yet it certainly is relevant to the issue and can legitimately be applied to it. What we have done is extend the explanatory paradigm of the *puncta extraordinaria*, in conjunction with the notion of *chate'u Yisrael* to *all* cases of discrepancy between peshat and derash. What we have thus done is make explicit what is left implicit in these rabbinic texts, forging an historical link between the neglect of the text through the process of *chate'u Yisrael* and Ezra's role in restoring the Torah to its original, uncorrupted configuration.

The Limitations of Ezra's Authority

But, as we have already stated, Ezra's authority was circumscribed.[35] We have seen in the quotation from *b. Sanh.* 21b, that according to Mar Zutra, Ezra recommended to the Israelites "Ashurith script and Aramaic language," but they selected "Ashurith script and Hebrew language." Ezra could not prevail upon the Israelites to accept his recommendation, for his authority was not unqualified. Similarly, he could not textually annul the process of corruption that had affected the Torah but could only work to ensure that authentic midrash be disseminated. This he did through the intermediary method of diacritical points indicating necessary changes. The corrupted peshat of these passages had already become textually anchored and could not be expunged, but Ezra possessed sufficient authority to impose revisionary and restorative derash upon the face of the text and, in effect, nullify the impact of the peshat. The notion of textual adulteration and Ezra's subsequent restorative activities, however, has not really tackled the larger issue of the reality of peshat/derash discordance that extends beyond the scope of the *Bemidbar Rabbah* passage. So far, we have maintained that in those instances where Ezra believed that the text had become corrupted through neglect, he used a system of indicators to signal the necessity for derash or omission, thereby initiating the process of consolidating the unity and authority of traditional interpretation. In these instances, derash will deviate from peshat because it *must*.

The Meaning of the Puncta Extraordinaria

But let us return to the examples of manifest peshat/derash discrepancy outlined at the beginning of the chapter, such as the cases of "an eye for an eye" and levirate marriage. Why don't these too bear the physical imprint of Ezra's restorative activities? In answering this question, we must accentuate a subtle, though essential, nuance in our proposed theory that modifies somewhat the historical picture presented till now. We have claimed that the *puncta extraordi-*

naria employed by Ezra reflected his industry in "purifying" the Torah of its textual impurities. This claim remains true, but must be qualified by the observation that these diacritical points represent marks of erasure only, and are *not* signifiers of more intricate or involved corrective midrash. These diacritical points remained Ezra's lone technical scribal device for identifying scriptural verses which had become blemished. Put simply, by placing a dot over a letter or word, Ezra was indicating that that letter or word was corrupt and should be read out of the text.

The rabbinic explanation of the *eser nekudot* alternates between interpreting them either as indicating spuriousness (i.e., as a mark of erasure) or as signaling various types of midrashic exegesis.[36] We now deviate from this relatively late rabbinic explanation by positing that the diacritical points employed by Ezra *always* denote erasure and *never* complex midrash. Excavation beneath the surface of the rabbinic sources reveals that the earliest stratum of the rabbinic interpretation of the *eser nekudot* corroborates our assertion. For example, the understanding of the word *rechokah* in Num. 9:10 ("When any of you or of your posterity who are defiled by a corpse or are on a *long* journey would offer a passover sacrifice to the Lord . . ."–one of the ten instances of *puncta extraordinaria*) provided in *m. Pesach.* 9:2 by R. Yose, "lo . . . vadai," a formula which usually denotes a derasha which deviates from peshat, is actually not a *derasha* at all. To claim, as R. Yose does, that the diacritical point over the letter "he" indicates that not actual instance is implied by *rechokah* but anywhere from "the threshhold of the Forecourt and beyond," is tantamount to the theoretical deletion of the entire word in Num. 9:10, in line with its absence in verse 13 of the same chapter. This pseudo-*derasha* of R. Yose confirms the original function of the diacritical points (represented in *Avot de-Rabbi Nathan*, second version), which was simply to signal erasure. By the time of R. Yose in the latter half of the second century some dots were interpreted to connote *derashot*, and in the period of the Gemara the dots were understood almost consistently in terms of full-fledged *derashot*.[37] Moreover, the *stam* (post-427 C.E.) in *b. Menach.* 87b apparently considered *derashot* derived from dots as idiosyncratic expositions that need not be universally honored. The *stam* therefore declared that R. Meir did *not* utilize dots for the purpose of derash.[38] This same sequence of ascent towards bonafide derash is embodied in the exegesis of the dot over the vav of *issaron* in Num. 29:15 (". . . and *one-tenth* for each of the fourteen lambs"), moving from implied spuriousness in *Sifrei* (the word *issaron* is repeated, and one *issaron* of the two needs to be excised) to robust midrash in *b. Menach.* 87b (one may not measure with a three-tenths measure the meal offering for a bullock or with a two-tenths measure for a ram). To continue, despite the rejection by someone like Origen (185–254 C.E.) of the notion that the dots over the word *va-yishakehu* (Gen. 33:4) signify deletion, and his assertion, rather, that the "wickedness of Esau is hereby hinted at by the Bible—he treacherously kissed Jacob"[39] (a similar interpretation of these dots is expressed in the *Sifrei*), it seems that the dots over the word *va-yishakehu* do come to inform us that Esau could not have kissed Jacob and that, in fact, the word must be deleted.[40] Our understanding of the *puncta extraordinaria* thus conforms to their original scribal function as symbols of deletion, rather than to the later rabbinic evaluation of these diacritical points as indicators of midrash. The rabbis of the Talmud grew increasingly reluctant to interpret the dots as indicators of deletion (because of the awkward theological implications of a "corrupt" text), and resorted instead to sophisticated midrashic techniques to "improve" the text. We, however, abide by the earliest stratum of rabbinic understanding of the *eser nekudot* which, with greater theological ease and readiness than the later strata of rabbinic sources, embraced the notion of the necessary deletion of certain scriptural letters or words. By clinging to the early rabbinic assessment of the dots (though repudiating the later), our theory remains firmly anchored in a rabbinic literary context.

Derash as a Remedy for the Insufficiency of Scribal Emendation

As in manuscripts throughout history, from the early Hellenistic period through modern times,[41] Pentateuchal diacritical points must therefore be seen as having been limited in scribal function and usefulness. Ezra's task was twofold: to isolate corruptions of the scriptural text and simultaneously to ensure the authenticity of its interpretation. The former task was partially fulfilled through the use of diacritical points, but only in instances when such a scribal mechanism was sufficient. The latter task, involving scriptural verses which had become so faulty that mere scribal emendation would be insufficient to ensure proper understanding of the text, was more formidable. Into this category fall the examples of "an eye for an eye" and levirate marriage. Diacritical points in these instances would not have conveyed the full scope and content of the proper interpretation of the scriptural text. More efficacious "emendation" of the text was necessary, beyond the usefulness of diacritical indicators.

Ezra's task in disseminating the true sense of these scriptural sore spots was accomplished through the oral communication and transmission of *derashot* that restored the genuine peshat of these verses. Though he could not physically purify the text because of his circumscribed authority, Ezra could resort to oral midrash when his written scribal resources were rendered inadequate. In other words, when the scriptural text required more than the mere "deletion" (in actuality, a diacritical cue of deletion) of a word or letter, the corrupt peshat of the text had to be accompanied, and corrected, by oral exegesis, i.e., by derash. For example, in the verse which discusses levirate marriage described above, the simple erasure of the words *asher teled* would not have yielded the desired meaning of *asher nolad* (i.e., as referring to the oldest brother of the deceased). Further midrashic accompaniment to the verse was necessitated. To crystallize this final subtlety of our proposal in capsule form, we maintain that a clear distinction must be drawn between (written) dots and (oral) *derashot*.

A word of methodological circumspection is appropriate here, in order to rebuff charges of historical gullibility. The apparent attribution to Ezra, in the passage from *Bemidbar Rabba* cataloguing the *puncta extraordinaria*, of the authority to emend the scriptural text through the deletion of spurious words, need not be read with utter historical credulity and literalism for the proper defense of my argument. The major contention of this chapter—that the scriptural text underwent a restorative process at the time of Ezra because of a prior period of textual corruption—is not damaged through the admission that this passage can be dealt with more historically loosely than literally. In fact, even if the attribution to

Ezra is historically unreliable, and can only legitimately be assessed as a product and function of the rabbinic documentary context in which it is found, the theological soundness of my overall thesis is not thereby undercut. The fact that in a later period of Jewish history it was deemed permissible and acceptable to attribute to Ezra such forceful powers of textual correction in regard to the Pentateuch, is itself theologically consequential and functional. It may even be appropriate to assert that the later in Jewish history this theological notion proved acceptable, the better for our theological purposes. If in the rabbinic period this attribution to Ezra of the capacity of textual emendation was valued as a viable and creditable theological option, it can still be so today.

Further Elucidation of "Chate'u Yisrael"

Our proposed resolution to the conflict of peshat and derash having now been presented,[42] it may be proper to reiterate a point that was intimated before. To repel the perception that our theory, which hinges on the notion of *chate'u Yisrael*, is somehow artificial or contrived, this very notion must be elaborated upon theologically and given historical materiality. As already suggested, the process of *chate'u Yisrael* strips the First Temple period of normative halakhic authority. Because the religious impulse that generates halakhic observance—the desire to achieve a closeness with God—was greatly vitiated during the First Temple period in the faltering Israelite struggle to embrace and champion monotheism, no halakhic or textual residue emerging from that period is binding. The importance of the First Temple period in the historical development of Judaism must not, however, be depreciated. The establishment of the foundational principles of Judaism, including the monotheistic service of God, lends this epoch undeniable historical significance and religious grandeur. This period was the era of the prophets and is thus certainly an integral link in the *shalshelet ha-kabbala* ("the chain of tradition"). The prophets, whose major function was to predispose the people to the undiluted and unattenuated service of God, were not law-givers, however, and their efforts towards elevating the religious standards of the people were not halakhic per se.[43] The legal foundations of the edifice of Judaism needed reinforcement in the time of Ezra. The halakhic implications of the theological notion of *chate'u Yisrael* for our assessment of the First Temple period are therefore clear. The observant Jew can owe it no real halakhic allegiance, for its religious character was uneven and not fully developed. Though crucial in the historical definition of the identity of Judaism, the First Temple period is not halakhically definitive.

Further Elucidation of Ezra's Role

The notion of *chate'u Yisrael* is thus a metaphor for the historical process of the inconstant maturation of Judaism and the tottering stability of its legal system.[44] This concept of *chate'u Yisrael* enables a religious Jew to handle the First Temple period in much the same manner as a critical scholar might—as a period of religious vacillation and scriptural mutability. In theological terms, the First Temple period is desacralized, divested as it is of abiding halakhic import. In turn, Ezra, to whom the important activity of canonization is attributed by many critical bible scholars,[45] is imbued, from a rabbinic theological perspective, with corrective and, indeed, revelatory authority. Even from a religious viewpoint, therefore, Ezra may legitimately be granted the power of "canonization," or in the terms of our theory, with the power of restoration. Ezra's role in the canonization of the prophetic books (including deciding, for example, that the prophecies of Obadiah would be confined to roughly a page and a half of written text, though he surely uttered more) is recognized by rabbinic sources and thus must have been, in the eyes of the religious Jew, tinged with prophetic insight.[46] The role of Ezra, as reflected in the *puncta extraordinaria*, indicates that the Pentateuch too was subject to canonization, contrary to the generally held traditional view that only the prophetic books went through the canonization process. The Pentateuch had to be cleared of the deleterious effects of the "chate'u Yisrael" period. By attributing to Ezra restorative powers, we merely accentuate Ezra's role in the stabilization of the text of the Pentateuch, which from a religious perspective must also be considered a prophetic endeavor.

Thus, while the concept of *chate'u Yisrael* deprives the First Temple period of binding halakhic value, Ezra's restorative and canonizing efforts are endowed with the status of revelation.

Therefore, should it be determined that the scriptural text was unstable during the First Temple period, this would not constitute a denial of revelation as such, but only serve to reinforce the qualification that during this period revelation was either incomplete[47] or humanly corrupted. This approach allows for the possibility that at a future date the text was rectified through further revelation. Indeed, as we have seen, it is plausible, and probable, that such a rectification of the scriptural text occurred during the time of Ezra and his successors.

Undergirding Theological Assumptions

It may be in order at this point to articulate the theological premises that have undergirded our discussion, so that our position that even the text of the Torah itself was subject to corruption and then restoration will be further clarified. Three theological claims are posited: first, the reality of the supernatural, of something beyond the ordinary human realm; second, the fact that revelation occurred in the past, that God broke into human history at some historical moment; third, that the Torah is the legacy of God's revelation. To put it differently, the theological assumptions consist of three major principles of faith: that there is a God, that God revealed Himself to man, and that the Torah is the result of that encounter. Without these principles, Judaism is not conceivable. With them, all that is left is commentary.

The Torah is thus the product of the encounter of the divine and the human in historical time; this location of revelation in time and space through the medium of the Torah has repercussions. Our discussion has made it clear that once the Torah was bequeathed to man, it was also exposed to human frailties and constraints. Indeed, it was exposed to man's corruptive capacities. The Torah became a "this-worldly" text, subject to the impermanence and inconstancy of this world. Though "maximalists" may want to deny this human element in the Torah, and assert that the Torah has remained an untainted island of divinity in the midst of the human experience, realism and textual evidence dictate otherwise. Revelation made the

Torah available and accessible to man, but also vulnerable to human exertion.

Strengthening the Argument of the Chapter

To dispel further the potential impression that the argument presented in this chapter is somehow artificial or contrived, let me point out that my contribution to the subject matter is relatively minor and not unconventional. My assertions about the First Temple period and about the role of Ezra vis-à-vis the Pentateuch are fairly standard and represent the scholarly consensus. The conclusion that during the First Temple period syncretism was prevalent and monotheism therefore unstable is an inescapable one, and emerges directly from the scriptural sources themselves. So does the negative assessment of Jewish religious behavior during this historical era. In such an atmosphere it is unlikely that the Jews cared enough to have preserved meticulously the Mosaic text, which to them was not the sole religious guide. Most scholars also agree that Ezra had some role to play in the canonization of the Scriptures. From a traditional Jewish theological perspective, this implies that he possessed revelatory powers, that his canonization decisions were in some way divinely inspired and guided. To the extent that a sense of retrieving a lost past (the Law of Moses) permeated Ezra's decision-making as to what to include and to exclude, canonization was an act of restoration. Add to this the fact that traces, or tracks, of midrashic activity—of derash—are discernible in the books of Chronicles and Ezra to which we have referred (indeed, as a canonizer, Ezra probably utilized midrash to reconcile contradictory constitutive texts), and the argument offered in this chapter is not so innovative. It merely applies these historical realities to the issue of the conflict of peshat and derash. In this way, by being correlated to each other, both these historical data and the problem of peshat and derash may be further illuminated.

Should someone object, saying: "Your thesis makes words say things that are not so (the words say, 'An eye for an eye,' for instance, and you say they do not mean that)," I would answer: "So do words that have *nekudot* over them (the words, for instance, in Gen. 19:13 say, 'He knew not when she lay down, nor when she arose,' and the nekuda makes them say, 'He knew not when she lay down but *he knew* when she arose')." Both changes in meaning are attributed to Ezra and his followers, who by virtue of their revelatory authority make these changes religiously legitimate.

Rejection of the Notion that the Oral Law "Uprooted" the Written Law

Finally, a potential demurrer to our proposal must be addressed. The occasional conflict of scriptural peshat and rabbinic derash that we have labelled theologically problematic may not be so evaluated by others. Why not posit, these readers ask, that the rabbis possessed the religious authority to (consciously) revise the meaning of the biblical text through their creative exegesis? Why should the occasional irreconcilability of peshat and derash be at all troubling? In fact, even traditional Jewish scholars have framed these questions in their own idiom, asserting that the glory of the oral law rests precisely in its capacity to "uproot" the written Torah. That is, they revel in the authority of rabbinic derash to deviate from scriptural peshat, to harness and manipulate the authorial intention of the biblical text.[48]

This attitude towards the problem of the conflict of peshat and derash, which in essence dissolves the problem before it can be confronted, is theologically unacceptable for three reasons. First of all, it illegitimately blurs the systemic distinction between the written Torah and the oral law. Despite the occasional hyperbolic, aggadic extolment of the *Torah shebe'al Peh* in Rabbinic literature,[49] the written Torah is, without doubt, granted superior and unchallengeable status within the Jewish legal system, particularly within its penal hierarchy. The entire substructure of the halakhic system attests to the rigidity of the distinction between written Torah and oral law. Doubt in matters of *de-oraita* legislation (i.e., of the written Torah) is always dealt with more stringently than similar issues of *de-rabbanan* halakha (i.e., of the oral law). Simply put, the theoretical right of the talmudic rabbis to casually amend and displace the peshat of the written Torah would nullify and invalidate a basic systemic principle.

Secondly, whether one claims that the rabbis possessed divine license to amend the plain meaning of the Written Torah or only that they adeptly adjusted the law to suit their changing socio-economic conditions, this type of unrestrained and assertive halak-hic revisionism, even on the part of the rabbis of the Talmud, sets a dangerous halakhic precedent. On the basis of such a precedent, every generation could claim the prerogative to amend the divine law as conditions and tastes may vary.[50] While such understanding of the character of rabbinic exegesis may please some, it is certainly not an accurate reflection of the intention of the rabbis of the Talmud.

The third consideration that renders theologically illegitimate the proposition that the rabbis of the Talmud possessed the exegetical license to annul the scriptural peshat as they saw fit is the unfeasible conclusion that the halakha that today governs behavior bears but slight resemblance to that commanded by God at Sinai. If rabbinic derash could simply render scriptural peshat obsolete and irrelevant, the contents of the Sinaitic revelation would then be buried in an irretrievable past, with no applicability to Jewish living in the modern world. A religious Jew must believe, rather, that rabbinic derash preserves the continuity of tradition and safeguards the content of the Sinaitic revelation which is the fountainhead of all halakha.[51]

A Short Recapitulation

It may be useful, as a final overview, to state once more the stance that was assumed towards the issue of the conflict of scriptural peshat and rabbinic derash and our objection to it. The apologetic stance denies that a conflict even exists. To an apologist bent on defending rabbinic derash at all costs, the very notion that there exists an occasional discrepancy between peshat and derash is offensive and perilous. For these apologists, the derash *is* the peshat, that is, the biblical verse means only and precisely what the rabbis say it means. This position, as our study clearly demonstrates, is untenable because it is uncritical. An honest and open investigation of the matter indicates that a discrepancy between peshat and derash does occasionally arise. Once these problematic discrepancies are recognized, they must be addressed, for they cannot be simply dissolved or ignored via apologetics. What we have attempted to accomplish in this theological section is to explain these deviations of derash from peshat through recourse to the paradigmatic concept of *chate'u Yisrael* and the historical role of Ezra. The process of textual rectification inaugurated by Ezra must be endowed with the authority and prestige of revelation. The period between Moses and Ezra, or the two revelations, recedes in halakhic and theological authority because of its record of behavioral and textual negligence. Yet, if one accepts the tradition of rabbinic interpretation as religiously binding, and thus claims for it the stamp of divine authorization, the relationship between the initial Sinaitic revelation and the Ezraitic-rabbinic revelation must be delineated. We have argued for a complementary relationship between the two: the latter revelation did not supersede or supplant the former, but reconstituted and regenerated it. Ezra's efforts served to reconstruct and restore—and not nullify or repeal—the form and contents of the initial revelation.

As we have continually stressed, our modern exegetical preference for peshat need not impinge upon the realm of practical halakha. A religious Jew may critically study the text of the Bible even with its occasionally disfigured peshat, yet his halakhic allegiance must be to rabbinic derash. In cases of his recognition of the radical discrepancy between peshat and derash, he must employ the theory of *chate'u Yisrael*—contingent upon a process of halakhic instability during the First Temple period followed by Ezra's remedial and restorative halakhic efforts—and rest assured that the canonization of rabbinic midrash has guaranteed the authenticity and veracity of halakha. For the religious Jew, the observance of *mitzvot* stimulates and promotes a closeness with God that is intimate and immediate.[52] Therefore, this assurance that his halakhic behavior accords with, and is sanctioned by, the divine will is indispensable. Even the doctrinal certainty that the text of the Torah is pristine can be dispensed with, indeed, *must* be, if such assurance can be earned.[53]

APPENDIX I

Mikan Samkhu Chakhamim and *Asmakhta Be'alma*

Contrary to the views of some medieval commentators, there is a difference in the degree of obligation between what is adduced through *asmakhta be'alma* (a mere support) and *mikan samkhu chakhamim* (the sages found a support). The former, employed by the *stammaim*, and also used once by R. Ashi (d. 427 C.E.), implies only rabbinic standing. The latter, in contrast, found only in *baraitot*, i.e., tannaitic material that was not included in the Mishnah, means that what was adduced is actually Biblically binding.[1] There are several proofs for this.

In *b. Ketub.* 10a, we find:

> It is written in the Torah (Exod. 22:16): "He [the enticer of a virgin] shall pay money according to the dowry of the virgins." This teaches us that the penalty paid for the enticement of a virgin is as much as the dowry of virgins . . . *mikan samkhu chakhamim* the rule that the *ketuba* [the money obligating the husband in the marriage contract] is biblical. R. Shimon the son of R. Gamaliel said: the *ketuba* of a wife is not biblically commanded but is only rabbinically ordained.

The first *tanna* who uses the expression *mikan samkhu chakhamim* disagrees with R. Shimon the son of R. Gamaliel, who maintains that a *ketuba* is rabbinically ordained, and claims that it is of Biblical origin. He derived that view from a *mikan samkhu chakhamim* of the verse about enticement, and that connection grants biblical status to the *ketuba* as well.

A similar proof can be found in the *Sifra Behar* (4.5). It is stated there:

> It is written (Lev. 25.20) "Behold we may not sow, nor gather in our increase." If we do not sow, what can we gather? Said R. Akiva: *mikan samkhu chakhamim*[2] the rule that the aftergrowth [which needs no sowing] is also forbidden [in the sabbatical year].

Again, R. Akiva's *mikan samkhu chakhamim* carries biblical force.[3]

155

Not so obvious, and therefore misunderstood by some commentators, is the proof from *b. Chul.* 106a:

> The washing of the hands for common foods . . . is a meritorious act. What is this meritorious act? Abaye [a fourth-century Babylonian scholar] answered: it is a meritorious act to hearken to the words of the sages. Rava [a colleague of Abaye] answered: it is a meritorious act to hearken to the words of R. Eliezer ben Arakh [a first-century Palestinian scholar] who said: it is written (Lev. 15:11) "without having rinsed his hands in water." *mikan samkhu chakhamim* the rule of wahsing the hands.

The difference between Abaye and Rava is that according to Abaye, the meritorious act is only rabbinically endorsed, whereas according to Rava, based on R. Eliezer ben Arakh's expression of *mikan samkhu chakhamim*, the meritorious act is biblically endorsed.[4]

This is true also in the case of *eruv tavshilin*, the "*eruv* of dishes," which allows one, on a holiday which falls on Friday, to prepare food for the Sabbath. (In general, cooking was permitted on the festival only for foods to be eaten that day, and not foods that would be enjoyed on another day.) *b. Betza* 15b employs the expression *mikan samkhu chakhamim* to convey the idea that according to R. Eliezer, the need for an *eruv tavshilin* is biblical. I say so despite the continuation of the discussion in the Palestinian Talmud, in the beginning of the second chapter of *Betza*, wherein it appears as if it is only rabbinically ordained. The Palestinian Talmud asks:

> If it is biblically forbidden, how can an *eruv tavshilin* permit it? Says R. Abahyu: by law, baking and cooking on the holiday for the Sabbath is permitted. But lest one mistakenly compare weekdays to Sabbath and incorrectly cook on the holiday for the upcoming weekdays, the rabbis instituted the *eruv tavshilin.*

In light of this discussion, it would appear that this is R. Abahu's view of R. Eliezer, leading us to conclude that already a fourth century Palestinian scholar, R. Abahu, resorted to *asmakhta*, though he did not mention it by name. However, a similar view is expressed in *b. Pesach.* 46b without reference to R. Eliezer. I take it that R. Abahu is expressing the view of those who disagree with R. Eliezer and who hold that the *eruv tavshilin* is rabbinic, whereas R. Eliezer himself who, in the Babylonian Talmud, uses the expression *mikan samkhu chakhamim*, holds that the "*eruv* of dishes" is biblical. A similar controversy exists according to *b. Betza* 15b, at the beginning of the discussion between Shemuel and Rava and R. Ashi.[5]

The peculiarity of *mikan samkhu chakhamim*, as compared to other *derashot*, is that the words of the biblical text do not *directly* imply the content. The latter is derived by way of analogy. It is similar to the content of the text but not contained in the text, either explicitly or derivatively. The Sages relied (*samkhu*) on the text but did not, as in the case of other expositions, directly extrapolate the content from the text. Yet even reliance on a text can provide biblical status.

In contrast, the content of an *asmakhta be'alma* is entirely *de-rabbanan*, i.e., rabbinic. The text is, as it were, merely ornamental, a rabbinic decoration with no biblical force. That was not so during earlier times. Then, even rabbinic ordinances had biblical force. A good example is the declaration made by the Talmud in several places that the *derasha* which includes a *chalutza*, a woman who received *chalitza* (the ceremony observed when the brother of a person who died childless refuses to enter into a levirate marriage with his sister-in-law), on the list of women forbidden to marry a priest is only an *asmakhta*. In fact, however, several tannaitic sources explicitly state (without the *derasha*) that a woman who received *chalitza* is in the category of women who are *biblically* forbidden to marry a priest.[6] Most likely, during tannaitic times, when the *derasha* originated, a *chalutza* was considered forbidden. Later on, for unknown reasons, she was only rabbinically forbidden. Still later, as a result, the Talmud was compelled to declare the *derasha* which included this woman in *asmakhta be'alma* sort of *derasha*.[7]

In short, earlier, the content of what was later called an *asmakhta be'alma derasha* was not much different from the content of a *mikan samkhu chakhamim* exposition. Both had biblical force. In the course of time, the forms split: *asmakhta be'alma* designated rabbinical ordinance, and *mikan samkhu chakhamimn* implied a biblical ordinance.[8]

APPENDIX II

Midrash and Modern Literary Theories

Scholars have recently drawn analogies between rabbinic mode of exegesis in midrash and some modern theories of literary criticism. The analogies are supposed to be quite comprehensive, affecting both the manner and the nature of interpretation. Great effort is being expended in some circles to show that what modern literary theorists are now discovering about textual exegesis was already practiced by the rabbis close to two millennia ago. The literature on the subject is growing rapidly, and may soon constitute an independent branch of scholarship in comparative literature. To summarize the positions here would take me too far afield of the scope and aim of this present study: the history of rabbinic exegesis. I will therefore concentrate on one aspect of the analogy only, the one most affiliated with the topic of reading in. Even this focus will be treated rather cursorily. The reader interested in a more detailed study of the analogies between the two different disciplines will have to consult the relevant literature directly.

I am referring to the affinity between rabbinic mode of exegesis and the modern emphasis on the reader's participation in meaning. Despite the differences of opinion that exist both among structuralists and deconstructionists,[1] the two major contemporary schools of literary criticism, they seem to unite in assigning to the reader a larger role in the formation of meaning.[2] The reader is not a passive agent receiving impulses from the author through the text. He is an active participant who actualizes the impulses and gives them coherence and structure. A text that is not read has no meaning (just as a sound that is not heard is not a sound). The reading is determinative of the meaning. The reading, however, has to be disciplined to comply with the prevailing conventions and be circumscribed by the interaction with the content, the mode of expression and genre of the text (even by the authorial intention). It was inevitable that sooner or later an analogy would be drawn to midrash, which although it everywhere cites Scripture is often not motivated or set in motion by Scripture, and is rarely supported by the "natural" meaning of the text. Midrash derives from the reader of Scripture, who is stimulated by the text—against the text's natural meaning—to indulge in imaginative comments. In midrash the reader is not passive. Most of his cues come from outside the text; the reader actively brings these cues to bear on the text and interacts with it. Midrash is a paradigm of text (author) and reading interacting, and to that extent modern theory coincides with Midrash.[3]

Midrash in this usually refers to midrash aggada, the nonlegal comments on the Bible. Its loose connection with the prooftext is well established, its extraneous nature generally assumed, so that the reader's imagination may well be deemed one of its many sources.

The situation is different with regard to midrash halakha,[4] the legal comments on the Bible. Legal comments in general are closer and more tightly bound to the text, more grounded in it than in nonlegal midrash. It is worthwhile noting here that the textual examples cited in the rapidly accumulating literature of the new literary theorists as illustrations of their position overwhelmingly come from nonlegal writings. Legal texts do not lend themselves so easily (despite recent attempts)[5] to the new modes of interpretation. Authorial intention will always play a more significant role in legal texts than in nonlegal texts. Midrash halakha remains less susceptible to modern theory than midrash aggada. Midrash Halakha's cues overwhelmingly come from within the text. The text is the principal guide in determining what constitutes proper halakha, the mode of behavior. The reader's (the interpreter's) role is much more limited. He interacts with the text, but what he brings to bear on it is much more impoverished. The hermeneutic principles at his disposal are fewer in number;[6] his maneuverability is restricted. The halakhist confronts the text; the aggadist joins the text. The halakhist submits to the text; the aggadist plays with it, as it were. The aggadist cooperates with the text (actively); the halakhist listens to the text (often passively)—except when reading into the text. Then, he is a determiner, a sharer in the making of the law; a co-author. He interacts with the text as an equal. What he brings to bear is weighty, decisive. He is not a passive recipient but an active begetter—a creator. In religious language, he is a partner in the divine creation of the law. Reading in introduces the reader (the interpreter) into the "inner chambers" of halakha, thereby broadening the resemblance with modern theory of literary criticism.

The resemblance, however, is far from complete. The rabbis of the Talmud, in the legal sections, most likely would not have conceded that they were reading into a text and would not have acknowledged reader's participation in the formation of meaning. De facto, the rabbis did give the reader-interpreter great leeway in shaping the meaning of a text. If asked, however, they would admit to little. They would most likely have sided with the opponents of the modern theorists and would have insisted that authorial intention is the sole criterion for true and reliable meaning, especially when that text is the Bible, whose divine authorship was universally accepted. If we still insist on resemblance it will have to be between the modern's conscious evaluation and the rabbis' unconscious practice.

My hesitation to state categorically that the rabbis of the Talmud did *not* think of themselves as reading into Biblical texts with respect to midrash halakha stems from the few instances where the rabbis gave admittedly nebulous expression to their powers of interpretation. I am referring to the famous story in the Babylonian Talmud when in the course of a halakhic dispute between R. Eliezer and R. Joshua, the former invoked a voice from heaven in his support. Thereupon R. Joshua stood up and declared: "One does not pay heed to a voice from heaven."[7] This was said in an environment where a voice from heaven on occasion decided practical matters, and was considered a true source of divine information.[8] There is also the even more bizarre story of when God in a halakhic dispute with the "Heavenly Academy" (the angels) about the laws of purity called upon a fourth-century Babylonian *amora* to decide between them.[9] The right of scholars to disagree with God Almighty on matters of Biblical interpretation, to ignore authorial intention, indicates that the rabbis of the Talmud had at least an inkling, unutterable as that might have been, that sometimes they created their own meaning and that as cocreators they had a right— seldom exercised, but exercised nevertheless—to disagree even with the Giver of the Torah. Legend has it that God Almighty studies Torah[10]— presumably meaning that He also abides by the rules of the game, the objective criteria employed by men, making it conceivable that men may even overrule Him.

Another dissimilarity that may disturb the resemblance between the rabbis of the Talmud and the modern literary theorists is that the rabbis may not have applied their mode of interpretation to any text other than the biblical one. The rabbis almost always justified reading in on some alleged superfluous phrase, word or even letter, allowing very little for stylistic repetition. That may be peculiar to a text considered divine, since the divine in their conception should be more parsimonious in expression and allow few precious words for stylistic niceties. In other, nonscriptural texts greater allowance is made for the human proclivity to indulge in extravagant verbal activity for the sake of stylistic beauty.[11] Needless to say modern theorists do not honor such a distinction.

It is difficult to know how the rabbis read and interpreted other, nonreligious texts. They just do not quote them. The book of Ben Sira (Ecclesiasticus)[12] is a written document that enjoys a special status in rabbinic literature; it is treated as, although not included in, Scripture. The only reference to a nonreligious text I could think of is that of the Mishnah in *Ketub.* 4:6 where it says that "R. Eliezer the son of Azariah thus expounded [the quotation from the *ketubba*-scroll] before the sages in the vineyard of Jabneh: The sons inherit and the daughters receive maintenance—just as the sons inherit only after the death of their father so the daughters receive their maintenance only after the death of their father." Already the Tosefta,[13] a tannaitic compilation (containing sayings of the sages who flourished before the end of the second century), noted that R. Eliezer the son of Azariah (in company with other *tannaim*, like Hillel and others) "expounded the language of a *hedyot* (a common man) as though it was a scriptural passage" (using the hermeneutical principle of analogy normally associated with scripture). If indeed the rabbis applied their mode of interpretation to other (secular) texts as well, the resemblance to modern literary theory is a bit strengthened. The argument that the *ketubba* is a semireligious document, and that its exegetical treatment cannot serve therefore as an example of nonreligious text, is not persuasive since the other *tannaim* mentioned in the Tosefta in conjunction with R. Eliezer the son of Azariah refer to other secular documents and contracts.[14] The evidence, however, is too flimsy to form a firm opinion. Yet even if one were to grant the dubious assumption that to the rabbis a divine text had to be didactic in all its elements, that every word, indeed every letter had to have an instructional function, with little attention to aesthetics, one may still argue that pertaining to reading in the rabbis would have drawn no distinction between sacred and profane literature had any been available to them. The mode of interpretation was the same.[15]

Finally, it should be added that the concession to the reader occasionally encountered in halakha was not an invitation to multiplicity of interpretation. Behavior had to be uniform. The concession was made once and the resulting content stands for all future generations. Had the rabbis acknowledged that each era has its own mode of interpretation, they would most likely have insisted that behavior be based on the interpretation expounded by those who received the initial revelation. God spoke to them in their own language, in their own mode of interpretation. Subsequent generations must defer. God could have chosen another generation to reveal Himself; in that case, a different mode of interpretation would have been followed. The fact that He chose whom He chose is not an accident, for those who believe in divine providence, but an indication that He wants us to follow in the footsteps of those to whom He chose to reveal Himself. The standard was set once and for all for all posterity. Aggada, on the other hand, was never standardized. It required no behavior, so there was less need to be uniform. It was from its very inception more individualistic, less threatened by diversity. It was always more flexible, less defined, and more hospitable to readers' input. Aggada speaks to temporary man; halakha to eternal man. Aggada edifies and heartens; halakha strengthens and fortifies. Halakha is less adaptable to change than is aggada. It cannot afford to grant each period a mode of interpretation in consonance with its contemporary state of mind. Halakha has a greater stake in stability and permanency, and when it makes a concession to the reader (interpreter) by allowing him to read into a text, it is a one-time concession. Timing was an integral part of the act of revelation. That further distances halakhic interpretation from modern literary theory. The latter is closer to aggadic midrash.[16]

In conclusion: the rabbis of the Talmud granted the reader significant interpretive powers. In aggada the powers were extensive and most likely conscious; in halakha they were occasional and unconscious. Taken together, one can legitimately claim that there is an affinity between the rabbinic mode of exegesis and some modern theories of literary criticism, though the similarity is quite limited, and of course the orientation is quite different. What to the rabbis at the beginning of their activity over two thousand years ago was part of their inner exegetical dictate became an analytical necessity to the moderns after all alternative modes were rejected, or more accurately found to be empty. What the rabbis, unconsciously perhaps, took for granted as part of the integrity of exegesis, the moderns consciously posit after the essence of traditional exegesis, authorial intention, was shown to be no longer defensible. What was to the rabbis a part of a larger exegetical commitment became to the modern a kind of salvage operation. Some aspect of textual communication had to be restored if textual meaning was to survive at all. If I may indulge in a conundrum—no rarity in modern literary criticism—I would say that the moderns had to endow meaning with meaningfulness in order to make meaning meaningful. To the rabbis, meaning had meaningfulness from the very beginning.

APPENDIX III

Minority Opinion and the Different Notions of the Revelation of the Oral Law

The governing systemic principle of *acharei rabim le-hatot*, of following majority opinion in matters of dispute, reflects the divinely sanctioned human factor in halakhic decision making. Man is thereby empowered and commissioned by God to consummate the process of revelation, to make tangible and exact what had been revealed only in outline. The issue of the status and serviceability of minority opinion within a system that is governed by majority rule becomes a thorny one, and is addressed explicitly in the Mishnah itself.[1] The rationale behind the preservation and continued teaching of dissenting opinions is questioned. If revelation is concretized and realized in accordance with majority opinion, why then should minority positions ever be recorded rather than simply discarded and forgotten? Why maintain for posterity a textual record of rejected opinions?

The Mishnah in *Eduyyot* offers two answers, the first anonymously and the second in the name of R. Judah. The first answer explains that the preservation of minority opinion justifies and legitimates the reversal of past decisions by future courts. An uncontested opinion could never be reversed. Therefore, the presence of a dissenting opinion creates an avenue of reopening the case and repealing a previous decision. A recorded minority position, though currently rejected, is thus not consigned permanently to halakhic oblivion. R. Judah assesses the value of the recording of minority opinion quite differently. His proposed rationale curtails the potential future usefulness of dissenting opinions. R. Judah explains that minority opinions are registered so that if a man shall say, "I hold such a tradition" (in opposition to the majority tradition), another may reply to him, "You have but heard it as the view of so-and-so." The "tradition" in

163

question can thus immediately and unambiguously be labeled a minority opinion, nullifying its claim to halakhic legitimacy. According to R. Judah, the recording of minority views is motivated not by a desire to maintain avenues of judicial discretion, but by a need to close them off. For R. Judah, the label of "minority opinion" renders a dissenting opinion not potentially halakhically viable, but halakhically disabled and disqualified.

In analyzing these mishnayot, R. Samson ben Abraham of Sens (late twelfth to early thirteenth century), one of the great French tosafists, understood these two answers to correspond to contrasting implicit conceptions of revelation.[2] The first answer correlates to what we may call a nonmaximalistic (this term henceforth encompasses both the intermediary and minimalistic rabbinic positions) conception of revelation. R. Shimshon of Sens explains that even though the minority opinion was not accepted previously, a later court may arise whose majority agrees with the minority position, and the dissenting opinion would then become legally binding. This halakhic reversal is systemically legitimate and viable because of the underlying notion of revelation encapsulated within the midrash in the name of R. Yannai discussed earlier: "The majority is to be followed—when a majority says it is unclean, it is unclean; when a majority says it is clean, it is clean." The avenues of judicial discretion must remain open because man's participation in the process of revelation is a continual one. The halakhic system was not revealed at Sinai *in toto*, and the legal process must therefore remain vibrant and active. Judicial recourse even to minority opinion must not be impeded.

According to R. Shimshon of Sens, the second answer offered in *Eduyyot*, that of R. Judah, corresponds to a maximalistic conception of revelation, which cannot tolerate the systemic viability of judicial reversal. Once the divine will has been clearly determined according to majority opinion, all divergent positions are rendered null and void. Minority opinions are preserved precisely so that they will be recognized as halakhically invalid, as nonrevelatory, and thus incapable of being legally resuscitated. Upon this conception of revelation as all-encompassing, and as reflective purely of the divine will, man's role in the judicial process is merely *pro forma*. Because revelation is comprehensive, judicial discretion—the human component—must necessarily be circumscribed.

The issue of the status of minority opinion is thus linked to, and governed by, varying notions of revelation. A maximalistic conception of revelation is allied to the proclivity to diminish the stature of minority opinion, to curb judicial discretion, in an effort to maintain absolute halakhic consistency and uniformity over time. A minority opinion must be branded an illegitimate halakhic alternative because it runs counter to the directives of revelation. But the very existence of dissenting opinion—

and of *machloket* in general—in a system governed by a maximalistic conception of revelation is troublesome and unsettling. The reality of controversy in the midst of a relevation that is supposedly comprehensive and enveloping in scope is obviously problematic. Theoretically, that which is determined to be the minority position should not be invested with any halakhic stature at all. In the introduction to his *Commentary on the Mishnah*, Maimonides states that nobody can disagree with a law claimed to be a *halakha le-Moshe mi-Sinai* (law given to Moses at Sinai). Based upon the logic of the maximalistic perspective, all the halakhic determinations of the oral Torah should be accorded the same treatment that Maimonides claims for a *halakha le-Moshe mi-Sinai*, for all these, too, are of Sinaitic origin. The halakhic preeminence and sanctity of majority opinions would then become inviolate, and minority opinions would become halakhic non-entities. Yet, if minority opinion within a *machloket* is granted any halakchic legitimacy, then a maximalistic conception of revelation can account for controversies that entail deviation from the revealed on the part of the minority position only through mystical transcendence of the law of contradiction. Somehow, though the majority position represents and reflects absolute divine truth, the minority opinion is yet partially true. A maximalistic conception of revelation is forced to admit, in practice, the reality of *machloket* and the continued record of minority views, even though, in theory, it cannot tolerate the persistence of dissenting opinion.

A nonmaximalistic conception of revelation can more smoothly account for the reality of controversy and accommodate the halakhic status of minority opinion. A recognition of the human component of the process of revelation can easily explain the reality of disagreement regarding the proper implementation of divinely revealed principles. No human judgment, even if it follows the dictates of majority opinion, can be unequivocally true or certain. Both sides to a *machloket* can retain a claim to truth if God offered Moses "forty-nine arguments by which a thing may be proved clean, and forty-nine other arguments by which it may be proved unclean." Even dissenting views can be subsumed under the legitimizing canopy of revelation.

The rabbinic principle of *Kedai hu R. Peloni lismokh alav bishe'at ha-dechak*[3] (Rabbi X is sufficiently worthy to be relied upon in time of great need) supports the notion of revelation as supple and adaptable, able to accommodate the halakhic merit of minority views. According to a maximalistic perspective of revelation, majority opinion is equivalent to absolute truth and minority opinion to absolute falsity—and an absolutely false position could never be justifiably relied upon.[4] The inclusion of the views of Beit Shammai in the Mishnah also constitutes evidence for an implicit nonmaximalistic conception of revelation. Despite the fact that by the time of R. Judah the Prince the supremacy of Beit Hillel was already well entrenched, the views of Beit Shammai, representative of the "losing" side of the halakhic competition, are nevertheless recorded. The language of the Mishnah itself gives no indication that the views of Beit Shammai are absolutely false, which would not be the case were the maximalistic conception of revelation regnant. Although the statement *Beit Shammai be-makom Beit Hillel eino mishna* (the view of Beit Shammai, when found side-by-side with that of Beit Hillel, is not even considered a legitimate teaching) can be found in the Gemara,[5] the evidence of the Mishnah does not favor the image of Beit Shammai as lacking all halakhic value. Indeed, the purposeful inclusion of the views of Beit Shammai in the Mishnah argues not for their halakhic triviality, but rather for their theoretical halakhic validity.[6]

Although a nonmaximalistic conception of revelation can more easily tolerate the dissemination of minority opinion than can the maximalistic position, because of its acknowledgment of the human, and thus fallible, aspect of revelation, there still exist systemic halakhic boundaries that limit the abrogation of majority views. The adoption of a nonmaximalistic perspective of revelation does not necessitate an adjunct approach to halakha that is anarchic or unrestrained. The realization that human reason, judgment and interpretation are integral elements of the implementation of divine revelation does not mandate a legal system that is unbounded and unbridled in its creative license. Though it may more naturally and successfully carve a legal niche for minority opinion within the halakhic system, the nonmaximalistic conception of revelation is still committed to the overarching principle of *acharei rabim le-hatot*, of following concensus in matters of dispute.

Recourse to an existent minority opinion is always a halakhic alternative, but the reversal of consensus practice in the absence of a minority option is unsanctioned by systemic guidelines. Even the nonmaximalistic position does not warrant the unchecked annulment of unanimous opinions. A consensus view on a legal issue that was not challenged by dissenting views when the issue originally arose cannot validly be declared inoperative by a later generation. Unanimous positions of a previous generation cannot simply be abolished. Only when a new legal issue arises, one that has not been addressed in previous halakhic discourse, does the requirement of recourse only to extant minority opinion become irrelevant. The nonmaximalistic conception of revelation does support the reopening of halakhic avenues in the face of changing historical or social circumstances, but the range of legitimate halakhic alternatives is bounded. The parameters of the original revelation, or in the formulation of the intermediary postion, the "forty-nine arguments by which a thing may be proved clean, and forty-nine other arguments by which it may be proved unclean," exercise a systemic restraint on halakhic innovation. Recourse to a minority opinion already encompassed and embedded within the system ensures that this halakhic alternative remains within the parameters of revelation, based on revelatory principles tacitly assumed within rabbinic halakhic discourse. Options within the framework of an "old" issue are thus limited to minority positions already ratified by past generations, for this safeguards against an interpretive free-for-all and halakhic chaos. Therefore, though the nonmaximalistic position respects the continued viability of minority opinion, it does not indulge an infinite range of halakhic possibilities.

APPENDIX IV

The Impact of Halakha on Peshat

Scholars have tended to classify traditional Jewish exegetes on the basis of their preference for, or indifference to, peshat. Such scholarly taxonomy of Jewish (primarily medieval) exegesis is useful, but is often perfunctory and inadequate, for it fails to address the vagaries of exegesis within the corpus of an individual exegete. Theoretically, a peshat orientation should or could be implemented on a consistent, regular basis. However, exegetes who display an affinity for peshat in certain contexts seemingly abdicate their commitment to peshat in others. Frequently the patronage of peshat within the work of a single exegete appears to be uneven. It seems as if there are certain identifiable factors that (pre)determine, or reinforce, a particular exegete's attachment to peshat, while in other instances different motivations may dilute an existent affinity for peshat in the work of that same exegete. Instead of simply dividing between *pashtanim* and others (which is often a reflection of the scholarly search for peshat "predecessors"), we will explore the fluctuating exegetical tendencies of individuals. The inconsistent allegiance toward peshat in the work of many medieval exegetes was not the function of a capricious hermeneutic, but rather of a quite reasonable, and even predictable, consideration, namely, the rules of halahkic decision-making. In other words, the fortunes of peshat within the work of medieval exegete (who is otherwise favorably disposed towards peshat) can be roughly correlated to the demands of pesak. Peshat was often sacrificed when pesak was on the line. Halakha, then, becomes a crucial variable in the makeup of medieval exegesis: solicitude for halakhic practicability often compromised an exegete's allegiance to peshat. Put simply, when halakha was an exegete's prime concern and consideration, peshat could often not be. A preference for peshat could often not be reconciled with the systemic constraints of practical halakha. The somewhat counter-intuitive thesis that we are suggesting is that halakha often has a greater impact on commitment to peshat than peshat has on the determination of halakha. This formative influence of halakha on exegesis has often been overlooked or underestimated.

Medieval exegetes like Ibn Ezra and Rashbam undoubtedly favored peshat over derash. Though not universal, the penchant for peshat was more prevalent during the medieval period than it had been previously. Indeed, our modern conception of peshat as the plain, natural meaning of a text historically follows upon the heels of this medieval awakening to the substantive integrity of the written word. Yet, if the Rashbam was an advocate of peshat, why is his commentary on the Talmud so unlike his commentary on the Torah, which is famous for its dedication to peshat even when anti-halakhic interpretation is the consequence? Why is the Rashbam willing to subordinate peshat to derash in the arena of talmudic, but not scriptural, exegesis?

The answer to these questions that we have already suggested is simple and straightforward, but also quite illuminating: when the systemic dynamics of halakhic decision-making are involved, an exegete's allegiance to peshat is often relinquished. The exigencies of life and law that inform halakhic thinking do not provide favorable circumstances for the flourishing of peshat. The need to harmonize conflicting sources of halakha (whether in the Bible or the Talmud), the requirement of adhering to systemic rules of authority and hierarchy (that place *tannaim* above *amoraim* and *mishnayot* above *baraitot*, etc.), and the condition of responding to the pressures and contingencies of daily halakhic living, constitute constraints on the recourse to peshat. Systemic guidelines used to resolve disputes between talmudic sages (e.g., that the law follow Beit Hillel over Beit Shammai except in specified cases, or that the law is according to R. Akiva or R. Yose when either disagrees with another Rabbi, but according to the majority when either disagrees with more than one), and principles invoked to grapple with halakhic predicaments (e.g., *hilkheta kevatrai*) may lessen the viability or feasibility of adhering to peshat. Peshat exegesis is often simply not conducive to the solution of halakhic dilemmas. In a sense, pilpul is endemic to halakhic exegetical maneuvering because halakha is at stake. Although as the Hatam Sofer rightfully claimed, pilpul is an unavoidable, inescapable dimension of the talmudic system, this is not because, as he claimed, "rationalistic" peshat reasoning is antithetical to halakhic "truth," but because halakhic jurisprudence often leaves peshat exegetically obsolete and irrelevant.[1]

When the Rashbam was engaged in the activity of halakhic reasoning, as he was in his Talmud commentary, the appeal of peshat receded. The dichotomization between the Rashbam's Torah and Talmud commentaries now becomes clear. The Torah, for him, was halakhically resonant and meaningful only through the prism of the Talmud. When read independently of its rabbinic (halakhic) manual, it could be subjected to the scrutiny of peshat. His disposition towards peshat could reign supreme in his Torah commentary—leading him, for example, to interpret the traditional scriptural prooftext for *tefillin* ("a sign on your hand and a reminder on your forehead" [Exod. 13:9]) metaphorically—because halakha was not jeopardized in the process. By contrast, in his Talmud commentary, when pesak halakha was the immediate backdrop to his interaction with the text, peshat could not be allowed to interfere with his task as halakhic mediator and negotiator. The same Rashbam who could interpret the prooftext for tefillin metaphorically, that is, according to peshat, in his Torah commentary, could not do so when the exegetical context was invested with halakhic significance. In a manifestly halakhic context, the explicit scriptural foundation of tefillin could not be denied. In *m. Sanh.* 11:3, in the discussion of the defiant behavior of a *zaken mamreh*, the scriptural basis of *tefillin* is presumed, as the *zaken mamreh* is punishable only if he rebels against something that is not explicit in the Torah, such as the number of partitions in the *tefillin*, but is not if he denies something that is explicit in the Torah, such as the existence of the precept itself ("if he says, 'There is no obligation to wear phylacteries' so that he transgresses the words of the Law, he is not culpable . . ."). In this setting, in which the Mishnah tacitly interprets the scriptural prooftext for *tefillin* literally and not metaphorically, the Rashbam must naturally abide by the Rabbinic derash. This context dictates that the *de-oraita* status of *tefillin* is indisputable; for the Rashbam, therefore, metaphoric peshat interpretation is an exegetical option neither defensible nor feasible. The Rashbam is not to be accused here of exegetical inconsistency, or of a disloyalty to peshat, for he is simply responding reasonably and judiciously to his exegetical setting.

In another illustration of his role as a halakhically responsive but anti-peshat Talmudic exegete, the Rashbam could declare that the Talmudic device of adding words to the text of a Mishnah (*chasorei mechasra*) was not a forced explanation (*ein zeh teirutz dachuk*), when clearly this maneuver violated the peshat of the Mishnah.[2] He could toe the talmudic exegetical line because he felt he *had* to, so that the halakhic stability and coherence that flowed from this talmudic *sugya* be preserved. An allegiance to peshat in this circumstance would be halakhically imprudent, even subversive. Only the halakhic "innocence" of the context of his Torah commentary allowed the Rashbam there to ignore the halakhic "perils" of his peshat exegesis. The metaphoric interpetation of the *tefillin* prooftext— which reflects the peshat of the scriptural verse—was halakhically anomalous but not halakhically threatening, precisely because its *context* was an exegetically liberating one. Because pesak was not on the immediate horizons of his Torah commentary, the Rashbam could freely and unhesitatingly exercise his preference for peshat. He could uphold the integrity of the scriptural text without doing damage to the authority of midrash halakha that deviated from peshat. The Rashbam's seemingly fickle attachment to peshat is understood, then, as a function of the motivational context of his exegesis. If his agenda is halakhic, his dedication to peshat must, of necessity, suffer.

In the case of the Rashbam, then, as our paradigmatic *pashtan*, the radical dissimilarity between his Torah and Talmud commentaries does not reflect a shifting or whimsical commitment to peshat, but is readily understood as a function of disjunctive exegetical contexts and concerns. The context of his Talmud commentary is halakhic, that is, his concern is with the ultimate determination of pesak halakha. His theoretical commitment to peshat at the time he wrote his talmudic commentary did not disappear. Rather, it was shelved because systemic rules often prompted "forced" interpretations. Even the artifice of *chasorei mechasra* could be defended—in obvious violation of the peshat of a Mishnah—if the flow of a *sugya*, and the halakhic implications that emerge from within it, demanded such a counter-peshat exegetical maneuver. The integrity and workability of halakha take primacy over the integrity of the mishnaic text. Halakhic reasoning sometimes necessitates *teirutzim dechukim* at the cost of abandoning peshat. In a palpable way, halakha interferes with the commitment to peshat, as can be clearly perceived from the Rashbam's Talmud commentary. In the domain of halakha, that is, in the context of talmudic *sugyot*, peshat is—and sometimes must be—expendable, if one's efforts are directed towards the determination of law.

This bifurcation between "halakhic" and "non-halakhic" exegesis, which helps contextualize shifting commitments to peshat, correlates to the dichotomization between the roles of jurist and historian. A jurist must work from within the parameters of a tradition of precedents and a system of regulations, and can therefore not always afford to uphold high ideals of interpretation grounded upon authorial intention. A critical historian, unencumbered by the pressures of tradition or system, can afford to embrace peshat at all costs. Equity is the aim of the jurist, truth is the domain of the historian. Changing conditions in society and shifting directions in consensus are factors which affect the jurist's legal interpretations. Ideally at least, the historian need not concern himself with the constraints of community or consensus. Scholarly debates are not adjudicated through reference to an authoritative body of scholarly tradition nor through compliance with contemporary consensus. The critical commitment to peshat is subject to the rigors of truth and falsity and, fortunately, not to the tides of authority and consensus. From the perspective of medieval Jewish exegesis, but in our idiom, Rashbam the scholar could afford to be

textually rigorous in his Torah commentary, but Rashbam the jurist had to
be halakhically sensible and wise in his Talmud commentary.

Jewish exegetes were not necessarily conscious of the impact of halakhic
considerations on their orientation towards peshat. The Rashbam did not
stray from peshat consciously in response to the pressures of *pesak*. Halakhic considerations were a natural, integral component of his "halakhic"
exegesis. In the face of a pre-existent record of precedents and decisions,
peshat could self-evidently not be the absolute arbiter of meaning. The text
had already been molded to fit the contours of halakha, and the process
could not be simply reversed or rerouted to suit the demands of peshat.

Other examples of exegesis that demands contextualization includes
that of R. Jonathan of Lunel (d. early thirteenth century), who distinguished between his commentary to *mishnayot* grouped as a cluster at the
beginning of a chapter, and his later commentary to a Mishnah when read
in conjuction with its attendant Gemara. When interpreting *mishnayot*
read in and of themselves, independently of their relationship to the
Gemara, R. Jonathan offered peshat exegesis. Once the Mishnah became
embedded within its talmudic context, however, the exegesis of the post-
mishnaic rabbis had to be respected and affirmed. R. Jonathan could not
simply disavow the exegesis of the *amoraim*, although he had implicitly
deviated from their exegesis of the same Mishnah when commenting on it
in a context divorced form Gemara.[3] Peshat had to succumb to the authority of established exegesis when in the shadow of that authority.

The exegetical differences vis-à-vis the Talmud between Rashi and
tosafot can also be understood in the light of contextualization. The
tosafists were more preoccupied with halakha than was Rashi, and often
faulted him for his apparently flagrant disregard of parallel Talmudic
sugyot. The tosafot often challenge Rashi's explanation of a *sugya* on the
basis of a conflicting *sugya* in another location. Rashi, however, could be
more firm in his commitment to peshat precisely because he was interested
in *ad locum* exegesis; his exegetical scope was purposefully restricted,
generally, to the *sugya* at hand. The tosafists, far more concerned with the
reconciliation of conflicting Talmudic sources—because their primary concern was for the determination and clarification of halakha—were forced
to abandon local peshat when Rashi was not. Because their exegetical
vision was attuned to the nuances of a broader halakhic landscape, the
tosafists were compelled sometimes to tamper with the peshat of *sugyot* so
that a broader, more encompassing halakhic harmony could thereby be
realized. Rashi could, without exegetical unease, interpret a *sugya* according to its peshat even when knowing that his interpretation ran contrary to
the Gemara in another location,[4] and he was almost certainly not unaware
of the conflicting talmudic sources which the *tosafot* referred to in object-

ing to his commentary. This can be discerned through his *responsa*, which, because of their obvious halakhic character, do take the full breadth of halakhic sources into account. His talmudic commentary, in contrast, was clearly not fundamentally impelled by halakhic motivations; its localized design was purposeful and strategic, and allowed him to focus on the peshat of discrete *sugyot*. The tosafists, because of their halakhic interests, could not afford themselves this exegetical luxury.

Though difficult to quantify, it is my impression that traditional exegetes, like the Ramban, Rashba and the Ritba, who were also *posekim*, were more prone to peshat commentary when *pesak* was not immediately involved. In *sugyot* where halakhic detail is not abundant, that is, where the impact of halakha is minimal, even these exegetes, not usually acclaimed for peshat tendencies, are more likely to approximate peshat exegesis. In an unselfconscious, uncontrived way, these exegetes also seem to be more exegetically "liberated" when secure from halakhic burdens. The ratio of peshat exegesis, across the board, seems to be in inverse proportion to halakhic concern. As the latter rises, the former falls. This is certainly not meant to demean "halakhic" exegesis. The demands of halakha are systemically ordained and mandated, and must be contended with by exegetes intent on *pesak*. Peshat and *pesak* are, at times, simply impossible to reconcile. It is apparent, then, that even within the work of individual exegetes, halakha sometimes is a potent, though perhaps not explicit, factor of exegesis, while at other times it is not. When it is, it can whittle away at an exegete's natural predilection for peshat. This dual-character, splintered exegesis can be operative within the commentary of the same exegete, depending on the immediate backdrop of the text. When the contingencies of law demand it, the jurist will forsake his scholarly commitment to peshat. For an exegete like the Rashbam, the cost of abandoning peshat for the sake of halakha was certainly not too high a price to pay.

NOTES

Chapter 1

1. Benedict de Spinoza, *A Theologico-Political Treatise*, trans. R. H. M. Elwes (New York: Dover Publications, 1951), pp. 114–19. See also I. Husik, "Maimonides and Spinoza on the Interpretation of the Bible," in *Philosophical Essays*, ed. M. C. Nahm and L. Strauss (Oxford: B. Blackwell, 1952), pp. 141–59.

2. A. Geiger, "Das Verhältnis des naturlichen Schriftsinnes zur talmudischen Schriftdeutung," in *Wissenschaftliche Zeitschrift für jüdische Theologie* 5 (1844): 234–59. See also D. Weiss Halvini, *Midrash, Mishnah, and Gemara* (Cambridge: Harvard University Press, 1986), p. 122, n. 17.

3. See in particular Saadya ben Joseph, *The Book of Beliefs and Opinions*, trans. Samuel Rosenblatt (New Haven: Yale University Press, 1948), pp. 157–58.

4. About allegorization, see n. 16.

5. K. Kahana in the introduction to D. Z. Hoffmann's *Commentary on Deuteronomy* (Tel Aviv: Netzach Press, 1960), p. 15 (in Hebrew).

6. Implicit in both the criticism and the upholding of rabbinic exegesis is the assumption that literal meaning most accurately reflects the intention of the author. Critics and traditionalists alike accordingly either claimed or feared that by abandoning literal meaning the rabbis of the Talmud misinterpreted the biblical intent, which to both was the objective of biblical study, though they disagreed who the author of the Bible was. This assumption may not meet with the approval of some of the present-day literary theorists (who will be discussed in greater depth in Appendix II). For them, to reduce meaning to "authorial intention" is to ignore the unique, creative contribution that each reader brings to a text, adding to its rich variety and idiosyncratic many-sidedness. Yet even to these present-day theorists, at least to most of them, meaning is not entirely separate from the intention of the author. Authorial intention remains an important component, perhaps the single most important component of any interpersonal communication. It may not exhaust all of the meaning. But neither is meaning meaningful without it. It remains central—cf. Jonathan Culler, *On Deconstruction* (Ithaca: Cornell University Press, 1982), p. 216—"Der-

rida's analysis does not dispense with the category of intention or ignore textual marks of intention." For an extreme position, see Calvin D. Schrag in Hugh J. Silverman and Don Ihde, eds., *Hermeneutic and Deconstruction* (Albany: State University of New York Press, 1985), pp. 29–30—"The proverbial 'every schoolboy' of our age knows that the author as the monarchical legislator of textual meaning has been effectively effaced by philosophers and theorists of literature. We have all cut our teeth on the intentional fallacy and have been apprized of the futility of chasing down the meaning of a text within the confines of authorial intention." Schleiermacher's exhortation "whenever a given text calls for a closer interpretation it must be determined and explained by the joint linguistic background of the author and his original public" (Friedrich Daniel Ernst Schleiermacher, *Hermeneutik*, ed. H. Kimmerle [Heidelberg: Carl Winter-Universitätsverlag, 1959], p. 90; my translation) is Spinozistic in origin. For Schleiermacher's theory of understanding a text, see H. G. Gadamer, *Truth and Method* (New York: Crossroad, 1986), pp. 157 and especially 168ff.

7. The literature on the subject is vast. For primary sources see *Mekhilta*, Tractate *Nezikin* (in reference to Num. 21:24), trans. J. Z. Lauterbach (Philadelphia: J. P. S., 1949), vol. 3, pp. 67–68; *b. B. Kam.*, pp. 83b–84a. For two similar cases see R. Vidal of Tolosa, *Maggid Mishnah, Genaiva* 9.8. Cf. N. M. Sarna, *Exploring Exodus* (New York: Schocken Books, 1987), p. 188. With regard to Deut. 19:18–19, 21, a witness may cause the defendant "to receive any of the mutilations listed" by testifying that the defendant has so mutilated another person.

8. *Sifrei Deut.* 289, p. 307 in L. Finkelstein's edition (New York: Jewish Theological Seminary of America, 1969); *b. Yevam.* 24a. See also Gen. 38:9.

9. *Mekhilta*, Tractate *Nezikin*, paragraph 15, see in particular p. 118; *b. B. Metz.* 94a. See also Halivni, *Midrash, Mishnah, and Gemara*, pp. 105–6.

10. *Sifrei Deut.* 280 (p. 297); *b. Sanh.* 27b.

11. E. Kant endorsed forced interpretations if they served moral ends. See his *Religion Within the Limits of Reason Alone*, trans. T. M. Greene and H. H. Hudson (New York: Harper Brothers, 1960), pp. 100–5.

12. This is a minimal definition that does not sufficiently delineate what constitutes plain meaning and what constitutes applied meaning. I will, therefore, refrain from using it, relying on examples that to me are clearly of one or the other category.

13. J. S. Preus, *From Shadow to Promise* (Cambridge: Harvard University Press, 1969).

14. See B. Smolly, *The Study of the Bible in the Middle Ages* (Notre Dame, IN: University of Notre Dame Press, 1978), pp. 1–37; and A. Ne-

metz, "Literalness and Sensus Litteralis," *Speculum* 34 (1959): 76–89. Thomas Aquinas (1225–1274)—*Summa Theologica*, Ia. I, 10, 2—takes for granted that "literal sense is that which the author intends."

15. Preus, *From Shadow to Promise*, p. 81. See also James L. Kugel and Rowan A. Greer, *Early Biblical Interpretation* (Philadelphia: Westminster Press, 1986), pp. 126ff.: "Christian Transformation of the Hebrew Scriptures."

16. Jewish allegorists (including Philo, but possibly excluding a few Hellenistic Jewish writers) did not negate the law, did not advocate disobservance (see the fine summary of allegory in Jewish tradition in A. Altmann's article "Bible," in *Encyclopaedia Judaica*, vol. 2, pp. 895–99). That is the main difference between Jewish and Christian allegorists. (There is very little allegorization or metaphorization of law in rabbinic literature even when no negation is intended. There is, however, negation of historical events like the David and Bathsheba affair or Reuben's involvement with his father's concubine—see *b. Shabb.* 55a–56a.)

The only instance of negation encountered in classical Jewish literture is when a legal text is read into, changing (though not completely displacing) its simple meaning. In this respect the rabbis of the Talmud are unique.

17. Gottlob Frege, "Über Sinn und Bedeutung," *Zeitschrift für Philosophie und philosophische Kritik* 100 (1892), makes the distinction, for philosophical purposes, between *sinn* and *bedeutung* which E. D. Hirsch (a critic of the new literary theory) adopted for literary criticism as a distinction between meaning and significance or understanding and explanation. (See E. D. Hirsch, *Validity in Interpretation* [New Haven: Yale University Press, 1967], pp. 211ff. In a later book, *The Aims of Interpretation*, [Chicago: University of Chicago Press, 1976], chap. 5, Hirsch modifies his position somewhat.) The distinction between reading in and adding to bears some affinity to Frege's distinction, in a negative way: reading in denies the natural *sinn* of a text whereas adding to denies the natural *bedeutung* of a text.

18. E. Von Dobschütz, *Vom vierfachen Schriftsinn, Die Geschichte einer Theorie* in Harnack-Ehrung (Leipzig, 1921), pp. 1–13.

19. See S. Lieberman in G. Scholem, *Jewish Gnosticism, Merkabah Mysticism and Talmudic Literature* (New York: Jewish Theological Seminary, 1960), pp. 118–26.

20. Sometimes called haggadah.

21. The best summaries of the various means and modes of aggadic interpretation are: Samuel Waldberg, *Darchei ha Shinuyim* (Lvov: 1870) and—written with greater modern sophistication—Isaac Heinemann, *Darchei ha-Aggada* (Jerusalem: Magnes Press, 1954).

22. See J. Goldin, "Freedom and Restraint of Haggadah," in *Midrash*

and Literature, ed. Geoffrey H. Hartman and Sanford Budick (New Haven: Yale University Press, 1986), pp. 57–76.

23. Louis Ginzberg, *Die Haggadah bei den Kirchenvätern und der apokryphischen literatur* (Berlin: S. Calvary, 1900).

24. For a discussion and statements of opinion on capital punishment, see J. Greenberg, *Judicial Process and Social Change: Constitutional Litigation* (St. Paul: West, 1977), pp. 421–540.

25. Outstanding among the apologists (more about them in chapter 2) was M. L. Malbim (1809–71), who in his introduction to the section on Leviticus in *Ha-Torah ve-ha-Mitzvah* (Bucharest, 1860), on the first page calls derash (applied meaning) "peshat [simple meaning] in depth," based on the rules of grammar known to the rabbis of the Talmud but subsequently forgotten. He felt compelled to write a commentary on the Bible— he tells us later on in the introduction—to counteract the Reformers (see above, note 2 for the statement of Abraham Geiger) who claim "that the rabbis of the Talmud did not know the plain meaning of the verses, did not know grammar, and followed a tortuous way of interpretation." On the relationship between the Malbim's exegesis and S. R. Hirsch's, see J. J. Neubauer, *Ha-Rambam al Divrei Sofrim*, (Jerusalem: Mossad ha-Rav Kook, 1957), pp. 168–73. Some Reformers were less harsh on the rabbis of the Talmud, and, like some medieval scholars (see below, n. 37), they held that the verses used in many an applied meaning were not intended to be the source of the law. Unlike the medieval scholars, however, they believed that the law was different in earlier times and that the rabbis of the Talmud changed it for social, economic, or ethical (and the like) reasons (so that they also have the right to change the law today whenever in their estimation social, economic, or ethical [and the like] reasons demand change). Cf. W. G. Plaut, *The Rise of Reform Judaism* (New York: World Union for Progressive Judaism, 1963), pp. 112–24.

26. I have in mind particularly R. A. Ibn Ezra (1089–1164), Exod. 21:8 (see below note 37). See U. Simon, "Tenach: Parshanut," *Encyclopedia Mikraith* (Jerusalem: Mossad Bialik, 1982), vol. 8, p. 674 (in Hebrew).

27. Michael Jehiel Sachs in *Die Poesie der Juden in Spanien*, 2d ed. (Berlin: Poppelauer, 1901), p. 161, arrived intuitively at a similar conclusion with respect to aggadah (nonlegal midrash). Heinemann, *Darchei ha-Aggada*, p. 3, calls this conclusion an "exaggeration" since aggada could almost always be considered an addition to peshat rather than in place of peshat; thus, there is no necessity to posit that the rabbis of the Talmud had no appreciation of peshat. Both probably would have been surprised to learn that the proof for this thesis is to be found not in the aggada but in halakha (legal midrash) in the occasions when the rabbis agreed to read into a text; when they attributed to Sadducees (the deniers of nonsimple

meaning) interpretations which are not in consonance with peshat, when they seriously inquire, offering possibilities and rejecting them, as to what the intention of the text is and end up with an interpretation far removed from peshat.

See also I. H. Weiss, *Dor, Dor, ve-Dorshav*, vol. 1 (New York-Berlin: Platt and Minkus, 1924), pp. 167–68. The idea that the rabbis' sense of peshat is different from ours has surfaced in the literature before Weiss, but almost always as a passing remark. Not much attention was paid to it. It was certainly not seen as a part of the history of exegesis in general. (Even Weiss attributes it to the rabbis' lack of language and culture.) See the brief entry by J. Z. Lauterbach, "Peshat," *The Jewish Encyclopedia*, vol. 9, pp. 652–53.

28. Found three times in the Babylonian Talmud: *Shabb.* 63a, *Yevam.* 11b and 24a.

29. In his commentary on the Pentateuch, edited by A. Grunbaum (Jerusalem: Mossad ha-Rav Kook, 1978), p. 478 (in Hebrew).

30. See for example *m. Sota* 8:5: "R. Akiva says, 'Fearful and faint-hearted' (Deut. 20:8) is meant literally (*kemishmao*)—he cannot endure the armies joined in battle or bear to see a sword drawn. R. Yose the Galilean says, 'Fearful and fainthearted' is that he is afraid for the transgressions that he has committed." Unlike R. Akiva, R. Yose the Galilean did not prefer there the plain meaning over the applied meaning.

To the Talmud's inquiry, how can R. Akiva of the *baraita* in a *gezera shava* "completely deprive the scriptural text of its plain meaning?" R. Nachman the son of Yitzak replied (*b. Ketu.* 38b) "read in the text that it is not a betrothed maiden"—a reading that changes the vocalization of the text and the understanding of the biblical word *orasa* in the later rabbinic sense rather than in the biblical sense (see below, chapter 3, n. 47).

Rava (a fourth-century Babylonian scholar) after criticizing the exposition of his colleague, Abaye, for "having dissected a biblical verse with a sharp knife" (*b. B. Bat.* 111b) goes on to offer a substitute exposition which is still very far from what we would consider the plain meaning.

31. R. Aaron ibn Chaim (b. 1560), *Korban Aharon* (Venice, 1609); R. Joseph Babad, *Minchat Chinuch* (Lvov, 1869), commandment 232. The former, however, does not say so explicitly.

32. See *Sifra*, Weiss edition, (1862) p. 88d; *b. Nid.* 57a.

33. See *b. Pesach.* 22b and parallels. For additional examples see C. H. J. Kasowski, *Thesaurus Talmudis* (Jerusalem: Jewish Theological Seminary of America, 1972), vol. 28, p. 299.

34. Not so to the postmedieval Bible commentators who eagerly sought a justification for excluding a physical stumbling block. See. R. E. Mizra-

chi (d. 1525), (Venice, 1527); Maharal (d. 1609), *Gur Arye* (Prague, 1578) (both are commentaries on Rashi); R. Aaron ibn Chaim, *Korban Aharon*.

35. Here classifying the different periods, rather that speaking of the rabbis as a whole, is highly desirable.

36. See the commentaries of the Ramban and Mizrachi on Lev. 23:11. Compare them with the lengthy discussion of Ibn Ezra.

37. Among them M. Maimonides in his introduction to his Mishnah commentary, Joseph Kafah, ed. (Jerusalem: Mossad ha-Rav Kook, 1963), p. 10; R. Yehuda Halevi, *Kuzari* 3.73 and R. A. ibn Ezra, in his commentary on Exod. 21:8.

38. L. Gersonides, *Peirush ha-Ralbag al ha-Torah* (Venice, 1547), p. 2c. For some other theories see "Asmakhta," in *Encyclopedia Talmudit*, vol. 2, pp. 106–7.

39. For a full treatment of the subject of which ordinances are biblical and which ordinances are rabbinical, see R. K. Miterani (1500–1580), *Kiryat Sefer*, (Venice, 1551).

40. Consider, for example, the eighteen ordinances enacted during the early years of the Shammaites and Hillelites (see my *Sources and Traditions* [Jerusalem: Jewish Theological Seminary of America, 1972], *Shabbat*, pp. 35–37), recorded in *m. Shabb.* 1:4.

41. The phrase in *b. Yoma* 74a is: "It is a rabbinical ordinance. The verse is merely an *asmakhta*." Even though this comes as a response to "Eteve R. Yochanan le-Resh Lakish," R. Yochanan asked a question of Resh Lakish, is not amoraic (by Resh Lakish) but stammaitic. See my *Midrash, Mishnah, and Gemara*, p. 70.

42. M. Guttmann, *Mafteach ha-Talmud*, (Breslau: Th. Schatzky, 1923) vol. 3, part 1, on the *asmakhta*, pp. 35ff. Whether a legal exposition based on Ginatriya (numerical value) is *ipso facto* an asmakhta, is not substantiated. Cf. *Seifer Hakritot*, ed. D. Sofer (Jerusalem, 1965), p. 145.

43. The question in *b. Avod. Zar.* 37b (at the bottom): "But nothing is written in the verse about fire?" (Which prompted the answer: "it is a rabbinical ordinance. The verse is merely an *asmakhta*.") is not to be understood as if the Gemara is implying that the *derasha* (which on the basis of Deut. 2:28)—"give me water for money that I may drink"—draws a comparison that one is allowed to buy from a heathen only the kind of cooked food that, like water, did not have its material changed by fire) is faulty because it violates the plain meaning. Understood that way, it would follow that the rabbis, at least in this instance, used the formula *asmakhta* to obviate the problem of reading in. Such an understanding seems to me to be incorrect. Earlier the Gemara was content with the *derasha* that drew the comparison to water more narrowly, "not having changed its natural form" (not necessarily "by fire"). Even this narrow exposition is not in line

with the plain meaning of the text. Reading in was not the rabbis' problem. They were accustomed to that. What bothered them there was that because the modification "by fire only" is not born out by the comparison to water—the heart of the *derasha*—the author had no right to limit the law and permit food cooked by a heathen that had not been changed by fire. The *derasha*, the comparison to water, is legitimate despite being read in. What is objected to is the *derasha*'s limited applicability. Since fire is not mentioned in the verse, the comparison to water should be made more inclusive. It should be like water that hasn't changed at all, by fire or otherwise. The discussion there is not a matter of peshat or derash, but how extensive the *derasha* should be—and as such is not reflective of any stance pertaining to our topic.

44. Cf. W. Bacher, *Die exegetische Terminologie der jüdischen Traditionsliteratur* (Leipzig: J. C. Hinrichs, 1905), s.v. *vadai*, p. 60. See also the gloss of R. S. Strashun to *Midrash Rabbah*, Genesis, Vilna edition, 98:4.

45. The exact meaning of Rava's interpretation is not clear. Even the explanation of the *Aruch*, s.v. *gara*, is not satisfying. What he probably meant was that when the Bible says that the closest relative shall inherit, it includes also the husband's inheriting the wife's property, since he is her closest relative.

46. See note 35.

47. For medieval times, See Halivni, *Midrash, Mishnah, and Gemara*, p. 153, n. 25.

48. Phylacteries were found in the Judean desert, dating back to the second century B.C.E., and according to *m. Meg.* 4:8 even heretics and "sectarians" put on phylacteries. So did members of the Beothusean sect, according to *b. Shabb.* 108a. See also *Letter of Aristeas* 159 and Josephus, *Antiquities* 4.8.13.

49. A very fine summary of the subject is to be found in "Tefillin," *Encyclopedia Mikrait*, vol. 8, pp. 883–95, written by J. Tigay (in Hebrew). The article is balanced and complete. It does not, however, mention that the question of whether to interpret the verses literally or metaphorically was raised again among nineteenth-century *maskilim* and that there exists a sizable literature for that period. As usual, A. M. Pineles' remarks in *Darka shel Torah* (Vienna, 1861), pp. 20–21, are perceptive and sensible. Cf., however, S. Poznanski, *Studies in Jewish Literature, Issued in Honor of Professor Kaufmann Kohler* (G. Reiner: Berlin, 1913), p. 250.

50. The Karaites nominally claim that they follow only the simple literal meaning of the text (a similar claim is made about the Sadducees). On the relationship between the Karaites and the Qumran sects see N. Weider, *The Judean Scrolls and Karaites* (London: East and West Library, 1962). Since they originated in early medieval times (ninth century), their sense of

distinction between peshat and derash is commensurate with the "interpretive state of mind" of that period.

51. Bruno Snell, *The Discovery of the Mind*, trans. T. G. Rosenmeyer (New York: Dover Publications, 1953), pp. ix–xii; 1–22; 227–29.

52. The purpose of the analogy is to strengthen the cogency of the timebound theory as applied to reading into a text by quoting analogous studies with similar conclusions in other fields. No analogy is perfect. This analogy too suffers from dissimilarities, both as to methods and to substance. Snell's argument is primarily from silence, from the failure of the *Iliad* and the *Odyssey* to mention the soul, the intellect, and the body. In this respect our case is stronger. We can quote scores of cases where the rabbis read into a text. On the other hand, Snell is dealing with very early epic, supposedly from the eighth century B.C.E. It is easier to accept the fact that people who lived less than three thousand years ago may be different from us than it is to accept the same for people who lived less than two thousand years ago. More importantly, Snell's theory affects the very fabric of thinking. Thinking is an essential part of the definition of man. We are instinctively reluctant to set ourselves apart from the people of the past with regard to such a basic human trait. That reluctance came to the fore when scholars, before even examining the anthropological data, rejected outright Levy-Bruhl's theory of the "prelogical" (see Lucien Levy-Bruhl, *Primitive Mentality*, Eng. trans. Lilian A. Clare [New York: The Macmillan Co.], 1923). Some philosophers went so far as to claim a priori that prelogical thinking is impossible, is a contradiction in terms. (See W. V. O. Quine, *Word and Object* [Cambridge: MIT Press, 1964], pp. 58ff. and p. 69.) No such outright strictures were hurled against Snell's theory. Yet, the feeling that this is improbable was expressed by some scholars (see Hirsch, *Validity in Interpretation*, n. 17, pp. 40ff.). I suspect that the cry of improbability will be raised against our thesis too. The modernness in all of us will stand up and revolt against such nonmodern concepts. I hope the analogy will soften the criticism slightly and that if it comes, it will be lighter than the criticism raised against Snell.

Chapter 2

1. For how a religious Jew commited to rabbinic interpretation justifies reading in even when peshat and derash are mutually exclusive, see chap. 5.

2. See Y. Kaufmann, *History of the Jewish Religion* (Jerusalem: Mossad Bialik; Tel Aviv: Dvir, 1960), vol. 4, pp. 331–38 (in Hebrew). See also below chap. 5, pp. 131–32.

3. See M. Fishbane, *Biblical Interpretation in Ancient Israel* (New York: Oxford University Press, 1985), pp. 135–37.

4. See *Mavo ha-Talmud*, attributed to R. Shemuel ha-Nagid (d. 1067), printed in the Vilna edition of the Talmud at the end of Tractate *Berakhot*, s.v. *ve-haggada*.

5. See above, chap. 1, pp. 4–5.

6. See note 5 above, and M. Kasher, *Torah Shelema*, vol. 17 (reprint, Jerusalem, 1984), p. 292, n. 3.

7. *T. Dem.* 2.24 (R. Nathan is not mentioned there), *b. Pesach.* 22b, and *b. Avod. Zar.* 6b. This statement of R. Nathan, as far as I know, is not quoted in the Palestinian Talmud, but it seems to be referred to in *p. Dem.* 3.1, p. 23b. That abetting wrongdoing is a violation of this verse is also indirectly stated in *m. B. Metz.* 5:11.

8. See also *b. Tan.* 3a; *b. B. Kam.* 65b; *b. Menach.* 17b; and the comments of the *tosafot* on the latter text.

9. See my note in D. Weiss Halivni, *Sources and Traditions* (Jerusalem: Jewish Theological Society of America, 1972), *Pesachim*, p. 392, note 2.

10. As can be seen from the parallel sources quoted in note 8.

11. The meaning of *ein mikra yotze middei peshuto* is discussed at length in chap. 3, pp. 54ff. See also ch. 1, pp. 10–12.

12. See D. Weiss Halivni, *Midrash, Mishnah, and Gemara* (Cambridge: Harvard University Press, 1986), p. 133, n. 25.

13. The *Sheiltot*, despite its arrangement according to Scripture, is actually either a book on the commandments or a book of *derashot*. See *Sheiltot*, ed. S. Mirsky (Jerusalem: Mossad ha-Rav Kook, 1960), pp. 1–2.

14. See U. Simon, "The Exegetical Method of R. Abraham Ibn Ezra as Revealed in Three Interpretations of a Biblical Passage," *Annual of Bar Ilan University* (1965): 3, 137, n. 166: "The evidence of J. Reifmann, it seems to me, should put an end to the long and excited discussion concerning Ibn Ezra's knowledge of classical Halakhic literature in favor of the negative." Further literature on the topic can be found there as well.

15. This was not enough of a concession to the rabbis for R. Shelomo Lurya who, in his book, *Yam shel Shelomo* (Prague, 1616), at the end of the introduction to Tractate *Bava Kamma*, attacks Ibn Ezra for ignoring talmudic biblical exegesis. Lurya did not know of the Rashbam's commentary on the Pentateuch, not published until 1705. It is worth speculating whether Lurya would have mounted a similar attack against one of his favorite *posekim* (adjudicators).

16. For a more detailed discussion and references, see chap. 3, pp. 81–82. R. J. Caspi (1280–1340), who generally followed the Ibn Ezra, apparently did not adopt the latter's submissive attitude toward the rabbis. In his introduction (patterned after the Ibn Ezra's) to *Mishneh Kesef Tirat Kesef*, ed. J. Last (Pressburg, 1905), passage 4, p. 6, he writes, "Let no person think that there is a contradiction in faith in composing interpretations of

the Torah in a manner different from the rabbis, may their memory be for a blessing." For interesting nonrabbinic interpretations (though based on *b. Chul.* 90b), see his comments on Exod. 12:29–30.

Also great "peshatists" were R. Josef Kara, a colleague of the Rashbam, and R. Eliezer of Beaugency, perhaps a disciple of the Rashbam. Their scholarly remains, however, contain little on the Pentateuch where commitment to peshat can best be tested in the conflict between peshat and derash in matters of halakha (see the fine evaluation of their works in S. Poznanski, *Commentary on Ezekiel and the Minor Prophets by R. Eliezer of Beaugency* [Warsaw: *Mekitze Nirdamim*, 1913], pp. 23–39; 125–64 [in Hebrew]). This is also true of R. D. Kimchi's (d. 1235) commentaries on the Pentateuch, of which only the one on Genesis has survived. (For a short, incomplete evaluation, see M. Segal, *Parshanuth ha-Mikra* [Jerusalem, 1944], pp. 86–90.) He often attributes to derash greater philological reliability than either the Rashbam or Ibn Ezra. See, for example, his comments to Josh. 4:11 and 6:25 and the interpretation of Y. Cooperman, *Le-Peshuto shel Mikra* (Jerusalem: Heskel, 1974), pp. 170–73. See also E. Z. Melammed, *Bible Commentators* (Jerusalem: Magnes Press, 1978), pp. 796–800 (in Hebrew). R. Isaiah de Trani (mid-thirteenth century) was a great halakhist, and the author of many *tosafot*. We do not have his commentary on the Pentateuch or on Chronicles. Of course, it is possible that he never wrote any. But it is also possible that he was prepared to study and write a commentary on the Prophets and the Hagiography according to peshat but not on the Pentateuch. The conflicts between peshat and derash in matters of halakha are by far more acute in the Pentateuch. Yet his comment on Ps. 51:2 in connection with David's sin may serve as a paradigm.

The closest to the Rashbam's commentary on the Torah is the commentary of his student, R. Joseph Bachor Shor (see Poznanski, *Commentary on Ezekiel*, pp. 55–75). He belongs in his league. Although he was not as daring in his commitment to peshat as was the Rashbam (compare the respective comments to Exod. 13:16 on the phylacteries) and the conflict between peshat and derash caused him greater tension, much of what we are saying about the Rashbam applies to him as well.

17. The great value of the commentary (or, as it was originally called, Midrash) by Rabbeinu Bachya, written around 1290, is in its encyclopedic scope; it contains quotations from sources that are no longer extant. His own exegetical contribution is minimal. As for R. Meyuchas, see below, chap. 3, n. 67.

18. The earlier commentators, however, knew his commentary and quoted him profusely. I will mention two here: R. Hezekiah the son of R. Manoach (mid-thirteenth century), the author of *Chizkuni* (see Ch.

D. Chavel's edition, [Jerusalem: Mossad ha-Rav Kook, 1981], Introduction, pp. 5–7, and *The Commentary on the Torah by R. Chaim Paltiel* (written around 1300), ed. R. I. S. Lange (Jerusalem, 1981), Introduction, p. 10.

19. See Ibn Ezra's censure of Rashi in *Sopha Berura*, ed. G. Lippmann (Furth, 1839), p. 5.

20. See also Mendelssohn's "opening" to *Parshat Mishpatim*.

21. Mendelssohn had access to the original Rashbam manuscript, which he often consulted because of the many mistakes and "misunderstandings of the copyist," as he says in his introduction. Among scholars, the Rashbam's commentary was apparently known—at least in Germany—as soon as it appeared. R. Y. Y. Falk, the author of the *Penei Yehoshua*, quotes him in *Kidd.* 16b, s.v. *Rashi*, in support of an interpretation which is according to the peshat, against the talmudic *derasha*. He justifies it on the ground "that no text can be deprived of its peshat." His commentary on *Kiddushin* was published in Amsterdam in 1739, and he died in Frankfurt in 1756.

22. Cf. Y. Heinemann, *Mekor ha-Chaim* (Berlin, 1833), Pentateuch, Introduction to Deuteronomy: "Mendelssohn related the derash to the peshat whenever it was needed, as in matters of law." See also P. Sandler, *Mendelssohn's Edition of the Pentateuch*, 2d ed. (Jerusalem: R. Mass, 1984), pp. 52–54 (in Hebrew). On the nature of this edition and the approbations contained there, see M. Hildesheimer, "Moses Mendelssohn in Nineteenth Century Rabbinical Literature," *Proceedings of the American Academy for Jewish Research* 55 (1988): 97–102. Compare, however, S. D. Luzzatto in his introduction to *Ha-Mishtadel* (Vienna, 1846).

23. Oxford, 1753. See Mendelssohn's *Gesammelte Schriften*, ed. G. B. Mendelssohn (Leipzig, 1843–45), pp. 171–210 and A. Altmann, *Mendelssohn* (Philadelphia: Jewish Publication Society, 1973), pp. 373–78, 409–13.

24. Similar to what R. Yehuda Halevi says in *Kuzari* 3.41: "Even if we concede to the Karaites in the meaning of the phrase 'from the morrow of the Sabbath' that it means Sunday, we will still add and say one of the judges or one of the priests or one of the kings who was accepted in the eyes of God finds it necessary to explain it thus [that it refers not to Sunday but to the second day of Passover] . . . and we are obligated to accept this determination as a commandment because it comes 'from a place that God selected' (Deut. 17:8) . . ." See also Y. Silman, *Thinker and Seer* (Ramat Gan: Bar Ilan University Press, 1985), pp. 283–85 (in Hebrew).

25. See what we wrote in *Sources and Traditions*, Introduction to *Nashim*, p. 8, n. 5. See also M. Flongyan, *Ben Porat* (Vilna, 1858), p. 14: "For the derash is distant from the peshat. The two will never get close to (each other.") Similarly, S. J. Fuen, *Kiryah Ne'emanah* (Vilna, 1860),

p. 144 ("Not to toil in vain, finding a basis in peshat for all the *derashot* of the rabbis . . ."). Already slightly before the Gaon, R. Chaim Itter (1696–1743) in his famous work *Or ha-Chaim*, in the introduction, unhesitatingly declared: "I will sometimes use my pen to explain the peshat of the verses in a way different from the expositions of the rabbis." In the beginning of *Mishpatim*, he writes: "Though the rabbis expounded *derashot*, one has to know also the peshat of the text." He frequently deviated exegetically from practical halakha, the list being first compiled by R. Margolioth in his *Biography of the Or ha-Chaim* (Lvov, 1928), pp. 62–70. Contrast Itter's and the Gaon's position with that of R. M. Sofer, the author of *Chatam Sofer* (d. 1839), who was also attracted to peshat but *suppressed* it. In a sermon he delivered on the eighth of the month of Tevet, published among his sermons, *Derashot ha-Chatam Sofer* (Grosswardein, 1929), p. 204, he says: "When the Torah was translated into Greek, the Jews began to taste the flavor of *peshuto shel mikra*, the flavor of peshat. And from then on heresy began to sparkle (i.e., flourish) and [the Jews] did not want to listen anymore to the voices of the rabbis and to their interpretations—as if, because of our great sins, he [Satan—see *b. Ber.* 51a and *Pesach.* 112b] is still dancing among us [meaning the situation has not abated]." People are attracted to peshat but it leads to heresy. In the same spirit he said in another place, *Chidushe Chatam Sofer* on tractate *Ketubot* (Satmar, 1908), p. 46, in connection with the study of the Talmud: "For the forced interpretations are mostly true while the plausibles and the discoveries are mostly false, and it is the latter which cover up the face of the truth." One ought not to follow peshat (forced interpretations are the opposite of peshat) irrespective of its attraction. It would lead to falsity. Cf. R. M. S. Glasner, *Dor Revii* (Klausenburg, 1921), Introduction, p. 4b, who attempts to explain this unusual statement of the author of the *Chatam Sofer*. See also *Sources and Traditions, Nashim*, Introduction, p. 10, n. 9.

In this connection, it is of value to refer also to the exhortation of Ibn Ezra in his second introduction to the Pentateuch, method 4: "Behold I am laying down a rule in explaining texts. In the Bible and in the Mishnah, in all tractates and in all *beraithot* and in all *mekhiltot*, if we find in any of the aforementioned books something that denies either one of the three following things: straightforward common sense, one verse contradicting another verse logically, or denying accepted tradition, then we should do our best to reconcile . . . and if we cannot truthfully reconcile, let us say then that this wisdom is concealed from us, that the means of our logic is narrow and the understanding of our generation is faulty." Particularly interesting here is the lumping together methodologically of the Bible and the Talmud.

26. For a short biography of Meklenburg, see D. Druck, *Horev* 4 (1937): 171–79. In Meklenburg's introduction *Ma'amar ha-Torah*, p. 21, he

says in rhymed verse: "The difference between peshat and derash is like the difference between the inside and the outside of a vessel. The outside (corresponding to peshat) could be seen with one look, everything revealed, open and spread out. The inside (derash) may be concealed in the first look, but a second look will reveal what is hidden there. See also below, note 29.

27. There exists a considerable literature on the Malbim. The latest full-length biography is that of N. Rosenbloom, *Ha-Malbim* (Jerusalem: Mossad ha-Rav Kook, 1988). For our topic, pp. 88–160 are of particular interest. See also *supra*, chap. 1, n. 25.

28. R. Naftali Zvi Yehuda Berlin. For biography, see his entry in the *Encyclopaedia Judaica* and the references given there. The purpose of his book, *Ha'emek Davar*, as he put it on the first page, is "to show that there are no changes and excesses, that everything is arranged according to peshat-in-depth . . . and also the *derashot* of the sages enjoy the splendor of peshat-in-depth." Like the Gaon, the Netziv will occasionally offer a different interpretation than the Gemara. See my *Sources and Traditions, Erubin*, p. 54, n. 9.

29. Some biographical material is attached to almost all of the Hebrew translations of his commentaries. I am including Hoffmann among the apologists because of the quality of his interpretations. He set forth his exegetical principles in his prefatory general remarks to Leviticus. Paradoxically, he accepted the notion of *asmakhta* (about *asmakhta*, see above, chap. 1, pp. 13–16) because he basically believed that his own *derashot* were superior to those of the rabbis. This is essentially also the approach of Meklenburg, Introduction to *Ha-Ketav veha-Kabbala* (Leipzig, 1839), n. 4. The latter divides biblical exegesis into two categories: one, the hermeneutical principles found in the Talmud that merely hover over the text, but do not inhere in it and which, like the *asmakhtot*, serve only as mnemonic devices (he calls them *siman zikhroni*) and two, the *derashot* that come out of the text itself and inhere in it (he calls them *siman muda'i*) and which "penetrate the depth of the roots of the language and the hiddenness of the style of Torah, so that from the language of the Torah itself one can understand the countless laws and their offspring found in the Talmud, to the extent that almost all of the oral law is revealed and explained in the books of Moses, with the result that the oral law is fully united with the written law."

Both Meklenburg and Hoffmann present us with the second category, whereas the Talmud explicitly gives us only the first. See also Gersonides, *Commentary on the Torah*, p. 2a.

30. There now exists a thoroughly annotated edition of *Meshekh Chokhma* by Y. Cooperman (Jerusalem: Heskel, 1983), prefaced with a long treatise on *peshuto shel mikra* in the spirit of the author of *Meshekh*

Chokhma. For our discussion of timebound exegesis and the conflict between peshat and derash, chaps. 8–11 of the preface hold special interest.

31. See Cooperman, *Meshekh Chokhma,* Chap. 4.

32. Enumerated in his introduction to Leviticus, named *Ayelet ha-Schachar.*

33. About levirate marriage, see chap. 1, p. 4: ch. 3, pp. 83–84.

34. Not quite consistent. See *Be'er ha-Gola,* the first *be'er,* and *Gur Arye,* on Gen. 28:11: "This is clear to every enlightened person (*maskil*). Only because they were pursuing peshat did they treat the Torah irresponsibly".

35. See chap. 2 of Dimitrovsky's fine phenomenological analysis of *pilpul,* practiced by some scholars of the sixteenth to eighteenth centuries, in "'*Al Derekh ha-Pilpul,*" *Festschrift in Honor of Salo Baron,* (Jerusalem: The American Academy for Jewish Research, 1975), pp. 111–81. Our concept of *pilpul* is wider. It embraces any farfetched interpretation, whether it meets the technical conditions uncovered by Dimitrovsky or not. Whether its references are exclusively to the local text or not, and whether the center of its concern is Rashi and *tosafot* or not—cardinal characteristics of the *pilpul* dealt with by Dimitrovsky—are not of much relevance to our discussion, as long as it superimposes itself on the text rather than alters the substantive meaning of the text. See also below, n. 42. For the subtle differences within the period between early and late scholars, see ibid., p. 148ff.

36. About the *stammaim,* see Halivni, *Midrash, Mishnah, and Gemara,* pp. 76–92.

37. Thoroughly studied by J. N. Epstein, *Introduction to the Mishnah* (Jerusalem: Magnes Press, 1948), pp. 510–88; 645–70 (in Hebrew).

38. He received it from his teacher R. J. Pollack. See Dimitrovsky, *Al-Derekh ha-Pilpul,* p. 116.

39. For a bibliography of "the scientific study of Judaism" (which, alas, includes little on the scientific study of the Talmud), see *Studies in Jewish Thought,* ed. A. Jospe (Detroit: Wayne State University Press, 1981), pp. 14–15.

40. Both how to read it and how to interpret it, which in those days was connected to establishing the proper text.

41. The statement of R. Isaiah di Trani, *Piskei ha-Rid,* (Jerusalem: Mossad ha Rav Kook, 1964), *Shabbat,* p. 229: "That the *amoraim* treated the Mishnah (exegetically) the same way the *tannaim* treated the Bible" applies more to the *stammaim* than to the *amoraim.*

42. The employment by late medievalists of the *kitzur* and *setira* modes (see Dimitrovsky, *Al-Derekh ha-Pilpul,* pp. 155ff.) has more to do with the order of the Talmud than with redundancy.

43. The Talmud in *Chul.* 70b presupposes that according to R. Yose the Galilean an animal with unparted hoofs (a *kalut*) born to an animal with parted hoofs is kosher. The principle is that if the mother is kosher, the offspring, irrespective of it possessing the kosher signs or not, is also kosher. The general outline of the tosafist argument is as follows: how can the Gemara assume that according to R. Yose the Galilean, a *kalut* is permitted to be eaten, when in Tractate *Bava Kama*, the same R. Yose the Galilean is listed among those *tannaim* who exposit *et*, and according to the Gemara in Tractate *Bekhorot*, those who exposit *et* actually prohibit *kalut*! Specifically, the tosafist asked: how could R. Yose the Galilean be of this opinion when *b. Kam.* 41b (in a totally different context) says: "For these *tannaim* who employ the phrase 'the owner of the ox shall be quit' [Exod. 21:28—the rabbis of the Talmud considered the phrase superfluous "since it was already said that the ox shall be surely stoned and its flesh shall not be eaten"] for deriving certain implications, whence do they derive the prohibition against making use of the skin [of an ox condemned to die]? They derive it [the Gemara answers] "from the auxiliary term in the Hebrew text [the accusative article] *et besaro*—his flesh (which is redundant), meaning together with that which is joined to its flesh, that is, its skin" (of which you are not allowed to make use). Since R. Yose the Galilean was one of those *tannaim* who employed the phrase "the owner of the ox shall be quit" for deriving certain implications, it follows that R. Yose the Galilean, together with the other scholars, saw every auxiliary term "*et*" as an extra word, and as such a source for a new exposition. Now, the tosafist argues, the Talmud in still a third tractate, *Bekh.* 6b, quotes the view of R. Simeon that "the word *camel* occurs twice (in the Bible, in connection with the forbidden animals): once in Lev. 11:4 and again in Deut. 14:7. One refers to a camel born from a camel and the other to a camel born from a cow (an example of an animal with unparted hoofs born to a kosher animal). The latter, too, is—according to R. Simeon—forbidden to eat. The Talmud (ibid.) continues: "According to the rabbis who differ with R. Simeon [that a camel born from a cow is permissible]—what is the purpose of the repetition 'camel, camel'?" The Talmud responds: "One comes to forbid itself and the other to forbid its milk. If so, from where does R. Simeon derive the prohibition of a camel's milk?" the Talmud persists. "He derives it from the auxiliary term *et* with the milk. And the rabbis? What do they do with the extra term *et*? They do not stress the word *et* occurring in the Scripture." The tosafist combined the two quoted tractates and concluded that R. Yose the Galilean, who in Tractate *Bava Kamma* stresses the accusative article *et* and applies it as a source for new expositions, must side with the view of R. Simeon in Tractate *Bekhorot* that the extra *et* of the verse about camels comes to teach that the

milk of a camel is also forbidden, thus freeing the repetition of the word *camel* to forbid a camel born from a cow. Why, then, asks the tosafist, does the Talmud in *Chullin* presuppose that according to R. Yose an animal with unparted hoofs born to an animal with parted hoofs is kosher?

All the inferences drawn by the tosafist in *Chullin* were oblique and indirect. The tosafist assumed that the *stam*, the anonymous author of the presupposition, was familiar with (if not actually the author of the expositions found in Tractate *Bava Kamma* and *Bekhorot*. The expositons, therefore, ought not contradict each other. While the Talmud (more accurately the Gemara, since all three places are anonymous and *Gemara* in our terminology designates the anonymous sections of the Talmud) in all three tractates was heftily expositing supposedly superfluous phrases or words of the Bible using the textual redundancy method, the tosafist, basing himself on the talmudic exposition, was using the oblique inference method to test the exposition's consistency. Each is using the respective method of its period. What makes the above example a bit unique is that the different methods come together and supplement each other.

44. See J. M. Greenspan, *Pilpula shel Torah*, vol. 1, (London, 1935), Introduction, p. 17: "It is the hallmark of the practitioner of *pilpul* to leave the substance of the sources intact, in its original shape, and through his *pilpul* to invent the different lines (characteristics) that separate the two subjects while the two sources remain abiding and complete." He almost defines *pilpul* in terms of this hallmark, whether it is farfetched or not. No wonder that he finds *pilpul* everywhere and in all times. See also above, n. 35.

45. Based on R. Ch. Soloveitchik, *Chidushe R. Chaim Halevi* (Brisk, 1936), pp. 10b–11a.

46. It is implied in the words of R. Judah: "Removal of *chametz* may only be by burning." Otherwise, there is no guarantee that the chametz will be removed.

47. P. 25

48. Despite the plea made by Greenspan, *Pilpula shel Torah*, Intro., p. 17ff, n. 5, to distinguish between the view of the author and the intention of the author. "The latter is the source of our difficulties with *pilpul*." For an opposing argument, see also my article "Contemporary Methods of the Study of the Talmud," *Journal of Jewish Studies* 30, (Autumn 1979): 196–97.

49. See Appendix II.

50. See, however, the books I quote in chap. 1, n. 6.

51. Medieval commentators assumed that a *tanna*, because of having lived earlier and because of his authoritative position, speaks in a more abbreviated manner than an *amora*. "A *tanna* does not need to explain his words; an *amora* does." See R. M. Hakohen, *Yad Malakhi* (Livorno, 1778),

passage 53. The *tosafot* (*Tem.* 30b, s.v. *mena*) make a similar distinction between a Mishnah and a *Baraita*.

52. See note 41.

53. See note 12.

54. A. Marks, Die Kelale ha-Talmud des R. Bezalel Ashkenazi, *Hoffmann Festschrift* (Berlin, 1914) p. 183.

55. See *tosafot* B. Kam., p. 106b, C. V. velishanei and what we wrote in *Sources and Traditions* (in ms.).

Chapter 3

1. I have in mind principally W. Bacher, *Die jüdische Bibelexegese vom Anfange des Zehnten bis zum Ende des Fünfzehnten Jahrhunderts* (Trier, 1982); idem, *Die Bibelexegese Moses Maimunis*, 1892. He neglected to record Maimonides' explanations of halakhic texts, however, as he himself says in the Introduction: "Many things were left out that I could not include here . . . such as Maimonides' biblical explanations of texts that affect halakha." Z. Karl, "Ha-Rambam ke-farshan ha-Torah," in *Tarbiz* 6 (1935): 152–63, added some of the halakhic material that Bacher left out. His overall view of Maimonides' position relevant to peshat and derash, however, is not acceptable to me. See below, pp. 83–88. See also L. Dobschütz, *Die einfache Bibelexegese der Tannaim* (Breslau, 1893).

2. *Papers of the Institute of Jewish Studies* 1 (1964); 140–86.

3. Jerusalem: Magnes Press, The Hebrew University, 1980.

4. Kamin's book also contains an extensive bibliography. I also benefited from P. Sandler's long summary article on exegesis in *Lexicon Mikrai* (Tel Aviv: Dvir, 1965), pp. 733–56, not mentioned in the bibliography.

5. Or authority. Loewe can point to no place in the Talmud where the use of *peshat* in this sense is confirmed without doubt. He claims, however, that this use "is a natural semantic development of the meaning 'extend'— namely, the extension of an opinion received by a teacher or elaborated by himself, over a wider body which, by acknowledgement thereof, *broadens* the currency of the authority of the course whence it emanates" (p. 158). See also N. H. Tur Sinai's note to E. Ben Yehuda's *Complete Dictionary*, s.v. *peshat*.

6. See in particular Kamin's book, pp. 31–32.

7. Tur Sinai (cited at the end of n. 5) and M. Gertner, "Terms of Scriptural Interpretation: A Study in Hebrew Semantics," *Bulletin of London School of Oriental and African Studies* 25, no. 1 (1962), pp. 20–22. Tur Sinai's note there is almost entirely incorrect, including his citation from the Palestinian Talmud.

8. The first version does not formulate its question symmetrically. (Ac-

cording to the sages "can a text be deprived of its peshat or not") but rather: "do we say that no text can be deprived of its *peshat*, or that once a text has once been torn away, it must in all respects so remain." Even the second possibility does not do away in principle with the dictum that "no text can be deprived of its peshat" (which, incidentally, is always quoted in Hebrew while the rest of the discussion is in Aramaic). Cf. *tosafot Sanh.* 50b s.v. *keshe-hu.* It takes the dictum for granted and assumes the case under discussion is an exceptional case—texts are usually not torn away—and inquires about the extent of the tearing away, whether it be complete or partial. Why is the text here "torn away" and not a regular case of a *derasha*, which transfers a part of its text to another subject but retains it locally as well? (See below, pp. 61–63, concerning the modification of the principle *im eino 'inyan le-gufo teneihu 'inyan le-.*) The Gemara does not say. But the tosafot and some other medieval commentators explain (though not specifically in reference to our question) that the sages held that the phrase "after she is defiled" doesn't fit at all the case of a husband's remarriage to his divorced wife, who after the divorce, married a second husband. Scripture would not call a legal marriage "a defilement." The phrase must be torn away from its original place—and the question arises: does the torn text leave enough of a trace to disqualify the other woman, the rival, from levirate marriage, or not?

9. This suggests that the dictum was older than Rava, and he therefore expressed surprise that it was ignored in this particular case.

10. Not so according to *Sifrei Deut.* 289. The reading there is not certain (see the Finkelstein edition, p. 307). Nevertheless, it seems that the *Sifrei* deduces this contextual incongruity from the phrase "succeed in the name of the brother," instead of "in the name of his father's brother," which it should have said had the subject been the newborn child. A similar deduction is made by the Babylonian Talmud. See *Tosafot Yevam.* 24a, s.v. *o eino*, and Ritba.

11. The medieval commentators point to another place in the Talmud where a *gezera shava* ignores the written context—b. *Yevam.* 70a, in connection with a *toshav* (sojourner) and a *sakhir* (hired servant), whom Exod. 12:45 forbids to partake of the paschal lamb. The Gemara was forced to ignore the written context of the paschal sacrifice, because it assumed that the *toshav* and *sakhir* were Jews, and there is no reason why Jewish sojourners or hired servants should not partake of the paschal lamb. But the verse in Exodus refers to non-Jewish sojourners or hired laborers, as was already noticed by the tosafists (see *Yevam.* 70b s.v. *ela*, and other places). And it is stated so explicitly in the *Mekhilta de R. Ishmael* on Exodus 12:45. It follows that we have no evidence that R. Eliezer (who lived during the late first century), whose statement the Gemara in

Yebamot is explaining, shared the view that a *gezera shava* can ignore a written context. See also note 45.

12. The Munich MS of the Talmud reads *lekulei talmuda*. *Talmuda* in the parallel talmudic sources refers to halakha only. Indeed, we do not possess aggadic statements in the name of R. Kahana (Rava's disciple).

13. In his glosses to *Shabbat*, 63a.

14. See chap. 1, pp. 19–20, concerning phylacteries.

15. I owe the analogy to Rava's statement in *Yevamot* to my son Rabbi Ephraim Halivni.

16. Observed already by the Ramban in his criticism of Maimonides' *Book of Commandments*, ed. Chaim Chavel (Jerusalem: Mossad ha-Rav Kook, 1981), root 2, p. 45 (in Hebrew).

17. *Sifrei Deut.* piska 321 and parallels. See also Rashi, *Sukka* 44a at the end. Most of the references given by R. Margolioth, *Ha-Mikra ve-ha-Masora*, (Jerusalem: Mossad ha-Rav Kook, 1964), p. 58, n. 2, are not relevant to our simile of sword.

18. See Rashi *Shabb.* 63a, s.v. *bedivrei*.

19. When R. Kahana said "but this verse refers to the words of Torah," he was referring to the second half of the verse, "your glory and your majesty," and not to the first half of the verse "gird you sword." The first half retains the meaning of a physical sword.

20. The Gemara in *Shabb.* 63a continues: "What does he [R Kahana] inform us? That a man should study and subsequently understand." The *stam*, the anonymous author of the Gemara, was not content with having R. Kahana merely express surprise at not having known the dictum that "a text cannot be deprived of its peshat" without thereby implying also something of didactic nature. (It is very much in line with the general thought patterns of the *stammaim* to see didactic reports in historical reports.) Not knowing the dictum is a sign that R. Kahana, despite his knowledge of the whole Talmud at the age of eighteen, did not really understand and digest the material taught to him. Yet they continued teaching him because learning, especially when one is young, is educationally beneficial even without full understanding of the material.

21. Employed frequently by the *Sifra* (see concordance, s.v. *'inyan*) belonging to the school of R. Akiva. It is a little surprising that we do not find explicit employment of this principle in the *Sifrei* to Deuteronomy, which also overwhelmingly belongs to the school of R. Akiva. See also *Yad Malakhi*, passage 2.

22. See *b. Yevam.* 95a: "It is written (in connection with a man who married a mother and her daughter) 'they shall be burned with fire, both he and they' (Lev. 20:14). Is the whole household to be burned? If this is not a case of burning (for the first wife whom he married lawfully should not be

punished because her husband has since entered into an unlawful marriage), then regard the text as indicating a prohibition (that he cannot live with either wife)." There, the old meaning of burning (explicitly stated in the text) was preempted by the new meaning, that of prohibition.

Similarly, in *b. Sanh.* 84b, the Gemara says: *Nefesh* is written in connection with one who smites an animal, that he has to make reparations (Lev. 24:18). Elsewhere, *nefesh* is associated with blood. But logic dictates that one who permanently impairs the strength of an animal by loading stones upon it (without wounding it) is also liable. "Since *nefesh* in connection with an animal is irrelevant, transfer its teaching to man." Again, the old meaning (*nefesh* written in connection with animals) was preempted by the new meaning (*nefesh* in connection with man only). Both these examples are embedded in stammaitic material. Yet their origin may be earlier. See also *Tosafot Betza* 20a, s.v. *limed* and R. Yom Tov Heller, *Tosafot Yom Tov, Bava Batra* 8.1, s.v. *vehaish.*

23. The book of faith covenant, Neh. 10:37. Cf. I. Weiss, *Dor, Dor, vedorshav* (New York-Berlin: Platt and Minkus, 1924), vol. I, pp. 43–54. Y. Kaufmann, *History of the Jewish Religion* (Jerusalem: Mossad Bialik; Tel Aviv: Dvir, 1960), vol. 4, pp. 334–35 (in Hebrew). See also M. Fishbane, *Biblical Interpretation in Ancient Israel* (New York: Oxford University Press, 1985), p. 214.

24. Tractate *Pischa*, pp. 161–62 in the J. Z. Lauterbach translation.

25. *Piska* 118 (p. 139, H. S. Horovitz's edition).

26. Apparently, that also happens whenever "the verses contradict each other and a third verse will *yakhri'a* between them." (The last of the thirteen hermeneutical principles, found in the beginning of the *Sifra* and in the prayer book.) According to R. Ishmael, this means (see my *Sources and Traditions* (Jerusalem: J. T. S. Press, 1982), Tractate *Shabbat*, pp. 111–12) that the third verse sides with one of the two contradictory verses, and by so doing, being two, prevail (*makhri'a*) over the contradictory one. But what happens to the contradictory one? Apparently it will be neutralized through a derash. It will be interpreted in a manner that would not contradict the other two verses. Compare the phrase in the Babylonian Talmud (*Pesach.* 59b and parallels): "Leave the verse, for it will still force itself to establish its own case."

27. See my article "Who Was the First One to Use the Phrase 'No Text Can Be Deprived of its *Peshat*'?" *Sidra* 3 (1987): 43–52.

28. And also by the authors of the readings of the Talmud that omit the word *mechalav* from R. Dimi's prooftext. (See *The Babylonian Talmud with Variant Readings,* ed. M. Hershler [Jerusalem: Institute for the Complete Israeli Talmud, 1977], Tractate *Ketubbot* II, p. 557, line 44. See also ibid., n. 114.) They realized that R. Dimi was not expositing this word.

29. Ibid., p. 558.

30. This method of expositing a word as if it is written twice is also found in Rashbam, Gen. 36:12, and in other Bible commentaries (see D. Rosin's edition of the Rashbam [Breslau, 1882], pp. 46–47, notes 10 [p. 46] and 14 [p. 47]). For the Mishnah, see *b. Tem.* 22a: "*avda . . .*"; Heller, *Tosafot Yom Tov, Taharoth* 9.3; the glosses of R. Eliyahu of Greiditz to *m. Tem.* 4:1 (found in the Romm edition of our Mishnah, p. 72); and *Sources and Traditions, Chagiga,* p. 584, n. 9.

31. See also *Eruv.* 23b and the commentaries on it.

32. See R. Eliyahu Mizrachi's comment on Exod. 27:18.

33. The exact connotation of *remez* in halakha is not clear. The places in the Talmud where *remez* appears were assembled by W. Bacher, *Die exegetische Terminologie der Jüdischen Traditionsliteratur,* (Leipzig, 1899), s.v. *remez.*

34. Quoted by N. N. Rabbinovicz and H. Ehrentreu, *Dikdukei Sofrim, Chullin,* p. 184a, n. 30.

35. See commentaries.

36. In *Eruvin* and *Kiddushin,* Abaye answers the question of what is the *peshatei dikra.* In *Arakh.* 8b, the Gemara asks, what is *peshatei dikra* according to R. Pappa and answers with a statement by R. Judah, who lived *before* R. Pappa. R. Judah is quoted by the *stam* as an alternative to R. Pappa's exposition.

37. See n. 36.

38. "Both expounded the same scriptural verse" is a favorite expression of R. Yochanan (see C. H. J. Kasowski, *Thesaurus Talmudis* [Jerusalem: Jewish Theological Seminary of America, 1978], vol. 39, p. 1068). It is therefore possible that this is actually a later exposition which was attributed to R. Yochanan because it is in his style. See n. 42.

39. R. B. Ashkenazi, *Shita Mekubetzet,* in the Vilna edition of the Talmud, quotes this version in the name of *sefarim acherim,* other books. In J. D. Ilan's edition of the *Shita Mekubetzet* (Benei Berak, 1976) p. 142, it is quoted in the name of *ketzat sefarim yeshanim* (some old books).

40. Ilan, *Shita Mekubetzet,* p. 143.

41. After R. Shemuel ben Chofni, who died in 1013.

42. Cf. n. 38. In *Zebach.* 113a, R. Nachman the son of Yitzchak seems to be saying both *kifeshatei dikra* (according to the manuscripts) and "Both expounded the same scriptural verse." Even if it is post-R. Yochanan, it could still be talmudic.

43. See *Aruch* in *Aruch Completum,* s.v. *gelidon,* vol. 2, p. 293.

44. Incidentally, the geonim (see *Otzar ha-Geonim, Sanhedrin,* ed. Ch. Z. Taubes [Jerusalem: Mossad ha-Rav Kook, 1966], p. 523) read there *lehavl* instead of *lechavla,* meaning "do not leave the skin in a place where

there is vapor (steam) heat so that it does not crumble." See also the commentary *Yad Remah, b. Sanh.* 100b.

45. See n. 11. The following statement of R. Shimon may constitute an exception. It is reported that he said (*b. Sota* 16b, *Tem.* 12b, and *Sifrei Num.* Piska 123 [p. 165]): "It is written [Num. 19:17] 'And for the unclean they shall take of the dust of the burning of the sin-offering.' Was it dust and not ashes? The text changes the expression [the *mishmao*], the plain meaning] to teach us a *gezera shava.* Dust is mentioned here as well as there [in the ceremony of the suspected woman]. Just as there the dust had to be placed over the water, so here too, the dust had to be placed over the water. The remnant of the sin-offering was actually ashes, but the Torah changed its expression to *dust* in order to indicate a *gezera shava.*" A *gezera shava* is such an integral part of the Torah that the Torah changed its expression because of it. Why, then, cannot a *gezera shava* sometimes change or modify a text?

The example of R. Shimon, however, is not decisive. Ashes and dust are sometimes interchanged in the Bible, as already noticed by the school of Hillel (*b. Chul.* in 88b): "We find ashes referred to as dust," and they go on to quote as a proof the above-cited verse (Num. 19:17). (See also 2 Kgs. 23:15.) Medieval commentators were hard-pressed to explain R. Shimon's exposition. In fact, he could have derived his conclusion that the ashes have to be over the water without saying that the Torah changed its expression. He could have employed the *gezera shava.* Perhaps that is really what he did. The saying is intended merely to give additional strength to the *gezera shava* by indicating that the word *dust* was employed—whereas in most parallel cases the word *ashes* was used—to indicate a gezera shava. There was really no change in the Torah's expression—only a less frequent usage—because of the *gezera shava.*

46. Extending, spreading out the Law, informing.

47. In English, in "A Note on *asher lo orasa*," *Journal of Biblical Literature* 81, no. 1 (1962): 69, n. 9; in Hebrew, in my *Sources and Traditions, Ketubboth*, p. 175, n. 1.

48. R. Nachman's suggestion is certainly not according to the plain meaning of the word *orasa.* Yet his aim is to show that R. Akiva of the *baraita* is not against the peshat. Peshat there is clearly not synonymous with plain meaning.

49. M. Jastrow's emendation in his *Dictionary of the Targumin, The Talmud Babli and Yerushalmi, and the Midrashic Literature,* s.v. *pesha'ta,* of *p. B. Bat.* 8.1, p. 16a to *peshatei* is incorrect. See E. S. Rosenthal, S. Lieberman, *Yerushalmi Nezikin* (Jerusalem: Israel Academy of Scribes of Humanitics, 1983), p. 213.

50. Bacher, *Die exegetische Terminologie der jüdischen Traditions literatur*, is still the best.

51. P. 168 in J. Z. Lauterbach's translation.

52. See chap. 1, pp. 11–13.

53. Cf. *m. Ya.* 4:7.

54. *Sifra* on Lev. 16:2 and *b. Yoma* 53a.

55. See M. Zucker, *Saadya's Commentary on Genesis*, (New York: The Jewish Theological Seminary, 1984), Introduction, p. 35ff (in Hebrew).

56. *The Biblical Commentary of Rav Shemuel Ben Chofni Gaon*, ed. A. Greenbaum, (Jerusalem: Mossad ha-Rav Kook, 1979), p. 478 (in Hebrew and Arabic). His son-in-law, R. Hai Gaon (939–1038), presumably hearing it from him, quotes it in his commentary to the Order of *Toharot*, ed. J. N. Epstein (Berlin: Mayer and Müller, 1915), *Kelim* 22.8, p. 62. However, Hai's authorship of this commentary is not certain—see Epstein's introduction. But see also B. M. Lewin *Otzar ha Ge'onim*: Berachot, Commentaries, (Haifa 1928), p. 93. Cf. also the quote from R. Y. ibn Bilam in *Perushei R. Saadya Gaon*, ed. J. Kafah (Jerusalem: Mossad ha-Rav Kook, 1963), p. 147.

57. *Sefer ha-Rikma*, vol. 1, ed. M. Wilensky (Berlin, 1929), Introduction, p. 19 (in Hebrew).

58. *Lekach Tov*, ed. S. Buber (Lvov, 1878) on Gen. p. 144, 232; Exod. p. 9; *Lekach Tov*, ed. A. Padun (Vilna, 1880) on Deut. p. 133.

59. Rashi quotes the dictum "No text can be deprived of its peshat" three times in his commentary on the Pentateuch—Gen. 15:10; 37:17; and Exod. 12:2—and once more in *Teshuvot Rashi*, ed. Elfenbein (New York, 1943), p. 293; whereas in his introduction to his commentary on *Song of Songs*, he quotes it "No text can be deprived of its *mishmao*" (see above, p. 000, on the meaning of the word *mishmao*). For a more comprehensive study, see Kamin, *Rashi's Exegetical Categorization*, pp. 122–30. Incidentally, Rashi also uses the expression *peshuto kemishmao*, "the peshat of the text is like its *mishma*" on Gen. 8:7; Exod. 2:12; Lev. 25:14 and at a few more places (see M. Banitt, *Rashi: Interpreter of the Biblical Letter* [Tel Aviv University, 1985], "Preliminary Remarks," particularly the notes to p. 2, as to where this expression comes from), which implies that sometimes the text's *peshat* is not like its *mishma*. For Rashi on the Talmud, see below, n. 61.

60. In his introduction to his commentary on the Pentateuch, method 5, and in *Sapha Berura*, ed. G. Lippmann (Furth, 1839), pp. 4–5.

61. For the appearances of the dictum in the *tosafot* (and Rashi on the Talmud), see R. S. Sussmann, *Meir Netiv* (Altuna, 1793), comment on *Shabb.* 63a (however, his references to the page numbers need to be

corrected); *The Talmudic Encyclopedia* (Jerusalem: Talmudic Encyclopedia Institute, 1982), vol. 1, p. 677, n. 7 (incomplete) and M. Kasher,
Torah Shelema., vol. 17, pp. 295–96.

62. For the Arabic sources, see Zucker, *Saddya's Commentary on Genesis*, pp. 42–96.

63. Both R. J. ibn Ganach (n. 57 above) and Rashi (in his introduction
to the *Song of Songs* and in his *responsa*; see also Iba Ezra, *Sophe Berura*,
pp. 4–)5, quote in the context of peshat and derash the statement in
b. Sanh. 34a concerning multiple teachings from the same verse. "Said
Abaye: The Scripture (Ps. 62:12) says 'God had spoken once, twice have I
heard this, that strength belongs unto God.' One biblical verse may convey
several teachings, but a single teaching cannot be deduced from different
scriptural verses. The students of R. Ishmael taught: 'And like a hammer
that breaks the rock in pieces' (Jer. 23:29)—just as the rock is split into
many splinters when struck [see what the tosafists on this passage and
parallels bring in the name of R. Tam], so also may one biblical verse
convey many teachings."

However, Ibn Ganach quotes these statements in support of the
right to teach peshat even when the rabbis of the Talmud adopted the
derasha, "for it is not impossible for a text to yield two or more distinct
correct meanings." Rashi, on the other hand, quotes these statements to
counteract the impression that all meanings are the same. "A verse may
convey many teachings." But "ultimately," says Rashi, "no verse can be
deprived of its *mishma*, of its plain meaning." Plain meaning remains
superior to applied meaning. It is always retained. In fact, many verses do
not have *derashot* and can be explained only according to the plain
meaning. For a thorough analysis of these statements vis-à-vis peshat and
derash, see Kamin *Rashi's Exegetical Categorization*, pp. 181–83.

Let me note that in discussing peshat and derash I did not mention
the famous statement attributed to R. Ishmael (quoted at *b. Sota* 16a,
Sifrei Deut. Piska 122 [p. 180], and *p. Kidd.* 1.2, p. 59d): "In three places,
the halakha crushes the scriptual text under its heel" (or, as it is in most
Palestine sources, "circumvents, or tears out, or bends the Scriptural
text"—see the variants in *Babylonian Talmud with Variant Readings*, Tractate *Sota* I, p. 238). This statement is not relevant to peshat and derash. It is
not a case of reading in, of changing the plain meaning. It is a case of
adding to the plain meaning, while preserving the latter. "The Torah states
with dust, and the halakha allows with anything; the Torah states razor and
the halakha says anything [that shaves]; the Torah states a book and the
halakha allows any form of document." The statement is basically saying
that in these three instances one does not have to follow the letter of the
Law. Something similar in nature is adequate—though not preferable.

Understood as such, the statement has no relevance to peshat and derash. See also Rashi *b. Sotah* 16a, s.v. *Torah*. The Rashbam, in his short introduction to *Mishpatim*, quotes it, however—in connection with peshat. Elsewhere (on Gen. 37:2), he also quotes in a similar context, the statement of R. Eliezer (*b. Ber.* 28b): "Keep your children from *higgayon*." For a fine history of the exegesis of this statement, see M. Breuer, *Michtam le-David*, (Ramat Gan: Bar Ilan University Press, 1978), p. 242ff.

64. Mention should also be made of R. Joseph Bechor Shor (twelfth century), one of the great rabbinic exegetes who followed the peshat. See what S. Poznanski wrote about him in *Commentary on Ezekiel and the Minor Prophets by R. Eliezer from Beaugency*, (Warsaw: Mekitze Nirdamim, 1913), pp. 55–78 (in Hebrew); J. Navo, "R. Joseph Bechor Shor—The Exegete of Peshat," *Sinai* 95 (1984): 268–77; idem, "The Relationship of R. J. Bechor Shor, Bible Exegete, to the Rabbis." *Tarbiz* 54 (1985): 458–62. In his commentary on the Pentateuch, he is close to the Rashbam's way of interpretation, but unlike the latter, he is troubled by the tension between peshat and derash.

65. See the perceptive observations made by U. Simon, "The Exegetical Method of R. Abraham Ibn Ezra as Revealed in Three Interpretations of a Biblical Passage," *Annual of Bar Ilan University* (1965): 130–38.

66. See for instance his comments on the interpretation of Lev. 22:22: "To sum up, we will lean on tradition and not rely on our faulty understanding"; Lev. 25:45: "The rabbis knew how to deduce correctly this conclusion. For our understanding is trifle in comparison with theirs"; Num. 5:7: "Their [the rabbis'] understanding is broader than our understanding."

67. Rashbam at the beginning Genesis. See also his comments on Gen. 37 (beginning) and to the end of the book of Exodus. For actual cases in which Rashbam applied this principle, see Poznanski, *Commentary on Ezekiel and the Minor Prophets by R. Eliezer from Beaugency*, pp. 41–42. To R. Meyuchas ben Elijah (1200?), redundancies and the opposite—lack of words or letters—are intimations of *sod*, mystical meaning, which he does not take up in his commentary. But he does take up peshat. He apparently thought that his commentary was entirely according to peshat. He says in his introduction to his commentary on Genesis, ed. A. W. Greenop and C. H. Titterton, (London, 1909): "They [the rabbis] wanted to let us know the way of peshat, which is essential and which teaches us the way we must walk and the way we must do" (the latter phrase is taken from Exod. 18:20). However, when one examines his commentary, one soon discovers that despite occasional disagreements with the rabbis (see Y. M. Katz, *Perush Rabenu Meyuchas a'l Sefer Devorim*, [Jerusalem: Mossad ha-Rav Kook, 1968], p. 20), to R. Meyuchas the standard meaning of the

text is almost always equal to the accepted halakha. See, for instance, his comments on Exod. 23:2; Deut. 24:16; 25:6.

68. These two terms are hardly distinguishable. See, for instance, Maimonides, *Mishnah Torah, Mamrim* 1.2.

69. Jerusalem: Mossad ha-Rav Kook, 1967. In the same book (pp. 163–68, n. 7), there is a very useful summary of the fierce battle that raged mainly in Germany (and in German) in the latter half of the nineteenth century concerning the rabbinic exegesis of the Bible.

70. The author of *Yad Halevi* (R. Yitzchok Horowitz?)—quoted in Chavel's edition of Maimonides' *Book of Commandments*, p. 33—is right when he says that according to Maimonides, "any exposition of the rabbis that does not agree with peshat is considered an *asmakhta* unless the rabbis themselves say that the exposition is part of essential Torah (*guf Torah*). According to the Rambam, it is the reverse. All expositions are a part of essential Torah unless the rabbis themselves say that the exposition is an *asmakhta*."

71. See R. M. Hakohen, *Yad Malakhi* (Liverno, 1778), "Rules of the Rambam," passage 4: "It is customary for the Rambam to select the exposition closest to the peshat even when it is rejected by the Talmud."

72. Cf. B. Z. Benedict, *Torah Shebe'al Peh* (Jerusalem: Mossad ha-Rav Kook, 1987), pp. 118–25.

73. See the comments of *R. Bahya on the Torah* (Jerusalem: Mossad ha-Rav Kook, 1968), Rambam, and *Gur Arye* on Deut. 24:4.

74. Maimonides does not accept the Gemara's decision "to subject the offense of marrying a *sota* to a negative precept." He therefore did not include this negative precept in his count of negative commandments—for which the Ramban took him to task in the section "the negative commandments that the Rambam forgot to count" in his comments on the Rambam's *The Book of Commandments* (Chavel's edition, p. 407).

75. I say this even though Maimonides completes the passage with a quotation from Exod. 21:19—"and shall cause him to be thoroughly healed"—which he quotes in *Mishnah Torah*, "Laws of Wounding and Damages" 1.5; 4.9 as proof that Torah requires monetary compensation, of which healing is one component. This verse from Exodus serves merely as a "support" and is not intended as real proof that "an eye for an eye" means money, for it is no proof. You pay money, including money for healing, when the injury is reversible; and you demand physical retribution when the injury is irreversible. This is in fact how R. Abraham the son of Maimonides, in his commentary *Perush Rabbeinu Abraham ha Rambam* on Exod. 21:24 (trans. Wiesenberg [London, 1959]) understood his father: "An eye for an eye-the peshat of the verse is clear [that it means physical punishment]; tradition [however] interpreted the meaning of the verse to be

'the money of a tooth for a tooth.' [Why did he skip the first example of an eye for an eye?] This tradition has support in the testimony of the text and in evidence arrived at through analogy [or logic, cf. Ibn Ezra]. R. Saadya wrote them [i.e., the testimony and the evidence] in his commentary. The testimony of the text is the verse [Exod. 21:25] 'a wound for a wound.' [It is not clear how this verse supports the notion of money. Cf. *b. B. Kam.* 84a.] It was already mentioned in this case or in a case similar to it that he is liable only to monetary punishment when He, may He be extolled, said [21:18–19]: 'And if men contend . . . only he shall pay for the loss of his time, etc. [and shall cause him to be thoroughly healed]." The latter verse serves merely as a support (*sa'ad*) and not as a real proof. R. Abraham continues: "My father, my teacher of blessed memory, in the *Guide* hinted here (*ramaz*) at an explanation which was transmitted orally and which contained a wonderful compromise between the tradition and the peshat of the text. I cannot write it down because he of blessed memory concealed it." What is this wonderful compromise? We do not know. But it preserves the integrity of the peshat. See also Seforno, *Biur al ha-Torah le-Rabbi Ovadiah Seforno*, ed. A. Darom (Jerusalem: Mossad ha-Rav Kook, 1980) on Exod. 2:24, p. 177.

76. The law has more force than an ordinary law from "Moses on Sinai" since it is rooted in the written law. See Maimonides' *Commentary on the Mishnah*, "Introduction," ed. J. Kafah (Jerusalem: Mossad ha-Rav Kook, 1963), pp. 9–10.

77. The word "appears" provoked this criticism from R. S. Lurya in his book *Yam shel Shelomo*, (Prague, 1616), at the beginning of chapter *Hachovel* in Tractate *Bava Kamma*: "I do not understand why he [Maimonides] has to resort to tradition. The Talmud adduces several *gezerot shavot* and expositions to that effect. He, however, has difficulty depriving the verse 'an eye for an eye' of its peshat because of a derash. Fearful of offering a place [of denial, and] a pretext to the heretics and Sadducees, he writes that it is a matter of tradition. That is also the view of Ibn Ezra in his commentary on the Torah. Behold their toil is in vain. One cannot say that 'an eye for an eye' is physical. . . ." cf. J. Levinger's article "A'l Torah Sheba'l Peh Behaguto Shel ha-Rambam," *Tarbiz* 37 (1968): 285–93.

78. See also *Mishnah Torah*, 1.3: "When the Torah says [Lev. 24:20]: 'as he has maimed a man, so shall it be rendered to him,' it does not mean to injure him the way he injured his friend but that he [the perpetrator] is worthy of having his limb removed or being injured the way he did"—a position a little closer to what he says in the *Guide*.

79. See note 70 above.

80. Cf. R. M. S. Hakohen, *Meshekh Chokhma*, ed. Y. Cooperman, Heskel, (Jerusalem, 1983), Lev. 19:14, pp. 484–87, and the editor's note, esp. n. 10.

81. See, for instance, his *Commentary on the Mishnah, Sanh.* 10:3, and also what I wrote in *Midrash, Mishnah, and Gemara* (Cambridge: Harvard University Press, 1986), p. 114. Of relevance is also R. Abraham the son of Maimonides, *Essay on Derashot Chazal*, ed. R. Margolioth (Jerusalem: Mossad ha-Rav Kook), pp. 83–89 (in Hebrew).

Part II: A Comment on Methodology

1. *B. Metz.* 59b, and parallel in *p. Moed Kat.*, beginning of the third chapter. For a bibliographical catalog of the literature on this story and interpretations of this phrase, see Y. Englard, *Shenaton ha-Mishpat ha-Ivri* (Jerusalem: The Institute for the Study of Mishpat Ivri, 1974), vol. 1, pp. 45–46.

2. For a striking example of the need felt by some commentators to reconcile sources which in reality are irreconcilable, see the interpretation of the phrase *nitna Torah le-Yisrael* ("the Torah was given to Israel," *b. Sanh.* 21b–22a) offered by R. Yom Tov ben Abraham Ishbili (Ritba, 1250–1330), discussed at greater length in chap. 5, n. 13. The Ritba, concerned about the theological daring reflected in the above talmudic source, was forced to reject the peshat of the phrase *nitna Torah le-Yisrael* and to interpret the phrase to refer not to the giving of the Torah to Moses, but to the popular use of the Torah. Only by offering a strained interpretation of this phrase could the Ritba reconcile this theological source with other rabbinic statements on the same topic. The peshat of the phrase (which undoubtedly refers to the Torah given to Moses), however, is corroborated by parallel uses of the phrase in other contexts, and therefore may not be legitimately abandoned. Despite the fact that the implications of this source may be chafing to someone of the theological bent of the Ritba, the (con)textual integrity and theological viability of this source must be respected.

3. We occasionally encounter a final halakhic determination in the Talmud which is not necessarily the most logical of the various options. For examples, see *b. Shabb.* 60b and *b. Yevam.* 67a. In these instances, strict logicality is not the absolute arbiter of halakhic propriety. Some ritual disputes in the Talmud are decided deductively rather than through the individual merits of the case. Whenever, for example, Abaye and Rava (two fourth-century Babylonian scholars) disagree, and they disagree hundreds of times if not more, the law is like Rava except in six places. Objectively it is unlikely that Abaye was wrong in all these instances. A criterion other than logic is the determining factor there.

4. I am referring, of course, only to the dynamics of the exposition of the oral law, as is the statement of R. Yannai quoted further on. In

contrast, the written Torah is immutable, and any willful change or tampering with its text is considered sinful. Human initiative and autonomy are only welcome and ratified within the arena of the oral law.

It is not exactly clear what Maimonides meant in *The Guide of the Perplexed* III, 41 (Chicago: University of Chicago Press, 1963) at the end of page 562: "Inasmuch as God, may He be exalted, knew that the commandments of this Law will need in every time and place . . . to be added to or subtracted from according to the diversity of places, happenings and conjectures of circumstances, He forbade adding to them or subtracting from them, saying: 'Thou shall not add thereto, nor diminish from it' (Deut. 13:1)." Is the "need in every time and place to be added to or subtracted from" not met at all, or is the need met in the oral law? Cf. *Sefer ha-Ikkarim*, III, 23. For a similar dichotomy, see R. N. S. Glasner, *Dor Revii* (Klausenburg, 1921), introduction, p. 3.

5. To put it differently, halakha strives to perfect a *torath chaim*, a living Torah, whose dual purpose is to stimulate man's emotions to be more receptive of the divine, and to make society more equitable and just. Like human experience in general, halakha remains inevitably subjective. Hashkafa, in contrast, strives to perfect a *torath emeth*, a Torah of truth, whose purpose is to achieve an accurate determination of reality, the way things are and were objectively for the sake of contemplation and manipulation. Like all objective truths, hashkafa aims to detach itself and keep aloof from human needs, desires, and subjective concerns.

6. This reality is reflected in a well-known story that often circulates in *yeshiva* circles. It is told of a *rosh yeshiva* who sends a halakhic query to another rabbinic scholar, but stipulates that he desires receipt only of the *pesak halakha* (the legal conclusion)—whether the item is kosher or not—without any accompanying halakhic argumentation. The rationale behind the *rosh yeshiva*'s somewhat curious request was that explanatory material might serve to cloud the issue rather than illuminate it, for halakhic reasoning is always susceptible to counterargumentation and thus to further uncertainty. The *rosh yeshiva* thus desired a black-and-white halakhic conclusion, free of the gray that usually attends halakhic decision-making. In so doing, he was opting, ironically, for an objective, *hashkafa*-like halakhic opinion.

7. The theoretical lines of demarcation between "truth" and "correctness" are not always so clear-cut. The comment of the twelfth-century scholar Rabad of Posquieres on Maimonides' claim about the heretical nature of anthropomorphic conceptions of God (Maimonides, *Mishnah Torah, Hilkhot Teshuva* 3.7) is relevant in this context: "And why did he call such a person a heretic? How many men greater and better than he [i.e., Maimonides] maintained such [anthropomorphic] views based on what

they read in biblical verses, and even more so, in aggadic passages that lead opinions astray." That is, in the view of the Rabad, anthropomorphic conceptions of God, though not objectively true, may nevertheless be "correct" and defensible theological tenets.

8. As an ironic aside in our discussion of the historical dimension of halakhic decision making, it should be noted that a modern Jew who maintains glatt kosher standards would not be able to eat in the medieval home of Maimonides, perhaps the greatest halakhist of Jewish history, because of the greater stringency of the halakhic regimen today.

9. See Maimonides' comments on *m. Sota* 3:3.

10. See J. Albo, *Sefer ha-Ikkarim*, vol. 1, ed. and trans. I. Husik (Philadelphia: Jewish Publication Society, 1929), pp. 44–47.

11. The various rabbinic conceptions of the revelation of the oral law, with their prooftexts, will be discussed and interpreted at greater length in the chapter to follow.

12. *p. Sanh.* 4.2 and *Midr. Pss.* 12:4.

13. The reality of the changing tides of halakhic legitimacy, and the usefulness of the intermediate conception of revelation, are to be noted in the purposeful inclusion of the views of *Beit Shammai* in the Mishnah with no accompanying explicit indication that these views are halakhically incorrect, despite the statement *Beit Shammai bemakom Beit Hillel eino mishnah* (the view of *Beit Shammai*, when found side-by-side with that of *Beit Hillel*, is not even considered a legitimate teaching) (*b. Ber.* 36b and parallels). The views of *Beit Shammai* (the classic representative of the minority view) were never declared absolutely false or deemed logically irredeemable. The Talmud consistently searches for, and then defends, the logic behind the opinions of minority as well as majority positions. *Beit Shammai*, although the perennial second-place finisher in halakhic debate, is accorded its measure of logical rationalization and justification nevertheless. This Talmudic propensity of defending the logical legitimacy even of rejected minority positions further sharpens the dichotomy between the realms of halakha and hashkafa. The Talmudic activity of officiating and deciding between halakhic opinions possesses a degree of inherent logical ambiguity that is not sanctioned in scientific speculation. In halakha, because minority positions are usually not rejected out of hand and discarded unceremoniously, but rather are often strenuously defended, the logical superiority of the majority view is sometimes not at all clearly or definitively drawn. The demarcation between truth and falsity becomes faint, the hierarchy of opinions somewhat shaky. The ultimate clarity and uncompromising finality that we usually expect from logical discourse are sometimes absent at the conclusion of a Talmudic halakhic argument, even if the debate has concluded, as expected, in favor of the majority view.

Though Talmudic reasoning is often very intricate, a certain logical fuzziness inheres in the very nature of halakhic argumentation, because of its habit of plumbing the logical depths of minority views. This distinguishes it from the very essence and aspirations of scientific discourse. In science, truth and falsity are rigorously distinguished and segregated. The objectives of science demand that true and false opinions be radically differentiated. The character of halakhic argumentation, in contrast, allows for a closer association of true and false, in the form of majority and minority opinions. The logical merits of minority opinions are usually not altogether repudiated. In fact, though a minority opinion will be ultimately rejected in practice, its theoretical value is usually enhanced through the give-and-take of halakhic disputation. In the process, however, the usual rigor and decisiveness of logic are somewhat compromised.

14. *Gen. Rab.* 44:1.

15. See the statement of R. Avin in *p. Ketub.* 1.2 concerning the link between a girl's physical maturity and a court's determination about a leap year. Objective time and physical reality are here subordinate to the halakhic accounting of the calendrical year.

16. For an intriguing distinction between the study of Torah and the study of philosophy, see Rosh (1220–1327) *Responsa*, rule 55, section 9.

Chapter 4

1. See below pp. 122–25 for a clearer explanation of what is meant by "initial revelation."

2. See R. M. Hakohen, *Yad Malakhi* (Livorno, 1768), "Rules of the *Rambam*," passage 4. Cf. also R. M. Margolit (d. 1781), *Mare ha-Ponim*, to *p. B. Kam.* 8a, s.v. *shem.*

3. See *p. Ber.* 3a. For a challenging view of the subject, see Chaim Hirschensohn, *Malki ba-Kodesh* (Hoboken, 1933), vol. 4, p. 80.

4. *Midrash, Mishnah, and Gemara* (Cambridge: Harvard University Press, 1986), pp. 105–6. See also p. 107 and pp. 148–50, n. 6 and 8.

5. As to which the rabbis considered more important, study or deeds, see Halivni, *Midrash, Mishnah, and Gemara*, p. 107 and pp. 148–50, n. 6 and 8.

6. "An Unscientific Postscript," in *The Seminary at One Hundred*, Centennial Volume of the Jewish Theological Seminary of New York (Jewish Theological Seminary of America, 1987), p. 276. I also said there that "a modern religious Jew must study Bible in a dual manner, according to the perception fitting the evolutionary rung of his or her ancestors and according to the perception fitting the evolutionary rung of its own. (Remember, Jewish philosophers, since the time of Philo, have urged us to study the

Torah dually according to the open meaning and according to the hidden philosophical meaning.)" For the kabbalists, see below, note 38.

To a religious Jew, evolution, too, is a divine creation ("In the beginning, God created heaven and earth"—He created everything, including the means of creation). God created the evolutionary mode of perception (which I call in this book a "time-bound" mode of perception), indicating to humans what He wants His Word to be intellectually understood by them in accordance with their respective evolutionary rungs (which we call in this book "interpretive states of mind"). Thus, to intellectually be a product of one's own age corresponds to the divine desire.

7. In his introduction to the book *Be'er Shave*, R. Y. Eilenberg (d. 1623), for entirely different reasons, says in the name of the old sages "that the study and occupation with the commandments that are inoperative today are more important and more recommended than the study of the commandments that are operative today."

8. See S. D. Luzzatto's *Commentary on the Pentateuch* (Padua: Dvir, 1871), Exod. 27:2, p. 360 (in Hebrew)—already noted by Ibn Ezra, *Safa Berura*, ed. G. Lippmann (Furth: 1839), p. 6a.

9. See, however, J. Goldin, "On the Account of the Banning of R. Eliezer ben Hyrcanus," *The Journal of Ancient Near Eastern Society* 16 (1984–85): 84–97, particularly 92ff.

10. See notes 14 and 15 below.

11. Cf. R. M. Hakohen, *Yad Malakhi* passage 526.

12. See *b. Sanh.* 88a–b.

13. Calendar differences set the boundary between remaining within the group and constituting a new sect outside the group. "I asked Yaqub Ibn Ifraim al Shami"—writes Al-Qirqasani, a tenth century Karaite scholar—"why do you [Rabbanites] favor the Isunians" (a small Jewish sect whose leader Abu Isa enjoined upon his followers the reading of the Koran and the Gospels) "and why do you intermarry with them although you know that they attribute prophecy to men who had nothing to do with it? He replied: because they do not differ from us in the observance of holidays." Qirqasani could not resist adding: "This answer of his indicates that according to them [the Rabbanites] manifestation of unbelief is more pardonable than manifestation of differences in observance of holidays." The text of Qirqasani was translated from the Arabic and published by L. Nemoy, "Al-Qirqisānī's Account of the Jewish Sects of Christianity," *Hebrew Union College Annual* 7 (1930): 382. See also L. Ginsberg, *An Unknown Jewish Sect* (New York: Jewish Theological Seminary of America, 1976), p. 105.

14. For the literature on this story, see Y. Englard, *Shenaton ha-Mishpat ha-Ivri* (Jerusalem: The Institute for the Study of Mishpat Ivri, 1974),

vol. 1, pp. 45–56. See also R. D. Lurya's *Introduction to Pirkei D'Rabbi Eliezer.*

15. The Palestinian Talmud at the beginning of the third chapter of *Moed Katan* raises the question, "Did not R. Eliezer know that one has to incline after the majority?" and answers: "He was very angry because they burned in his presence all the objects that R. Eliezer declared clean." It is not clear how the burning of the objects justified R. Eliezer's defiance of the majority. Perhaps it means—akin to what I said—that the burning of the objects caused R. Eliezer to lose his audience, deprived him of his right to advocate his dissenting view, thus exceeding the Law, which commands to incline after the majority only in matters practical. It should be mentioned that according to the Palestinian Talmud, God was more on the side of R. Eliezer. The Palestinian Talmud does not report that God said, "My children have defeated me." Also, in the Palestinian Talmud the miracles took place after the excommunication.

16. This is how the statement should be understood and not the way most authors of "rules of the Talmud" understood it. I am basing my assertion on parallels, particularly *Yoma* 36b and *Ber.* 37a. See also *Ketub.* 21a and the *Responsa of the Rashba,* vol. 1, no. 44.

17. See also *p. Sota* 5.2, 2a (at the end). "The rabbis of Caesarea said: R. Joshua praised R. Akiva's *derasha,* his exposition. But he did not follow R. Akiva's opinion." The two references, to *b. Ketubot* and *p. Sota,* I took from R. Margolioth's notes to "R. Abraham, the Son of the Rambam," *Milchamot ha-Shem* (Jerusalem: Mossad ha-Rav Kook), p. 88. Also see *Sifra Metzora,* chap. 5, p. 77b; R. Yose and R. Shimon said: "R. Eliezer's opinion appears to be more acceptable than R. Joshua's, and R. Akiva's opinion more acceptable than both. Yet the law is like R. Eliezer."

18. See, for instance, *tosafot, Sukk.* 3a, s.v. *deamar,* quoting R. Amram Gaon to the effect that in six instances the law is like the Shammaites.

19. R. Yom Tov Heller (1579–1654), *Tosafot Yom Tov, Ned.* 9:1, s.v. *im.*

20. R. Chaim Itter (1696–1743), *Pri Toar* (Solkiew, Poland, 1770), chap. 119, n. 1. See also Halivni, *Midrash, Mishnah, and Gemara,* p. 154, n. 32.

21. If the purpose of mentioning the minority view is to make it easier for future generations to reopen the case (cf. *m. Ed.* 1:5), analyzing and explaining that view may have practical value. Moreover, the Gemara sometimes identifies the author of the Mishnah's anonymous or majority view and goes on treating it as a minority view, ignoring the Mishnah's codificatory classification, ultimately concluding against it. (See D. Weiss Halivni, "The Reception Accorded to Rabbi Judah's Mishnah," in *Jewish and Christian Self-Definition,* ed. E. P. Sanders et al. [Philadelphia: For-

tress Press, 1981], pp. 204–12). Yet one has the distinct impression that when the Gemara is analyzing and explaining a minority view, its purpose is purely intellectual, to make that view as palpable and attractive as possible.

22. See, however, the commentary of R. Shimshon of Sens (d. 1230) found in the standard edition of the Talmud.

23. *b. Shabb.* 55a and parallels.

24. In his commentary on the Torah, in the latter half of the passage.

25. See also the Ramban's comment in his criticism of Maimonides' *Book of Commandments*, root 1, (ed. Chaim Chavel [Jerusalem: Mossad ha-Rav Kook, 1981] p. 16a [in Hebrew]): "If they hold that something is forbidden or that something is allowed . . . and he thinks the opposite, he is obligated to quash his own opinion and believe in what they say . . .", and the comments of R. E. Mizrachi, Mizrachi, and Maharal, *Gur Arye*, on Deut. 17:11.

26. For a fuller discussion of the topic by posttalmudic rabbis, see the insightful article by J. Silman, "Torah Elohit 'she-lo ba-Shamayim hi,'" *Annual of Bar Ilan University* 22–3 (1988): 274ff. As is to be expected, the Abravanel (1437–1508) sees in the view of the Ran (d. 1380) and the author of *Ha-Chinuch* (around 1400), passage 508, that one has to follow the majority even if they are mistaken a denial of the notion that God's Torah is true. See also Albo, *Sefer ha-Ikkarim*, vol. 3, p. 23.

27. See Karl Lowith, *Meaning in History* (Chicago: University of Chicago Press, 1970).

28. The author of *Mahdura Batra le-Marharsha*, R. Moses b. Yitzchat Bonmesh (who was the son-in-law of R. S. E. Eidls, 1555–1631 [the Maharsha]) in his comments on *b. B. Metz.* 59b (86a).

29. I am not the first one to use the phrase "double verity" or "double-tiered theory." It was used before by historians of medieval philosophy referring to faith and reason. See, however, H. A. Wolfson, "The Double Faith Theory in Clement, Saadia, Averroes, and St. Thomas," *Jewish Quarterly Review* 33 (1942): 213–64. They usually mean that there are multiple sources of information or truth which cannot and should not contradict. I mean by it the allowing of free intellectual inquiry even when that inquiry leads to conclusions different from the ones on which practical behavior rests. Logically they contradict. They can be implemented only when applied to different spheres.

30. Whenever a verse (or a fracton thereof), or a word, or a letter quoted in the Talmud disagrees with the way we have it in our Bible text, the Masora (a partial list was collected by R. A. Eiger [d. 1837] in his gloss to the *tosafot Shabb.* 55b), there exists a double textual truth, one for study-

ing the *derasha* which the Talmud has based on its own reading and one for the writing of the *Sefer Torah* (the Holy Scroll) which must comply with the version found in the Masora. Medieval scholars (among them the Rashba [1235–1310], in his *responsa*, falsely attributed to the Rambam, no. 232) wondered already why in matters of version we do not accept the authority of the Talmud. They realized the conflict, which has not been resolved to this day. We continue to study the respective places in the Talmud and, of course, continue reading from our *Sifrei Torah*. For a daring responsum, see R. Chaim Hirschensohn, *Malki de-Kodesh*, vol. 2 (Hoboken, N.J., 1921), pp. 215–49. See now also J. Ta-shema, in *Sidra 3* (1987): 87 (English abstract, p. vii) on the conflict in eleventh-century Germany between the laws as stated in the Babylonian Talmud and as practiced in custom: "The final result of this process, which is basically a compromise, was an ambivalent stance towards the Babylonian Talmud in general at that time. The Babylonian Talmud was the central and undisputed source of Torah with respect to fulfilling the commandment of studying Torah, which was the first and foremost commandment for the German Jew at the time, along with its secondary role as an instrument for *pesak* of practical law."

For the double theory of Torah in Jewish kabbala see G. Scholem, *On the Kabbalah and its Symbolism* (New York: Shocken Books, 1965), pp. 32–87, and the very learned essay by I. Tishbi, *Mishnat ha-Zohar* (Jerusalem: Mossad Bialik, 1975), vol. 2, pp. 363–98.

31. For a slightly different and larger description of "man's role in revelation," see my "On Man's Role in Revelation," in *From Ancient Israel to Modern Judaism: Essays in Honor of Marvin Fox* [out of which Appendix III is taken], edited by J. Neusner, E. S. Frerichs and N. I. Sarna, Atlanta: Scholars Press, 1989), vol. 2, part 6, pp. 29–49.

32. R. Yom Tov Heller, in the introduction of *Tosafot Yom Tov*, argues that the implication of this statement is only that God showed it to Moses for his private edification not to transmit it further to the people. Otherwise the language would not have been "he showed Moses" but rather "he gave Moses" the minutiae of the Torah to transmit them further.

33. Even though the text says "*vatik*," which here means rather a fledgling student, a beginner (that even his comments were revealed before). *Leherot* certainly does not mean to render practical decisions, for a student is not allowed to render practical decisions in the presence of his teacher (without permission). See *b. Eruv.* 62b–63a. See also *b. Ber.* 5a and *Tanchuma*, ed. S. Buber, Ki Tissa, p. 116.

34. In the beginning of *Mavo ha-Talmud*, attributed to R. Shemuel ha-Nagid (d. 1067), printed in the Vilna edition of the Talmud after Tractate

Berakhoth, the author says: "The commentary of the Mishnah can be divided into two parts, confirmed halakha and rejected halakha. The confirmed halakha is the one we learned from Moses our teacher, may he rest in peace, and Moses learned it from God Almighty." The rejected halakha is one that was not learned from Moses.

35. See also *b. Bekh.* 26b; and R. A. de-Boton (1545–88), *Lechem Mishnah, Shabbat* 21.1.

36. See M. Zucker, *Rav Saadya Gaon's Translation of the Torah* (New York: Philip Feldheim, 1959), p. 219.

37. *b. Shabb.* 10a, 119b speaks of men "becoming a partner to God in creation." Similarly, a man may become a partner to God in Torah or in revelation.

38. The kabbalistic references were quoted and discussed eloquently by G. Scholem in his book *The Messianic Idea in Judaism* (New York: Schocken Books, 1971), pp. 282–303, in a chapter titled "Revelation and Tradition as Religious Categories in Judaism." The rabbinic texts contained therein, however, need further elucidation.

39. The full statement says: "If the words of the Torah were given clear-cut, the foot would not have had a base to stand on"—i.e., the world could not have existed because there would have been no justification for the many subsequent controversies. The commentators, however, give a different explanation.

40. See *p. Ber.* 1, 4 (end), and D. Weiss Halivni, *Sources and Traditions* (Jerusalem: Jewish Theological Seminary 1982), *Eruvin*, pp. 12–13.

41. In his *Rules of the Talmud*, later attached to the book *Halichot Olam* by R. Yeshua Halevi (fifteenth century) (Saloniki, 1598), gate 5, chap. 1. See also R. S. Algazi (1610–1683), *Yavin Shemua* (also later attached to the *Halichot Olam*) (Venice, 1639). The connection between the statement "these and those are the words of God" and the intermediate position that only the arguments were revealed to Moses, is generally assumed to have been first made by the Ritba (at the beginning of the fourteenth century) on *Eruvin* 13b in the name of the sages of France. However, Algazi there quotes a book by the name of *Mishpetei Shemuel*, which in turn quotes the connection in the name of R. Chananel (eleventh century). For a lengthy discussion, cf. Chida (eighteenth century), *Rosh David* (Mantua, 1776), p. 14a and b.

42. I am referring in particular to the *Derashot of R. Nissim of Gerondi* (d. 1380) ed. L. Feldman (Jerusalem; 1974), pp. 44–45, 84–88, 110–16. See also *Ha-Chinuch* (author uncertain although the book was composed not later than the fourteenth century), passage 508; R. A. J. Hakohen, *Ketzot Ha-Chosen*, and *Kova Yeshua* by R. M. B. Lurya (Warsaw, 1888), Introduction.

43. In defense of Maimonides, who followed the view of the Heavenly Academy, R. Joseph Karo in his commentary on the laws of defilement of leprosy, *Kesef Mishnah* 2:9, says "that since Rabba sided with God while the soul was abandoning him [while he was dying], it is considered as if he was already in heaven and as such the stricture that the Torah is not in heaven applies." See also Chida, *Rosh David*, pp. 77a–78a.

44. In fact, dichotomy is practiced whenever *acharonim* (later scholars) interpret a text or answer a question differently than did the *rishonim* (earlier scholars)—something they would not do for the purpose of affecting practical law. R. M. Sofer, the author of *Chatam Sofer*, chided the young authors of *Meforshei ha-Yam* (R. Y. S. Natansohn and R. M. Z. Etinga)—and they humbly conceded to him (see R. Moshe Y. Heschel *Yam ha-Talmud* [Halberstadt, 1862], pp. 74a and 75a)—for having dared to deduce a new law on the basis of their answer to a *tosafot*'s question. "Are you friends or collegues of the *tosafot*?'" he inquires ironically. "If the *tosafot* asked the question, that is an indication that your answer is false. Otherwise, the *tosafot* would not have asked the question. The views of later scholars are null and void when they stand in contradiction to the slightest inclination (literally: the nails) of the early scholars." R. D. Pardo (1710–92) wrote a monograph (it is included in his book *Lamnatzeach le-david* [Saloniki, 1765]) to obviate all the difficulties concluded in the Gemara with the word *kashya*. Needless to say, his obviations have no practical halakhic standing. It is done merely for intellectual edification. The gaonic distinction between *kashya* and *teyuvta* is well known. See *Aruch*, s.v. *teyuvta*.

45. See my article "Revelation and Tzimtzum," *Judaism* 21, no. 2 (1972): 205–10.

46. *b. Ketub.* 30a and parallels.

47. According to Scholem, *The Messianic Idea in Judaism*, p. 363, 8, "this thesis seems to first have been stated by Moses Graf of Prague; see his *Va-Yakhel Moshe* [Dessau, 1699], pp. 45b and 54a." I have found in *Alfei Menasseh* by R. Manasseh of Ilya (1767–1831) [Vilna, 1822], p. 48b, passage 159, the same thesis in the name of R. Y. Lurya (1534–72).

Qirqasani (Nemoy article, n. 13 above), p. 328 reports that "the people of Babylonia accepted the system of the school of Hillel, while the people of Palestine accepted that of the school of Shammai." I know of no rabbinic parallel to this division of behavior between Babylonia and Palestine and can think of many places in rabbinic literature that contradict it; yet, it resembles the kabbalistic view inasmuch as Palestinian behavior (the pattern set in the Holy Land) fits more appropriately the behavior of the "days to come." I subsequently saw L. Finkelstein's article "The Persistence of

Rejected Customs in Palestine," *Jewish Quarterly Review* 29 (1938/1939): 179ff. and S. Lieberman's explanation in *Shekiin* (Jerusalem, 1939), pp. 21–22.

48. Or—according to R. M. Sofer, *Chatam Sofer*, *Pesach*. 3b—"to another place or to another incarnation." See my note in *Sources and Traditions*, *Eruvin*, p. 31.

49. See, for instance, his commentary on *m. Sanh*. 10:3.

50. *b. B. Kam*. 27b and parallels.

51. *b. Yoma* 84b. The author of this statement is Shemuel (a third-century Babylonian scholar) who, according to the *b. B. Kam*. 46b, also holds that "one does not follow the majority in matters of money." The two statements are connected. Shemuel is consistent.

52. *Tosafot Yoma* 85a, s.v. *ulefakeiach*. In close to ten places in the Babylonian Talmud (see *b. Ber*. 9a and parallels) it says that the minority view is worthy, "to be relied on in a case of emergency"—further indication that majority evidence is not certain evidence. In posttalmudic times, one who was in possession of an object had the right to say *kimli*, I follow the minority opinion. For the literature, see P. Ch. Medini, *Sedei Chemed*, vol. 3, pp. 505–12; vol. 4, pp. 480–81.

53. R. Shimshon of Sens in his *Tosafot Shanz* rightly connects the view of *m. Ed*. 1:3 that a majority decision is subject to change with what we called above "the nonmaximalistic notion of revelation." According to the "maximalistic notion of revelation," every major religious decision is predetermined by revelation, and once decided it is irreversible. See Appendix III.

54. See, however, M. S. Glasner, *Dor Revii*, (Klausenburg, 1921), Introduction, p. 4. For a short biography of Glasner, see N. Katzburg, *Memorial Volume for the Jews of Cluj-Kolozsvar* (New York, 1970), pp. 48–60. It is appropriate to mention here that the widespread belief that R. Eliezer held the view that an eye for an eye meant a physical eye for an eye is based on an erroneous understanding of *b. B. Kam*. 84a. See my forthcoming *Sources and Traditions*, Vol. 5.

55. See *b. Yoma* 69b, *San*. 64a, and also *Shabb*. 88a. This is contrary to Y. Kaufmann's view that syncretism ceased after the reign of Manasseh. See his *History of the Jewish Religion*, (Jerusalem; Mossad Bialik; Tel-Aviv: Dvir, 1960), vol. 3, pp. 348ff. Hebrew. See also below, pp. 134–35.

56. Halivni, *Midrash, Mishnah, and Gemara*, p. 15. See Y. Kaufmann, *History of the Jewish Religion*, vol. 4, pp. 327–38.

57. Y. Elman, "R. Zadok Hakohen On the History of Halakha," *Tradition*, 21, no. 4 (1985): 5.

58. Ibid., p. 15.

59. On the relationship between the cessation of prophecy and midrash, see Halivni, *Midrash, Mishnah, and Gemara*, pp. 15–16.

60. *b. Taanit* 17b and parallels. Cf. R. Z. Chayes, *Torat Neviim* (Zolkiew, 1838).

61. Cf. *Kuzari III*, 54–63. See I. H. Weiss, *Dor, Dor, ve-Dorshav* (Berlin-New York: Platt and Minkus, 1927), vol. 1, the first six chapters; and for a contrary view, Y. I. Halevi, *Dorot ha-Rishonim*, vol. 6 (dealing with the Bible) (Jerusalem, 1939), p. 42.

Chapter 5

1. For references to only several representative critiques of rabbinic exegesis, see the beginning of chapter 1.

2. See *Mekhilta*, vol. 3, Tractate *Nezikin* (in reference to Exod. 21:24), trans. Lauterbach, pp. 67–88; and *b. B. Kam.* 83b–84a.

3. See *Sifrei Deut.* 289, p. 307 in Finkelstein's edition and *b. Yevam.* 24a.

4. See *Mekilta*, vol. 1, Tractate *Pischa*, parsha 4, pp. 28–33.

5. For details on the implementation of this principle, see my *Mekorot u-Mesorot* (Jerusalem: Jewish Theological Seminary, 1982), *Shabbat*, pp. 110–13, and above, chapter 3, note 26.

6. See *Mekilta*, vol. 1, Tractate *Pischa*, parsha 4, p. 32.

7. See *b. Bav. Bat.* 15a.

8. For the former, see Neh. 8:17 and for the latter, see 2 Kgs. 23:22.

9. For a recent scholarly view of the historical period of Ezra and Nehemiah, including a discussion of the historical origins of the oral law, see Aharon Demsky, *History of the People of Israel*, ed. Chaim Tadmor (Jerusalem, 1983), pp. 40–65 (in Hebrew). For a similar notion to "Chate'u Yisrael," but from a different perspective (Zadok instead of Ezra), see the *Zadokite Documents*, V, lines 1–5.

10. This understanding of *kohanim* as the teachers/guardians of Scripture is not a singular occurrence. For further compelling evidence for this usage, see Jer. 2:8: "The *kohanim* never asked themselves, 'Where is the Lord?' The guardians of the Torah ignored me." For other examples, see also Mal. 2:7 and Hag. 2:11.

11. For relevant Muslim legends, see H. Z. Hirschberg, *Le-Shoneinu* (1947): 130–33. See also 4 Esd. 12.

12. *b. Sukk.* 44a. This historical explanation of R. Abahu is transferred by the *stammaim*, the anonymous (post-427 C.E.) redactors of the Talmud responsible for most of its discursive material, to parallel discussions in *b. Yoma* 80a and *b. Meg.* 2b–37a. The theological differences between the views of the *amoraim* and the *stammaim* that are evident in these *sugyot* must be recognized, however. The *stammaim*, unlike the *amoraim*, were uncomfortable with innovation even in the nonhalakhic realm. The phrase

from the last verse of Leviticus (27:34)—"These are the commandments
. . ."—is brought by the *stam* in the latter *sugyot* to forestall and deny any
post-Mosaic innovation even when the realm of practical halakha is not
affected. Note the comment in *Sifra* on this phrase (i.e., *ele ha mitzvot*"):
she-ein navi rashai lechadesh devar me-ata ("no prophet was destined ever
to introduce an innovation hereafter"). This caveat against innovation is
extended even to nonhalakhic matters by the *stam*, and the historical
concept of "they were forgotten and then established anew" is employed to
substantiate and uphold this principle in the face of apparent innovation.
The *stam*, perhaps, considered script a matter of practical halakha since it
affects the way a scroll is written. If this is so, then R. Yose, who stated that
Ezra changed the script, either denies that a prophet cannot introduce an
innovation, or—and this is more in line with the tenor of this chapter—
asserts that Ezra constitutes an exception. The opening statement of
R. Yose ("had Moses not preceeded him, Ezra would have been worthy of
receiving the Torah for Israel") supports the latter contention. Compare
also the statement in *b. Shabb.* 14b: "they wanted to exclude the book of
Ezekiel from the canon because its words [its halakha; see *Rashi*] contradict the Torah," with the statement in *b. Makk.*: "Moses had said, the Lord
is . . . visiting the iniquity of the fathers upon the children and upon the
childrens' children. . . . Ezekiel came and annulled that, declaring 'the soul
that sins, it shall die.'" He annulled a non-halakhic decree. For further
Talmudic grappling with the reality of innovation, in apparent violation of
the principle "no prophet was destined ever to introduce an innovation
hereafter" which clearly prohibits halakhic novelty, see *b. Meg.* 7a, where
special dispensation must be located for the new halakhic directives found
in *Megillat Esther*. Also see *p. Meg.* 1.5. My own theory about Ezra's role
in reinstituting derash, incidentally, does not violate the principle of *she-ein
navi rashai lechadesh* . . . because we posit not innovation of Ezra's part
but rather rectification and restoration, and we limit this textual jurisdic-
tion to Ezra alone. In fact, the historical process of *chate'u Yisrael* followed
by Ezra's restorative efforts is not unlike the process of forgetting and
reinstitution connected to the rite of the willow branch in *b. Sukk.* 44a and
in the analogous references brought above.

13. I feel compelled to add in this context that R. Yom Tov ben Abraham Ishbili (Ritba, c. 1250–1330), in his commentary on *b. Meg.* 2b,
blunted the theological edge of the phrase *nitna Torah le-Yisrael* ("the
Torah was given to Israel") by stating that it refers *not* to the giving of the
Torah to Moses, but to the popular use of the Torah by the people of Israel.
By explaining the phrase in this way, the Ritba could maintain that the
"true" Torah was given in the Ashurith script, the identical script that we
find the Torah in today, thus dissolving the connotations of change. The

interpretation of the Ritba was followed by many traditional scholars, including Ibn Habib (1460–1516), the author of *Ein Ya'akov*, in his commentary on *b. Meg.* 2b, and by modern *maskilim* like S. Refaeili, *Jerusalem*, vol. 10 (Jerusalem, 1904), p. 279; Y. Bachrach, *Ishtadalut im Shadal*, vol. 1, p. 187ff.; and R. Margolioth, *Ha-Mikra ve-ha-Masora* (Jerusalem: Mossad ha-Rav Kook, 1964), pp. 30–34. However, the Ritba's interpretation does not accord with the peshat of the phrase *nitna Torah le-Yisrael*, which undoubtedly refers to the giving of the Torah by God to Moses, as it does in contexts in *b. Shabb.* 63b and 86b, *Yoma* 4b, *Betza* 25b, and *Zevach.* 116a. (The tension reflected in the Ritba's grappling with this phrase demonstrates once again that the ultimate choice is between interpreting verses contrary to their peshat and maintaining the prevailing view of the text of the Torah, or modifying this view in accordance with the reality of peshat). In addition (besides the fact that neither *t. Sanh.* 4.7 nor *p. Meg.* 1:7 had the word *le-Yisrael*), further evidence against the Ritba's interpretation can be adduced from the statement of R. Eleazar of Modi'im that continues the passage quoted above from *b.* Sanhedrin: "This writing [of the law] was never changed, for it is written, 'The vavs [i.e., hooks] of the pillars.' As the word *pillars* had not changed, neither had the word *vavim* [hooks]." This statement, as already recognized by R. S. Yafeh Ashkenazi (sixth century) in his commentary, *Yafeh Mare*, on *p. Meg.* 1.7, must necessarily refer to the giving of the Torah to Moses. On the interpretation of the phrase, "the Torah was given to Israel," also see Azariah de Rossi, *Meor Einayim*, ed. D. Cassel, end of chap. 58. Cf. Radbaz, *Responsa*, vol. 3, no. 442, where the evidence which runs counter to the Ritba's interpretation is challenged.

14. The Tosefta and Palestinian Talmud mention here, in accord with the statement of Mar Zutra, that both script and language were changed by Ezra.

15. Having been idolatrous throughout the First Temple period—Rashi. *b. Ned.* 22b supports Rashi's interpretation. See, however, Neh. 9:32, *Otzar ha-Geonim*, and the comments of the Ran (R. Nissim ben Reuben Gerondi, d. 1380), (Chidushei ha-Ran), on Sanh. 21b.

16. The order of the opinions in this passage is arranged neither chronologically—for R. Judah ha-Nassi was the youngest of the latter three rabbis—nor according to the sequence of the biblical verses quoted. It seems that it was arranged, rather, according to the (decreasing) "radicalness" of the opinions. The most radical opinion is that of R. Yose, who claims that Ezra changed the script of the Torah. A bit less radical is the claim of Rabbi that Ezra merely *restored* the old script. The most conservative opinion is, of course, that of R. Eleazar of Modi'im, that "this writing [of the law] was never changed." It is important to note in this context the

difference in attitude in regard to this issue between the *geonim* and the late medieval scholars like the Ritba. R. Sherira Gaon (906–1006 C.E.) and R. Hai Gaon (939–1038 C.E.) (in *Otzar ha-Geonim, Sanhedrin,* ed. C. Taubes, pp. 161–63) share the Ritba's theological discomfort with the position of R. Yose and even with that of Rabbi (which explains the harsh rejection of R. Yose's prooftext reflected in their statement: "ve-ein bah mamash," i.e., "[R. Yose's proof] has no substance"), but ease this discomfort in a different manner from the Ritba's. They could rest content—while the Ritba apparently could not—with emphasizing repeatedly that this tannaitic dispute is decided in favor of R. Eleazar of Modi'im. They reach this conclusion partially through the dubious claim that R. Eleazar was the teacher of the other rabbis mentioned ("they are all his [R. Eleazar of Modi'im's] disciples"). These *geonim* felt no obligation to accord the opinions of R. Yose and Rabbi theological validity. The Ritba and those who followed in his footsteps, however, reacted more vehemently, and felt that the notion that Ezra changed even the script of the Torah was so theologically repellent that it could not be maintained on any account—even as a minority view. This theological antipathy towards the proposition that Ezra played such a determinative role in the textual history of the Pentateuch is vented in even more strident tones in the *responsum* of the Radbaz quoted below in n. 34.

17. There are also rabbinic passages, as in *Sifrei* Deut. 48, *t. Sota* 13, 3 and parallels, *b. Sukk.* 20a, and *Lev. Rab.* 2, 11, which implicitly minimize Ezra's role vis-à-vis the text of the Torah by comparing it to the roles of Hillel, R. Akiva, and R. Chiya and his sons (in the *Sifrei* passage, Ezra's role is also compared to that of Shaphan, Josiah's scribe who read to the king the "scroll of the Torah" that had been discovered by the priest Hilkiah) rather than to that of Moses. See also *b. Zevach.* 62a. Josephus, *Antiquities* vol. 11, par. 136–59, calls Ezra the reader of the laws of God.

18. The passage is quoted from *Bemidbar Rabbah* because this text is the preferred one. Cf. *Avot de-Rabbi Nathan* I, chap. 34, 50b, and II, ch. 27, 49a, ed. Schechter (London, 1887); *Sifrei Num.* piska 69, pp. 64ff., ed. Horovitz (Leipzig, 1917); *Midrash Mishle* XXVI 24, 50a, ed. Buber (Vilna, 1893). Also see *Batei Midrashot,* vol. 2, ed. Wertheimer (Jerusalem: Mossad ha-Rav Kook, 1953), p. 490.

19. For our interpretation of what these dots signified prior to their talmudic exposition, see below, pp. 145–46. There are five more instances of dotted words in the Hebrew Bible, but these lie outside the Pentateuch: 2 Sam. 19:20; Ezek. 41:20 and 46:22; Isa. 44:9, and Ps. 27:13. In Ezek. 41:20, *ha-heikhal* is mentioned twice, and the dot over the first indicates erasure. In Ezek. 46:22, as well as in Isa. 44:9 and Ps. 27:13, the words

could be deleted and the sense of the verse still be retained, but the deletion of the dotted word in 2 Samuel 19:20 (*yatza*) would disturb the flow of the verse.

20. That the first opinion, i.e., everything preceding the *ve-yesh omrim*, belongs to R. Yose (the same R. Yose who affirms Ezra's revelatory stature in the passage from *b. Sanh.* 21b quoted above) is proven in *Ginzei Mitzrayim*, ed. E. Adler (Oxford, 1897), pp. 38–39. One may correctly assume that even for the first opinion, which grants less exegetical license than does the second, the dots were, in fact, instituted by Ezra.

21. The matter of these ten dotted words is different from the case of the three Torah scrolls mentioned in *Sifrei Deut.* 356 and parallels, in which simply the correct reading, and not the proper meaning, of certain words is at stake. In the event of contradictions between the scrolls, the authority of two is favored over that of one in the cause of ascertaining the correct and authentic reading. In the case of the ten dotted words, in contrast, all the available pentateuchal texts contain the same ten words, which all require dots to indicate that their peshat is somehow problematic. The ten words are common to all versions of the scriptural text. The dots, however, minimally signal that, across the board, the peshat of these words must be disowned (or, as I will prove later, erased).

22. My interpretation of the significance and implications of the ten *puncta extraordinaria* as understood by the rabbis of the Talmud generally follows that of Horovitz in his commentary on the passage in *Sifrei*. The plausibility of his rabbinic summary (with modifications; see below nn. 37 and 40) of the significance of these diacritical points has been confirmed by several scholars. Among the important scholarly discussions of the *puncta extraordinaria* are L. Blau, *Masoretische Untersuchungen* (Strasbourg, 1891), pp. 6–34; Christian Ginsburg, *Introduction to the Massoretico-Critical Edition of the Hebrew Bible* (London, 1897), pp. 318–31; Romain Butin, *The Ten Nequdoth of the Torah* (1906, reprint New York, 1969 with a prolegomenon by Sh. Talmon; and Saul Lieberman, *Hellenism in Jewish Palestine* (New York: Jewish Theological Seminary of America, 1962), pp. 43–46, in which attention is called to the Greek parallels to the rabbinic treatment of these critical marks. Shemaryahu Talmon, in his prolegomenon to Butin's book, discusses the relevance of *puncta extraordinaria* in the Qumran literature to a proper understanding of the pentateuchal *nekudot*.

23. The most prominent example among the ten of a *shelo kepeshuto* interpretation, in which derash deviates from peshat, is the instance of the dot over the he in the word *rechokah* in Num. 9:10. Cf. *M. Pesach.* 9:2, where the phrase *lo . . . vadai* is applied to *rechokah* as the standard tannaitic term for a *shelo kepeshuto* interpretation. We will return to this

Mishnah further on. The statement of R. Shimon ben Elazar in *Gen. Rab.* 78:9 (and in *p. Pesach.* 9:2) is relevant: "Whenever you find the plain writing exceeding the dotted letters, you must interpret the plain writing; if the dotted letters exceed the plain writing, you must interpret the dotted letters." Whether one interprets (*doresh*) the plain writing or the dotted letters, one engages in the same activity—making *derashot.*

24. Azariah de Rossi, *Meor Einayim,* chap. 19, p. 232.

25. In *Iggerot Moshe, Yoreh Deah,* vol. 3, nos. 114–15, R. Moshe Feinstein cateogrizes this passage, from *Avot de-Rabbi Nathan,* as spurious and heretical. Apparently, however, he was not aware of the location of this rabbinic passage in several parallel sources, including the *Bemidbar Rabbah* version noted above. R. Feinstein was evaluating this passage as found in *Piskei Tosafot* (*Menachot,* no. 231), which is an abridged paraphrase of the text and is thus not a complete source, as was already correctly recognized by R. Eleazar Fleckeles (d. 1826), in a *responsum* in *Teshuva me-Ahava,* section 3, no. 391. R. Feinstein's reaction can be contrasted frutifully to that of the Netziv, Rabbi Naftali Z. Y. Berlin (1817–93), the great ninteenth-century scholar, who, in his *Emek ha-Netziv,* on *be-ha'alotekha,* p. 219, only described the passage as "peculiar" (and not heretical), was familiar with its location in parallel sources, and thus realized that is excision was not a legitimate or defensible option. See also Eliyahu Schulsinger in *Yad Eliyahu,* vol. 3, (Jerusalem: Mossad ha-Rav Kook, 1956), p. 114, who was aware of the quotations of the passage in tosafistic literature and linked the passage to the discussion of changes in the language and script of the Torah found in *b. Sanh.* 21b.

26. See *Pirkei de-Rabbenu ha-Kadosh,* vol. 3, ed. L. Greenhut (Jerusalem, 1898), p. 86; and *Midrash Chaserot ve-Yeteirot,* ed. A. Marmorstein (London, 1918), pp. 23–33; and *Aruch,* s.v. *nakud;* and *Machzor Vitry,* ed. S. Horowitz, (Nurnberg, 1933), p. 685. See also *Hadar Zekenim* (Livorna, 1840), which consists of *Baalei ha-Tosafot* and *Perushei ha-Rosh,* for two references to the passage in tosafistic literature. Both references quote the *Avot de-Rabbi Nathan* version of the passage and, in fact, deduce halakhic rulings based on this reading. Incidentally, the reading in these versions substitutes "Moses" for "Elijah."

27. Y. F. Lisser, *Binyan Yehoshua* (Dyhernfurt, 1788). Lisser based his own commentary on what R. Meir Eisenstadt (1670–1744), the author of *Panim Meirot,* wrote in his book *Kotnot Or,* where the relevant *Avot de-Rabbi Nathan* passage is quoted and explained.

28. *Beit Talmud,* vol. 1, eds. I. H. Weiss and M. Friedmann (Vienna, 1881), pp. 234–38. Also see Chaim Hirschensohn, *Malki ba-Kodesh,* vol. 2 (Hoboken, 1921), p. 215.

29. Cf. the eighth principle of Maimonides' thirteen principles of faith as stated in his *Commentary on the Mishnah Sanhedrin*, chap. 10 and the somewhat modified form in *Mishnah Torah*, Laws of Repentance 3, 8.

30. It should be added (since Ish Shalom failed to mention it) that the phrase *Moshe mipi atzmo* does not *always* mean "of his own volition" without divine approbation. *b. Meg.* 31b distinguishes between the curses in Lev. 26 and the curses in Deut. 28, saying that the former were given *mipi ha-Gevura* and the latter were given by *Moshe mipi atzmo*. Both are divine, the difference being only in formulation: the curses in Leviticus are addressed by God in the first period, whereas the curses in Deuteronomy are addressed by God in the third person. A similar distinction was established in Ibn Ezra and others in their commentaries on Exod. 20:1 between the first Decalogue in Exodus and the second Decalogue in Deuteronomy. Even such a modified interpretation was considered inappropriate by many a biblical commentary, including the *Zohar* ve-Etchanan 265a, which offers its own interpretation based on the word *mipi*. Some versions, however, do not have the word *mipi* in the text. Such a reading is supported by *b. B. Bat.* 88b. For a posttalmudic reaction to the above-quoted text in the Talmud, see A. J. Heschel, *Torah min ha-Shamayim*, vol. 2, (London: Soncino Press, 1972), pp. 204–10. See also J. S. Levinger's "Maimonides' Commentary on *b. Meg.* 31b" in his *Malmonides as Philosopher and Codifier*, (Jerusalem: Bialik Institute, 1989), pp. 172–76.

31. See especially Ibn Ezra on Deut. 1:2. But see also Y. L. Krinsky, *Mechokekei Yehuda*, in *Karnei Or*. For R. Judah the Hasid's designation of non-Mosaic scriptural verses, see his *Perushei ha-Torah le-Rabbi Yehuda ha-Chasid*, ed. Y. S. Lange (Jerusalem, 1975), p. 64 (Gen. 48:20—written either by Joshua or by people of the High Synod); p. 138 (Lev. 2:13); pp. 184–85 (Num. 21:17—removed to Psalms); p. 198 (Gen. 36:31 and Deut. 2:8—by the people of the High Synod). Also note the comments of Ramban and Abravanel on Num. 21:1 and Radak, Josh. 21:7.

It is generally assumed, following *Tzofnat Pa'aneach* (see next note), that Ibn Ezra's condemnation of Isaac Israeli the Elder's (c. 855–955?) assertion that the passage in Gen. 36:13–43 ("These are the kings who reigned in the land of Edom before there reigned any king over the children of Israel. . . .") was written during the time of Jehoshaphat, is an expression of Ibn Ezra's rejection of the possibility of the presence of an entire passage (i.e., more than just a few words which may serve an explanatory function) of non-Mosaic material in the Pentateuch. This interpretation is uncertain, however. From the quotations of Ibn Ezra it is not clear why Isaac Israeli attributed this passage to the time of Jehoshaphat, nor is it clear how Israeli reconciles this claim with his thesis that Hadar, the last of the Edomite kings (Gen. 36:39), is identical to Hadad, mentioned in I Kgs. 11:14, of the time of Solomon. It is unlikely that Israeli was referring to the midrash quoted also by Rashi, that the eight Edomite kings are mentioned to contrast them with the eight Israelite kings during whose reigns no king reigned in Edom. More likely, Israeli arrived at his conclusion through the emendation of the text, and this drew the wrath of Ibn Ezra. An almost identical condemnation (*chalila, chalila,* "the book ought to be burned") is employed by Ibn Ezra in his book *Tzachot,* ed. G. Lippmann (Berlin, 1769), p. 72a, against emendations (whether he is referring there also to Israeli or to Ibn J. Yanach, is a controversy among scholars). See also Ibn Ezra's *Short Commentary* on Exod. 21:8. For a strange explanation, which can also serve as a defense of Israeli, by none other than the author of the *Tossafot Yom Tov,* R. Yom Tov Heller, see now *Maamar Yom Tov* (Jerusalem, 1989), p. 63a.

32. R. Joseph b. Eliezer Tob Elem, *Tzofnat Paaneach* (Berlin, 1912), pp. 91–92, in his supercommentary on Ibn Ezra's commentary on Gen. 12:6 ("The Canaanites were then in the land").

33. Moses Alashkar, *responsum* no. 74.

34. The general reluctance on the part of medieval Jewish scholars (the case of Moses Alashkar being among the rare exceptions) to attribute scriptural license to Ezra can be traced to the Jewish sensitivity to the Muslims' accusation that Ezra had falsified the scriptural text. This reluctance is particularly evident in a *responsum* (vol. 4, no. 101) of the Radbaz, R. David ibn Abi Zimra (1479–1573), who responds to a petition to emend the text of the Torah on the basis of the *Zohar.* Radbaz writes: "You shall not make our Torah as two *torot,* especially when we are in the midst of this nation [i.e., the Muslims], who claim that we have made changes in the Torah—adding to it, deleting from it, and emending it as we have seen fit. And what would they say if they saw our Torah scrolls conflicting with one another?" R. Tob Elem had expressed similar sentiments reflecting Jewish-Muslim polemical considerations, before Radbaz, in *Tzofnat Paaneach,* p. 93: "This secret [Ibn Ezra's hint that certain verses are non-Mosaic] must not be disseminated in public so that the words of the Torah should not be degraded, for an unenlightened person does not know to distinguish between verses which embody laws and those which are merely narrative. But [this is so] also because of the nations [i.e., Muslims] who say to us, 'Your Torah was once true but you have wrought changes in it.'" For an overview of these polemical circumstances, see Chava Lazarus-Yafeh, "Ezra/Uzir: The Development of a Polemical Motif," in *Tarbiz* 55, no. 2 (1986), pp. 359–79. These polemical considerations, however, need no longer bear on Jewish theology in the modern times.

35. The scope of Ezra's authority vis-à-vis the scriptural text may be compared to that of Rabbi Judah ha-Nasi vis-à-vis the Mishnah. The latter had extensive powers of revision and redaction (despite the Talmudic dictum of *mishna lo zaza mimkoma*), but still had to grapple with the reality of an entrenched, "normative" Mishnah that preceded his own. While Rabbi was not hesitant in making changes in the halakhic landscape of this normative Mishnah, he generally retained its syntactical and linguistic structures in the dissemination of his own Mishnah. On authority in regard to the scriptural text, see Josephus, *Against Apion*, 1. 37–43. Ezra, because of his special status, constitutes an exception.

36. This explains the inconsistencies and contradictions that can be discerned within the biblical and talmudic commentaries concerning the significance of the *eser nekudot*. For examples of such inconsistency, compare Rashi's comment on *b. Pesach.* 93b, s.v. *nakod* with his comment on *b. Bar. Metz.* 83a, s.v. *limda*; and comments of R. E. Mizrachi, and Maharal, *Gur Arye* on the respective verses.

37. Interestingly, in regard to the presence of the dot over the letter he of *rechokah*, the *Sifrei* offers a very complex *derasha*. It interprets the dot to signify that if a person is near the Temple court but is *tame*, i.e., defiled with the brand of defilement that lasts only till sunset—so that during the slaughtering of the Passover lamb, which is performed during the day, he cannot enter the Temple court but is able to partake of it in the evening—he does not celebrate the first passover. This was correctly understood already by R. Hillel (twelfth century), based on *p. Pesach.* 9.2; but see also R. D. Lurya's gloss to the parallel *Bemidbar Rabbah* passage. Regarding the later rabbinic understanding of the function of the dots, Talmon (in Butin, *The Ten Nequdoth of the Torah*, p. 21) writes that the "*puncta extraordinaria* could be employed not only to mark a required deletion of a letter or of a word but also for other purposes, as seems to be the case also in Massoretic tradition." By "Massoretic" he is making reference to the talmudic interpretation of the dots. See below n. 40.

38. Of interest also is the commentary of Ramban on Num. 9:10.

39. Quoted by F. Field in his edition of the *Hexapla* a. 1, n. 6 (to Gen. 33:4), first noticed by Blau, *Masoretische Untersuchungen*, p. 22.

40. The dots in Deut. 29:28 also connote deletion. Exactly what should be deleted is not clear. The unclarity is compounded by the divergence of interpretations recorded in *b. Sanh.* 44b and by the observation made already by Rashi that it is not respectful to dot God's name. Nevertheless, I am inclined to follow Horovitz's suggestion, in his comments on the *Sifrei*, that the omitted words should be *lanu u-levaneinu*. It should be pointed out that a single dot over a word deletes not only that word but also the words connected with it syntactically. Thus the dot over the word *et* in Gen. 37:12

deletes also the words *tzon avihem*, and the verse is thus read as if it said: "and the brothers went to pasture [themselves] at Shechem." (The *Sifrei* does not state which letter of the word is dotted, and according to Ginsburg, *Introduction to the Massoretico-Critical Edition of the Hebrew Bible*, pp. 318–31, there was a general tendency as time went on to reduce the number of dotted letters.) Similarly, in Gen. 18:9, the whole text integrally connected with the question of the angels—"Where is your wife Sarah?"—is to be deleted. (Later sources, including *b. B. Metz.* 87a, retained the words but employed a *derasha* to make sense of the text). In Gen. 16:5, the entire phrase "The Lord decide between you and me" should be deleted because, as the *Sifrei* states, "She [Sarah] complained only about Hagar" and not about Abraham, though the word *chamasi* may suggest otherwise. *T. Sota* 5.12 does not mention that this verse is dotted and treats it therefore as a regular verse. This was correctly understood by R. David Pardo in his commentary *Chasdei David*. Cf. S. Lieberman, *Tosefta Kifshuta, Sota* (New York: Jewish Theological Seminary, p. 664. As to Num. 21:30, the oldest tradition had the words *asher ad* dotted, and came to inform us either that, as the *Sifrei* says, the destruction (*va-nashim*) extended beyond Meidva, or that, as in the second version of *Avot de-Rabbi Nathan*, the desolation did not even reach Meidva.

My analysis bears out Butin's conclusion even as I disagree with him in the interpretation of the meaning of individual *nekudot*. At the end of *The Ten Nequdoth of the Torah*, Butin concludes that the *puncta extraordinaria* "were devised by their author or authors, to condemn, as spurious, the words or letters over which they were placed" (p. 117). Sh-Talmon's analogy between the *puncta extraordinaria* and the diacritical marks employed in the Qumran writings ("Prolegomenon" to *The Ten Nequdoth of the Torah*, p. xvi) needs to be re-examined.

41. See Blau, *Masoretische Untersuchungen*, p. 8, and Lieberman, *Hellenism in Jewish Palestine*, p. 44, n. 51, 52. Butin, in *The Ten Nequdoth of the Torah*, p. 24, attributes the dots "to that dark period known as the times of the Soferim or of the Great Synagogue." The rabbis, in fact, reckoned Ezra among the *anshei kenesset ha-gedola*, the People of the Great Synod. See Targum to the Song of Songs 7:3 and H. Mantel, *The Men of the Great Synagogue* (Dvir, Israel, 1983), p. 261, n. 17. Mention should be made of the strange continuation of the "chain of tradition" (Aboot 1, 1) found in *Midrash Otiyot D'Rabbi Akiva*, included in A. S. Wertheimer's collection of *Batei Midrashot*, vol. 2, p. 355 (Jerusalem: Mossad ha-Rav Kook, 1953), that "the people of the Great Synod transmitted the Torah to Ezra the scribe, Ezra the scribe to Hillel the elder(!), Hillel the elder to R. Abahu(!), R. Abahu to R. Zeira(!)." Also see Blau's review of Butin's book in *Jewish Quarterly Review* 19 (1907): 413.

42. The lack of unambiguous talmudic *proof* for our theory may be unsettling or dissatisfying to some readers. Our conception of timebound exegesis, however, can help explain why there is no clear-cut (that is, more clear-cut than the rabbinic sources I have catalogued) talmudic reference to the historical sequence of *chate'u Yisrael* that we have described, and Ezra's restorative midrashic efforts. In other words, our recourse to analogy through the illustrative paradigms offered by these rabbinic sources underscores the absence of *direct* talmudic reference to the precise details of our theory; this absence, nevertheless, is explainable. The notion of timebound exegesis that we have delineated posits the increasing exegetical allegiance, through time, to the plain sense of the text. Equipped with our modern exegetical sensibility, we perceive more acutely than did the rabbis of the Talmud the problem of the occasional discrepancy between peshat and derash, because our commitment to peshat is more thorough. The conflict between peshat and derash, when it arises, is therefore for us more serious and more problematic than it was for the rabbis. If the conflict had been more pressing for them (that is, if the integrity of peshat had been more inviolable than it in fact was), there probably *would* have been more explicit and direct talmudic reference to the historical sequences we have outlined. With our recognition of the dynamic of timebound exegesis, we must be satisfied with the evidence of our theory yielded by analogical reasoning, for we cannot hope for definitive proof.

43. See *b. Taan.* 17b and parallels for the talmudic assertion that the origin of a law cannot be traced to a prophet (in this case, to Ezekiel), but must be attributed to Moses. The rabbis maintained the principle that the (post-Mosaic) prophets could not have created halakha of their own accord.

44. The incident of the golden calf illustrates quite strikingly the fickleness of Israelite faith in and allegiance to the God who had rescued them from Egypt. A generation that could worship the golden calf following so closely upon the heels of the Exodus and in the context of the Sinaitic revelation was obviously not predisposed to, or capable of, taking upon themselves the Torah's detailed halakhic regulations. If the immediate presence of God could be so easily forgotten, the text of the Torah stood little chance of careful preservation. If laws could be so quickly abandoned, the text that embodied them was bound to be neglected. As to the theological feasibility of such a reversal, see below, n. 53. For an interesting aggadic discussion of the many laws forgotten even as soon as the death of Moses, although here as the result of mourning over his death, see *b. Tem.* 16a.

45. For the latest scholarly treatment of the subject of Ezra's hand in the canonization of the Pentateuch, see John Barton, *Oracles of God* (New York: Oxford University Press, 1988), p. 23: "Nearly all modern scholars

agree that the . . . Torah was the first of the three divisions to be accorded canonical status, and in this, many would think Ezra may well have been at least partially instrumental, though naturally the authority of most of the Pentateuch was agreed upon before this work." As to the immediately ensuing centuries, the fourth and third centuries B.C.E., it is still well to quote (despite the caveats raised recently by the editors M. E. Stone and D. Satran of *Emerging Judaism: Studies on the Fourth and Third Centuries B.C.E.* (Minneapolis: Fortress Press, 1989), p. 2) the conclusion of J. Bright in his *History of Israel*, 3rd ed. (Philadelphia: Westminster Press, 1981), p. 428: "Through the obscurity of the fourth and third centuries, development continued along the lines laid down (by Ezra and Nehemiah) until, by the time of the Maccabean revolt, Judaism, though still in process of development, had assumed in all essentials the shape characteristic of it in the centuries to come."

46. See *b. Meg.* 15a and parallels. See also *Kuzari*, III, 65. For Ezra as a prophet in other traditions, see E. R. Kraft, "Ezra," in Wolfgang Haase, ed., *Aufstieg und Niedergang der Romischen Welt* 11, ch. 19 (Berlin: Walter De Gruyter, 1979), pp. 119–36.

47. This concept of an "incomplete" revelation may be understood, aggadically, along the lines of the discussion in *b. Shabb.* 88a about the question of choice versus compulsion in the Israelites' acceptance of the Torah. According to R. Avdimi bar Chasa, the Israelites were compelled at Sinai to accept the Torah under duress: "'And they stood at the nether part of the mount'. . . This teaches that the Holy One, blessed by He, tilted the mountain over them like a cask and said unto them: 'If you accept the Torah, well and good; and if not, there shall be your burial.'" Rava adds the following important footnote to R. Avdimi bar Chasa's controversial statement: "Even so, the generation in the days of Ahasuerus accepted it [anew]." Rava's rejoinder accentuates the significance of the voluntary and wholehearted acceptance of the Torah in the time of Mordechai and Esther during the crisis of the Purim episode. At the time of Mordechai (traditionally considered a member of the High Synod), the Jewish re-acceptance of the Torah was done willingly, and thus represented a more lasting, authoritative, and decisive acceptance of Torah. Only then could the revelation be considered "complete," for its acceptance by the Jews was finally voluntary and permanent.

It ought also to be stated briefly that the idea of "Chate'u Yisrael," the central theme of this chapter, is not compatible with R. Zacharias Frankel's notion that what the whole community agrees upon has revelatory status and "is worthy to be recognized no less than that which comes directly from God" (*Zeitschrift für die religiösen interessen des Judenthums* [2]: 15). Frankel's notion ultimately led either to a dispensing altogether with revelation and embracing only "peoplehood," or to making the people the guide as to what halakha to keep and what not to keep. For a sympathic exposition of Frankel's theological views, see I. Heinemann, *Ta'amei Hamitzvot*, vol. 2 (Jerusalem, 1956), pp. 161–82.

48. For an example of this type of traditionalist theology, see the commentary of the Gaon of Vilna in his *Aderet Eliyahu*, at the beginning of *Mishpatim*. See also above, chapter 2, note 24.

49. See *p. m. Ber.* 1.4 and parallels for this type of exaggerated praise for the authority of the oral law in relation to the written Torah. See also *Biurei Hagra*, Avod. Zar. 2:5 (printed in the standard Romm edition of the Mishnah).

50. Indeed, early leaders of the Reform movement in the nineteenth century perceived themselves as heirs, and successors, to the rabbis of the Talmud, and claimed the mantle of halakhic assertiveness. It is no wonder that the most perceptive and learned Reformer, Abraham Geiger, saw in the work of the Reformers "the organic continuation of the activities of the rabbis" (I. Heinemann, *Ta'amei ha-Mitzvot*, vol. 2 [Jerusalem, 1956], p. 171).

51. D. Z. Hoffmann (in his general introduction to his *Das Buch Leviticus* [Berlin: M. Poppelauer 1905–1906]) insists that a religious Jew must consider the oral law as contiguous with the written law, and whenever there is a contradiction between the two it should be resolved the same way as contradictions within the written law are resolved. Besides blurring the distinction between written and oral laws, his suggestion is of value only if one follows R. Akiva's interpretation of R. Ishmael's last hermeneutic principle ("if two biblical passages contradict each other, they can be determined only by a third passage"), according to which the third passage acts as a harmonizer between the first two contending passages. R. Ishmael, however, interprets this hermeneutic principle to mean (see note 5 above) that you follow two against one and relegate the minority passage to derashic interpretation. If the minority "passage" happens to be the oral law, according to Hoffmann's insistence, one ought to act contra peshat and behave against standard halakha, a concession that Hoffmann cannot make.

52. See Halevi, *Kuzari*, III, 23, 53; Franz Rosenzweig, *Briefe* (Berlin: Schocken Books, 1935), 520; and N. Arieili, *R. Judah Halevi's Concept of Halakha* (in Hebrew), *Da't*, 1 (1977): 40ff.

53. In connection with Chate'u Yisrael, referring primarily to idol worship during the First Temple, one would have expected revelation to have wiped out idolatry among the Israelites. It did not. Israel clung tenaciously to idolatry centuries after the giving of the Torah. Why did God tolerate Israel's idolatrous obdurancy? Why did He not put an end to Israel's sinful inclinations? A similar question was asked by Maimonides, *The Guide of*

the Perplexed, III, 32, in connection with animal sacrifice the purpose of which was to wean man away from idolatry. Why this stronghold of idolatry even after revelation that an antidote (animal sacrifice) was necessary to counteract it? The answer Maimonides gives fits our questions too, namely, that revelation did not change human nature; it merely afforded man an opportunity to change himself. Revelation did not turn men into supermen; only into superior beings capable of infinite improvement, religiously and morally. Self-improvement takes a long time to achieve. Therein lies the explanation for the discrepancy between the biblical description of the natural order and modern man's perception of reality. Biblical description reflects man's conception of reality as of that particular historical juncture. That conception changed gradually. While revelation was a factor in that change, it was not revelation's primary aim. I touch upon this very complicated subject in order to forestall a possible objection to "Chate'u Yisrael," lest one assumes *a priori* that Israel could not have sinned so gravely after revelation. It could and it did.

Appendix I

1. Cf. *p. Shev.* 10.2, p. 39c: *"mikan samkhu le-peruzbol shehu min hatorah"* (*mikan samkhu* that peruzbol is biblical. See also the continuation there and my interpretation of it in D. Weiss Hallivni, *Sources and Traditions* (Jerusalem: Jewish Theological Seminary of America, 1972), *Gittin*, p. 539, n. 1. (There you will find also references to some of the literature. I will mention here two sources: *tosafot Sota* 27b, s.v. *ish*, and Ramban at the end of his commentary to *Ketubot*.) *P. Ketub.* 5.4, p. 29d that added to the statement of R. Judah the son of Betheira (not found in the parallels) the phrase *vesamkhu lehen mikra* held that it is biblical—as it is suggested by *p. Yevam.* 9.5, p. 10b. Cf. S. Lieberman, *Tosefta Kifshuta* (New York: Jewish Theological Seminary, 1967), *Ketubot*, p. 258. See also *p. Yevam.* beginning of chapter 12. Rashi, in his comment on Exod. 16:29 seems, however, to have employed *mikan samkhu chakhamim* for a rabbinic ordinance. The sources from which Rashi took his expositions do not have there the phrase *mikan samkhu chakhamim*. They probably held, like many other authorities (see, for instance, *b. Eruv.* 17b) that *Eruvei Techumim* (the *eruv* of boundaries) too is biblical. See also *m. Sota* 5.3.

2. Not found in the parallel source, *b. Pesach.* 51b.

3. Cf. J. Guttmann, *Mafteach ha-Talmud* (Breslau: Th. Schatzky, 1923), pp. 2–4.

4. See, however, the medieval commentaries ad. loc., including the *tosafot* s.v. *mitzva*.

5. See Rashi, *b. Betza* 15b, s.v. *ma tama*, to the effect that according to Rava the verse quoted as the source for *"eruv* of dishes" is *asmakhta be'alma* which indirectly implies that according to Shemuel it is biblical.

6. CF. Y. T. Heller, *Tosafot Yom Tov, Yevam.* 9.3, s.v. *vechalutza.*

7. See Y. Gilat, "Chalutza-De-Rabbanan hi?" in Y. Gilat, Ch. Levine, Z. Rabinowitz, eds., *Studies in Rabbinic Literature, Bible and History* (Ramat Gan: Bar Ilan University Press, 1982), pp. 135–42.

8. It should be mentioned that there are also those who deny that the Talmud when it employs an *asmakhta* meant to say that the verse does not bear out the content of the *derasha.* "Let this be silenced and not repeated, for it is heresy," said that Ritba (around the fourteenth century) in his commentary on *b. Rosh Hash.* 16a. According to the Ritba, *asmakhta* means that biblically the content is desirable but not obligatory, and the rabbis made it obligatory. "The rabbis do not make up things." They merely strengthen what is already expressed in the text. This sentiment is also shared by Maharal, *Gur Arye,* on Exod. 19:15. He too feels that it would be almost immoral to attribute a content to a text for ulterior motives, like to add authority or to use it as a mnemonic device. To him, *asmakhta* is also biblical, except that it is not contained in the actual words. It merely leans on them (and therefore is a part of them) although the text does not directly express it. (Why then is its content considered as if it were rabbinically ordinated?) The author of *Gur Arye* treats an *asmakhta* similar to the way we treat a *mikan samkhu chakhamim.* See also *p. Shev.,* at the beginning.

Appendix II

1. For a brief history of deconstruction see Christopher Norris, *Deconstruction* (London: Methuen, 1982), pp. 1–89.

2. See Roland Barthes, *Image, Music, Text* (New York: Hill and Wang, 1977), p. 148, and Culler, *On Deconstruction* (Ithaca Cornell University Press, 1982), pp. 31ff.

3. The literature which deals with the similarities between midrash and modern literary criticism, like S. A. Handelman, *The Slayers of Moses* (New York: The State University of New York Press, 1982), particularly pp. 66ff. See also D. Stern, "Literary Criticism or Literary Homilies?" in *Prooftexts* 5 (January 1985); 96–103; Jose Faur, *Golden Doves with Silver Dots* (Bloomington: Indiana University Press, 1986), particularly chapter 4; Hartman and Budick, *Midrash and Literature,* pays insufficient attention to the reader's role in forming meaning. The reader's role represents the strongest similarity between midrash and modern literary criticism. Read-

ers' participation in the meaning of a text is indisputably a characteristic of midrash (see Y. Heinemann, *Darchei haAggada* Jerusalem: (Magnes Press, 1954) p. 3: "Derash [= midrash] endows the interpreter with greater freedom of action in line with his personal idiosyncracies than does peshat") and reader's participation is a common assumption of the modern literary critics. All the other similitudes are problematic either because they are not expressive of the literary school as a whole, or because they are not accurately describing the nature of midrash.

4. R. Travers Herford's slightly romantic description of the "devout student" who "would find that many thoughts came into his mind as a result of meditating on some text, and such thoughts would remain associated with that text, though he hardly knew whether the text had suggested the thoughts or was only a helpful reminder of them" (in the preface to I. Frankel's book *Peshat* [Toronto: LaSalle Press, 1956], p. 20) applies best to aggada. In halakha, the student knew—or thought he knew—that the text suggested the thoughts. Otherwise he would not have considered them binding.

5. See Mark Kleinman, *A Guide to Critical Legal Studies* (Cambridge: Harvard University Press, 1982).

6. The number of halakhic hermeneutic principles is usually given as either seven (*t. Sanh.* 7.11, in the name of Hillel) or the more popular number of thirteen (found also in the prayer book in the name of R. Ishmael); whereas the standard number of aggadic hermeneutic principles is thirty-two (found in the Vilna edition of the Babylonian Talmud at the end of tractate *Berakhot*, in the name of R. Ishmael, the son of R. Yose the Galilean).

7. B. Metz. 59b.

8. For a summary of "heavenly voices" in rabbinic literature, see R. Margolioth, *Questions and Answers from Heaven* (in Hebrew) (Jerusalem: Mossad ha-Rav Kook, 1957), pp. 27–35.

9. *B. Metz.* 86a.

10. *b.* Avod. *Zar.* 3b. See the perceptive words of S. Rawidowicz, "On Interpretation," *Proceedings of the American Academy For Jewish Research* 26 (1957); 96: "only a God who learns Torah, who loves interpretation can give an open text—in order to encourage learning . . . only He can entrust man with a multifaceted code—deficient from the perspective of the most perfect giver—the validity of which will depend on man . . . on the many . . . who . . . will be able to form the majority in any dispute to arise."

11. N. H. Weisel, a principal collaborator of Mendelssohn's *Biur*, wrote in the introduction to Gan Naul, (Lvov, 1806), vol. 1, p. 9: "It is no doubt

that God's intention was not to increase words for the sole purpose of beautifying the language or to adorn it. . . ." See also Rashi, *Sota* 49a, s.v. *batal*.

12. See M. Segal in his critical edition of Ben Sira (Jerusalem: Mossad Bialik), 1959, pp. 12–13.

13. *Ketub.* 4.9–13.

14. The linguistic conservatism of contracts is well known. It is possible that because of their binding nature, contracts were treated as quasi-religious documents.

15. Of some relevance is the current debate with respect to "original intent." Advocates of original intent claim that the United States Constitution ought to be interpreted according to the intention of the original authors, the framers of the document, even when the wording of the Constitution suggests to us otherwise. Opponents of original intent either entirely ignore the opinions of the originators or hold that the original intention was that each generation should interpret the Constitution according to its own mode of interpretation—the former argument is inapplicable to a canonized text claiming divine authority, and the latter would have been unacceptable to the rabbis. For a lively and popular discussion of original intent, primarily from the perspective of the opponents, see Mark Tushnet, "The U.S. Constitution and the Intent of the Framers," in *Tikkun: A Quarterly of Jewish Critique of Politics, Culture, and Society* 1, no. 2 (1986): 35–40; and Jack N. Rakove, "Mr. Meese, Meet Mr. Madison," *The Atlantic*, December 1986, 77–86.

16. Our distinction between halakha and aggada with respect to authorial intention is similar to R. Posner's distinction between literature (aggada) and law (halakha) in his book *Law and Literature*, (Cambridge: Harvard University Press, 1989), pp. 204ff., with respect to intentionalism. The book is studded with references and quotations. Little, however, is taken from the Bible and nothing from the Talmud. It would be a desideratum to do the same for the latter literatures.

Appendix III

1. *m.* Ed. 1:5–6.

2. R. Shimson of Sens *Tosafot Shanz, m.* Ed. 1:5–6.

3. *b. Ber.* 9a and parallels.

4. "Maximalists" later tried to curtail the applicability of this principle by limiting it to cases in which the entire *issur* is *de-rabbanan*, and to cases in which the relevant law has not yet been codified.

5. *b. Ber.* 36b and parallels.

6. Cf. the Netziv's introduction to the Shiltot, sec. 1 par. 10. The introduction represents a beautiful example of a non-historical, semi-homiletical overview of learning, especially of the biblical period.

Appendix IV

1. For reference to the Hatam Sofer, see my *Sources and Traditions* (Tel Aviv: Dvir, 1968), "Introduction" to Seder Nashim, p. 10, no. 9.

2. *b. B. Bat.* 93b.

3. R. Jonathan of Lunel, *b. Ketub.* 58b.

4. See *Sources and Traditions*, Seder Nashim, on *b. Kidd.* 20a, p. 643, n. 13.

Index of Citations

Name Index

Aba the son of Kahana, 73
Abahu, 213n.12
  cooking on the holiday,
    commentary on, 156
  the law of the willow branch,
    commentary on, 137
Abaye, 109
  the book of Ben Sira, commentary
    on, 73–74
  on the length of the Tabernacle's
    court, 65–66
  meritorious acts, commentary on,
    156
  multiple teachings from the same
    verse, commentary on, 198–99n.63
  on enticement to worship idols, 67
  Safra's dream, commentary on, 69–
    70
Abiathar; on God having doubts, 116
Abraham the son of Maimonides,
    200n.75
Abravanel, I., 28
Aderet Eliyahu, 30–31
Akabya Ben Mahlel, 106–7
Akiva, 169, 179n.30
  fining a divorcee's seducer,
    commentary on, 75–76
  on sowing, 155
Albo, J., 203n.4, 204n.10
Alashkar, Moses, 142–43
Amaziah the son of Joash, 124
Aquinas, Thomas, 5
Aruch, 181n.45

Ashi, 155
  and asmakhta, 15
  discrepancy between logic and
    acceptance, 109
Ashkenazi, Bezalel, 51
Avdimi Bar Chasa, 224n.47
Avot de-Rabbi Nathan, 141–42, 145

Babylonian Talmud, 10
  reading in, 160
  on scholarly disputes, 116
Bacher, W., 191n.1
Barton, John, 223n.45
Bechor Shor, J., 184n.16, 199n.64
Beit Talmud, 142
Ben Chofni, Shemuel
  commentary on peshat, 10, 79–81
Ben Gabbai, Meir, 114–15
Ben Kipper, Yose. *See* Yose the son of
    Kipper
Berachya, 73
Bet ha-Bechira, 51
Binyan Yehoshua, 141–42
Biur, 29
Blau, L., 217n.22
Bonmash, Moses, 112
Book of Beliefs and Opinions, 79–80
Book of Commandments, 80–81, 88
Bright, J., 224n.45
Butin, R., 217n.22, 222nn.40, 41

Caspi, J., 183–84n.16
Chajes, Z. H., 59

Note: This index is selective only.

Subject Index

Adornment
wearing a sword on the Sabbath,
58–61
". . . After that she is defiled . . .", 54–
56, 84–85
Agent of another person, culpability
of, 40–41
Aggada, 6, 14, 161–62
and halakha, 228*n*.16
Allegory
allegorists, 177*n*.16
reading in, 3–7
Amoraic period, 47, 51
literature: the meaning of
"beferush", 77–78
stammaim, theological differences
with, 213–14*n*.12
textual implication during, 25–27
Analogy
Homeric, 20–22
rabbinic theology, as a means of
extracting, 90–92
Animal sacrifice, 225*n*.52
Animal with unparted hoofs born to
an animal with parted hoofs,
189*n*.43
Appetite
"Put a knife to your throat, if you
are a man given to appetite", 68–
69
Arabic sources of peshat, 79–81
Ashes, 196*n*.45
Asmakhta (biblical support for
rabbinic law), 13–16, 81, 226*n*.8
be'alma, 155–57
talmudic references to, lack of, 15–
16

Beferush; its meaning in amoraic
literature, 77–78
Behavior. *See* Dichotomy between
practice and intellect
Biblical description of reality, 225*n*.52
Biblical exegesis
amoraic period, 25–27
eighteenth century, 29–31
evolution of: summary, 46–48
fourteenth to eighteenth centuries,
28–29
Gaon of Vilna's commentary on the
Torah, 30–31
historical survey, 23–35
Mendelssohn's *Biur*, 29–30
Middle Ages, 27–28
nineteenth and twentieth centuries,
31–33
reading in. *See* Reading in
stages of: summary, 33–35
textual implication, 25–27
twentieth century, 31–33
The blind; "Thou shall not put a
stumbling block before the blind",
10–12, 24, 88

Calf, golden, 223*n*.44
Capital punishment, 6
Chametz, disposal of, 43–44
"Chate'u Yisrael", 132–35, 148–49,
151–52, 222–23*n*.42. *See also*
Conflict of peshat and derash
Ezra's role in, 149–53
oral law, role of, 152–53
in rabbinic literature, 136–38
theological assumptions, support of,
150–51

243